First World War
and Army of Occupation
War Diary
France, Belgium and Germany

29 DIVISION
Divisional Troops
Gloucestershire Regiment
9th (Service) Battalion Pioneers
1 May 1919 - 31 October 1919

WO95/2294/4

The Naval & Military Press Ltd
www.nmarchive.com
Published in association with The National Archives

Published by

The Naval & Military Press Ltd

Unit 10 Ridgewood Industrial Park,

Uckfield, East Sussex,

TN22 5QE England

Tel: +44 (0) 1825 749494

www.naval-military-press.com

www.nmarchive.com

This diary has been reprinted in facsimile from the original. Any imperfections are inevitably reproduced and the quality may fall short of modern type and cartographic standards.

© **Crown Copyright**
Images reproduced by permission of The National Archives, London, England, 2015.

Contents

Document type	Place/Title	Date From	Date To
Heading	WO95/2294 29 Div 9 Btn Gloucestershire Regt (Pioneers) May 1919 Oct 1919		
Heading	Rhine Army Southern Division Late 29th Division 9th Bn Gloster Regt (Pioneer Bn) May-Oct 1919 From 66 Div		
War Diary	Leichlingen	01/05/1919	31/05/1919
Miscellaneous	Battalion Order By Lt. Col. R.I. Rawson Cmmg. 9th Bn. Gloucester Rgt (Pioneers) May 1st 1919		
Miscellaneous	Battalion Order By Lieut Col. R.I. Rawson Cmmg. 9th Bn. Gloucester Rgt May 2nd 1919		
Miscellaneous	Battalion Order By Lt. Col. R.I. Rawson Cmmg. 9th Bn. Bn Gloucester Rgt May 3rd 1919		
Miscellaneous			
Miscellaneous	Battalion Orders By Lt. Col. R.I. Rawson Cmmg. 9th Bn. Gloucester Rgt. May 5th 1919		
Miscellaneous	Battalion Orders By Lt. Col. R.I. Rawson Cmmg. 9th Bn. Gloucester Rgt. May 6th 1919		
Miscellaneous	Battalion Orders By Lt. Col. R.I. Rawson Cmmdg. 9th Bn. Gloucester Rgt. May 7th 1919		
Miscellaneous	Battalion Orders By Lt. Col. F.P. Smyly Cmmdg. 9th Bn. Gloucester Rgt. (Pioneers)	06/05/1919	06/05/1919
Miscellaneous	Battalion Orders By Lt. Col. F.P. Smyly Cmmg. 9th Bn. Gloucester Rgt. (Pioneers)	09/05/1919	09/05/1919
Miscellaneous	Battalion Orders By Lieut. Colonel. F.P. Smyly Cmmdg. 9th Bn. Gloucester Regt.	10/05/1919	10/05/1919
Miscellaneous	Battalion Orders by Lt. Col. F.P. Smyly. Cmmg. 9th. Bn. Gloucester Rgt., (Pioneers)	12/05/1919	12/05/1919
Miscellaneous	Bt. Col. F.P. Smyly Commanding. 9th Bn. Gloucester Rgt.	13/05/1919	13/05/1919
Miscellaneous	Battalion Orders By Lt. Col. F.P. Smyly Cmmdg. 9th Bn. Gloucester Ret. (Pioneers)	14/05/1919	14/05/1919
Miscellaneous	Battalion Orders By Lieut-Colonel. F.P. Smyly Cmmdg. 9th Bn. Gloucestershire Regt	15/05/1919	15/05/1919
Miscellaneous	Battalion Orders By Lieut. Colonel. F.P. Smyly Cmmdg. 9th Bn. Gloucestershire Regiment (Pioneers)	16/05/1919	16/05/1919
Miscellaneous	Battalion Orders By Lt. Col. F.P. Smyly Cmmdg. 9th Bn. Gloucestershire Regt (Pioneers)	17/05/1919	17/05/1919
Miscellaneous	Battalion Orders By Lt. Col. F.P. Smyly Cmmdg. 9th Bn. Gloucestershire Regt (P)	20/05/1919	20/05/1919
Miscellaneous	Battalion Orders By Lt. Col. F.P. Smyly Cmmdg. 9th Bn. Gloucestershire Regt	21/05/1919	21/05/1919
Miscellaneous	Battalion Orders By Lt. Col. F.P. Smyly Cmmdg. 9th Bn. Gloucestershire Regt (P)	22/05/1919	22/05/1919
Miscellaneous	Battalion Orders By Lt. Col. F.P. Smyly Cmmdg. 9th Bn. Gloucestershire Regt (Pioneers)	23/05/1919	23/05/1919
Miscellaneous	Battalion Orders By Lt. Col. F.P. Smyly Cmmdg. 9th Bn. Gloucestershire Regt (P)	24/05/1919	24/05/1919
Miscellaneous	Battalion Orders By Lt. Col. F.P. Smyly Cmmdg. 9th Bn. Gloucestershire Regt (P)	26/05/1919	26/05/1919

Miscellaneous	Battalion Orders By Lt. Col. F.P. Smyly Cmmdg. 9th Bn. Gloucestershire Regt (P)	27/05/1919	27/05/1919
Miscellaneous	9th Bn Orders By E F Smyle Commanding Gloucestershire Rgt	28/05/1919	28/05/1919
Miscellaneous	Battalion Order By Lt. Col. F.P. Smyly Commanding 9th Battn. Gloucester Regt	29/05/1919	29/05/1919
Miscellaneous	Battalion Order By Lt. Col. F.P. Smyly Commanding 9th Battn. Gloucestershire Regt. (Pioneers.)	30/05/1919	30/05/1919
Miscellaneous	Battalion Order By Major H.B. Spear Commdg 9th Bn. Gloucestershire Regt. (P)	31/05/1919	31/05/1919
War Diary	Leichlingen	01/06/1919	19/06/1919
War Diary	Burschied	21/06/1919	28/06/1919
Miscellaneous	Battalion Order By Major H.B. Spear Commanding 9th Bn. Gloucester Rgt. (Pioneers)	02/06/1919	02/06/1919
Miscellaneous	Battalion Order By Major H.B. Spear Commdg 9th Bn. Gloucestershire Regt. (P)	03/06/1919	03/06/1919
Miscellaneous	Battalion Order By Major H.B. Spear Commanding 9th Bn. Gloucester Regt. (P)	04/06/1919	04/06/1919
Miscellaneous	Battalion Order By Major H.B. Spear Commdg 9th Bn. Gloucestershire Regt. (P)	05/06/1919	05/06/1919
Miscellaneous	Battalion Order By Major H.B. Spear Commdg 9th Bn. Gloucestershire Regt. (P)	06/06/1919	06/06/1919
Miscellaneous	Battalion Order By Major H.B. Spear Commdg. 9th Bn. Gloucestershire Regt. (P)	07/06/1919	07/06/1919
Miscellaneous	Battalion Order By Major H.B. Spear Commanding 9th Bn. Gloucester Rgt.	09/06/1919	09/06/1919
Miscellaneous	Battalion Order By Major H.B. Spear Commanding 9th Bn. Gloucester Rgt. (P)	10/06/1919	10/06/1919
Miscellaneous	Battalion Order By Major H.B. Spear Commanding 9th Bn. Gloucester Rgt. (Pioneers)	11/06/1919	11/06/1919
Miscellaneous	Battalion Order By Major H.B. Spear Commdg 9th Bn. Gloucestershire Regt. (P)	12/06/1919	12/06/1919
Miscellaneous	Battalion Order By Major H.B. Spear Commdg 9th Bn. Gloucestershire Regt. (P)	13/06/1919	13/06/1919
Miscellaneous	Battalion Order By Major H.B. Spear Commdg 9th Bn. Gloucestershire Regt. (P)	14/06/1919	14/06/1919
Miscellaneous	Battalion Order By Major H.B. Spear Commdg 9th Bn. Gloucestershire Regt. (P)	16/06/1919	16/06/1919
Miscellaneous	Battalion Order By Major H.B. Spear Commdg 9th Bn. Gloucestershire Regt. (P)	17/06/1919	17/06/1919
Miscellaneous	Battalion Order By Major H.B. Spear Commdg 9th Bn. Gloucestershire Regt. (P)	18/06/1919	18/06/1919
Miscellaneous	9th Bn. Gloucestershire Regt. (Pioneers)	18/06/1919	18/06/1919
Miscellaneous	Battalion Order By Major H.B. Spear Commdg. 9th Bn. Gloucestershire Regt. (P)	19/06/1919	19/06/1919
Miscellaneous	Battalion Order By Major H.B. Spear Commdg. 9th Bn. Gloucestershire Regt. (P)	20/06/1919	20/06/1919
Miscellaneous	Battalion Order By Major H.B. Spear Commdg. 9th Bn. Gloucestershire Regt. (P)	21/06/1919	21/06/1919
Miscellaneous	Battalion Orders By Lieut.-Colonel J. Fane, D.S.O., Commdg. 9th Bn. Gloucestershire Regt. (Pioneers)	23/06/1919	23/06/1919
Miscellaneous	Battalion Order By Lieut.-Colonel J. Fane, D.S.O., Commdg. 9th Bn. Gloucestershire Regt. (P)	24/06/1919	24/06/1919
Miscellaneous	Battalion Order By Lieut.-Colonel J. Fane, D.S.O., Commdg. 9th Bn. Gloucestershire Regt. (P)	25/06/1919	25/06/1919

Miscellaneous	Battalion Order By Lieut.-Colonel J. Fane, D.S.O., Commdg. 9th Bn. Gloucestershire Regt. (P)	26/06/1919	26/06/1919
Miscellaneous	Battalion Order By Lieut.-Colonel J. Fane, D.S.O., Commdg. 9th Bn. Gloucestershire Regt. (P)	27/06/1919	27/06/1919
Miscellaneous	Battalion Order By Lieut.-Colonel J. Fane, D.S.O., Commdg. 9th Bn. Gloucestershire Regt. (Pioneers)	28/06/1919	28/06/1919
Miscellaneous	Battalion Order By Lieut.-Colonel J. Fane, D.S.O., Commdg. 9th Bn. Gloucestershire Regt. (Pioneers)	30/06/1919	30/06/1919
War Diary	Burschied	01/07/1919	01/07/1919
War Diary	Leichlingen	02/07/1919	31/07/1919
Miscellaneous	Battalion Order By Lieut-Colonel J. Fane D.S.O., Commdg 9th Bn. Gloucestershire Regt. (Pioneers)	01/07/1919	01/07/1919
Miscellaneous	Battalion Order By Lt,Col J. Fane D.S.O., Commdg 9th Bn. Gloucestershire Regt. (Pioneers)	02/07/1919	02/07/1919
Miscellaneous	Sports Committee Meeting		
Miscellaneous	Battalion Orders By Lieut.-Colonel J. Fane, D.S.O., Commdg. 9th Bn. Gloucestershire Regt. (Pioneers)	03/07/1919	03/07/1919
Miscellaneous	Battalion Orders By Lieut.-Colonel J. Fane, D.S.O., Commdg. 9th Bn. Gloucestershire Regt. (Pioneers)	05/07/1919	05/07/1919
Miscellaneous	Battalion Orders By Lieut.-Colonel J. Fane, D.S.O., Commdg. 9th Bn. Gloucestershire Regt. (Pioneers)	07/07/1919	07/07/1919
Miscellaneous	Battalion Orders By Lieut.-Colonel J. Fane, D.S.O., Commdg. 9th Bn. Gloucestershire Regt. (Pioneers)	09/07/1919	09/07/1919
Miscellaneous	Battalion Orders By Lieut.-Colonel J. Fane, D.S.O., Commdg. 9th Bn. Gloucestershire Regt. (Pnrs)	10/07/1919	10/07/1919
Miscellaneous	Battalion Orders By Lieut.-Colonel J. Fane, D.S.O., Commanding. 9th Bn. Gloucestershire Regt. (Pioneers)	11/07/1919	11/07/1919
Miscellaneous	Battalion Orders By Lieut.-Colonel J. Fane, D.S.O., Commdg. 9th Bn. Gloucestershire Regt. (Pioneers)	18/07/1919	18/07/1919
Miscellaneous	Battalion Orders By Lieut.-Colonel J. Fane, D.S.O., Commdg. 9th Bn. Gloucestershire Regt. (Pioneers)	14/07/1919	14/07/1919
Miscellaneous	Battalion Orders By Lieut.-Colonel J. Fane, D.S.O., Commdg. 9th Bn. Gloucestershire Regt. (Pioneers)	15/07/1919	15/07/1919
Miscellaneous	Battalion Orders By Lieut.-Colonel J. Fane, D.S.O., Commdg. 9th Bn. Gloucestershire Regt. (Pioneers)	16/07/1919	16/07/1919
Miscellaneous	Battalion Orders By Lieut.-Colonel J. Fane, D.S.O., Commdg. 9th Bn. Gloucestershire Regt. (Pioneers)	17/07/1919	17/07/1919
Miscellaneous	Battalion Orders By Lieut.-Col. J. Fane. D.S.O., Commdg. 9th Bn. Gloucestershire Regt. (Pioneers)	16/07/1919	16/07/1919
Miscellaneous	Battalion Orders By Lieut.-Col. J. Fane. D.S.O., Commdg. 9th Bn. Gloucestershire Regt. (P)	21/07/1919	21/07/1919
Miscellaneous	Battalion Orders By Lieut.-Col. J. Fane. D.S.O., Commdg. 9th Bn. Gloucestershire Regt. (P)	22/07/1919	22/07/1919
Miscellaneous	Battalion Orders By Lieut.-Col. J. Fane. D.S.O., Commdg. 9th Bn. Gloucestershire Regt. (P)	23/07/1919	23/07/1919
Miscellaneous	Battalion Orders By Lieut.-Col. J. Fane. D.S.O., Commdg. 9th Bn. Gloucestershire Regt. (P)	24/07/1919	24/07/1919
Miscellaneous	Battalion Orders By Lieut.-Col. J. Fane. D.S.O., Commdg. 9th Bn. Gloucestershire Regt. (P)	25/07/1919	25/07/1919
Miscellaneous	Battalion Orders By Lieut.-Col. J. Fane. D.S.O., Commdg. 9th Bn. Gloucestershire Regt. (P)	26/07/1919	26/07/1919
Miscellaneous	Battalion Orders By Lieut.-Col. J. Fane. D.S.O., Commdg. 9th Bn. Gloucestershire Regt. (P)	28/07/1919	28/07/1919
Miscellaneous	Battalion Orders By Lieut.-Col. J. Fane. D.S.O., Commdg. 9th Bn. Gloucestershire Regt. (P)	29/07/1919	29/07/1919

Miscellaneous	Battalion Orders By Lieut.-Col. J. Fane. D.S.O., Commdg. 9th Bn. Gloucestershire Regt. (P)	30/07/1919	30/07/1919
Miscellaneous	Battalion Orders By Lieut.-Col. J. Fane. D.S.O., Commdg. 9th Bn. Gloucestershire Regt. (P)	31/07/1919	31/07/1919
War Diary	Leichlingen	01/08/1919	30/08/1919
Miscellaneous	Battalion Orders By Lieut.-Col. J. Fane, D.S.O., Commdg. 9th Bn. Gloucestershire Regt. (P)	01/08/1919	01/08/1919
Miscellaneous	Battalion Orders By Lieut.-Col. J. Fane, D.S.O., Commdg. 9th Bn. Gloucestershire Regt. (P)	02/08/1919	02/08/1919
Miscellaneous	Battalion Orders By Lieut.-Col. J. Fane, D.S.O., Commdg. 9th Bn. Gloucestershire Regt. (P)	05/08/1919	05/08/1919
Miscellaneous	Battalion Orders By Lieut.-Col. J. Fane, D.S.O., Commdg. 9th Bn. Gloucestershire Regt. (P)	06/08/1919	06/08/1919
Miscellaneous	Battalion Orders By Lieut.-Col. J. Fane, D.S.O., Commdg. 9th Bn. Gloucestershire Regt. (P)	07/08/1919	07/08/1919
Miscellaneous	Battalion Orders By Lieut.-Col. J. Fane, D.S.O., Commdg. 9th Bn. Gloucestershire Regt. (P)	08/08/1919	08/08/1919
Miscellaneous	Battalion Orders By Lieut.-Col. J. Fane, D.S.O., Commdg. 9th Bn. Gloucestershire Regt. (P)	09/08/1919	09/08/1919
Miscellaneous	Battalion Orders By Lieut.-Col. J. Fane, D.S.O., Commdg. 9th Bn. Gloucestershire Regt. (P)	11/08/1919	11/08/1919
Miscellaneous	Battalion Orders By Lieut.-Col. J. Fane, D.S.O., Commdg. 9th Bn. Gloucestershire Regt. (P)	12/08/1919	12/08/1919
Miscellaneous	Battalion Orders By Lieut.-Col. J. Fane, D.S.O., Commdg. 9th Bn. Gloucestershire Regt. (P)	13/08/1919	13/08/1919
Miscellaneous	Battalion Orders By Lieut.-Col. J. Fane, D.S.O., Commdg. 9th Bn. Gloucestershire Regt. (P)	14/08/1919	14/08/1919
Miscellaneous	Battalion Orders By Lieut.-Col. J. Fane, D.S.O., Commdg. 9th Bn. Gloucestershire Regt. (P)	15/08/1919	15/08/1919
Miscellaneous	Battalion Orders By Lieut.-Col. J. Fane, D.S.O., Commdg. 9th Bn. Gloucestershire Regt. (P)	16/08/1919	16/08/1919
Miscellaneous	Battalion Orders By Lieut.-Col. J. Fane, D.S.O., Commdg. 9th Bn. Gloucestershire Regt. (P)	18/08/1919	18/08/1919
Miscellaneous	Battalion Orders By Lieut.-Col. J. Fane, D.S.O., Commdg. 9th Bn. Gloucestershire Regt. (P)	19/08/1919	19/08/1919
Miscellaneous	Battalion Orders By Lieut.-Col. J. Fane, D.S.O., Commdg. 9th Bn. Gloucestershire Regt. (P)	20/08/1919	20/08/1919
Miscellaneous	Battalion Orders By Lieut.-Col. J. Fane, D.S.O., Commdg. 9th Bn. Gloucestershire Regt. (P)	21/08/1919	21/08/1919
Miscellaneous	Battalion Orders By Lieut.-Col. J. Fane, D.S.O., Commdg. 9th Bn. Gloucestershire Regt. (P)	22/08/1919	22/08/1919
Miscellaneous	Battalion Orders By Lieut.-Col. J. Fane, D.S.O., Commdg. 9th Bn. Gloucestershire Regt. (P)	23/08/1919	23/08/1919
Miscellaneous	Battalion Orders By Lieut.-Col. J. Fane, D.S.O., Commdg. 9th Bn. Gloucestershire Regt. (P)	25/08/1919	25/08/1919
Miscellaneous	Notice Aquatic Sports		
Miscellaneous	Battalion Orders By Lieut.-Col. J. Fane. D.S.O., Commdg. 9th Bn. Gloucestershire Regt. (P)	26/08/1919	26/08/1919
Miscellaneous	Battalion Orders By Lieut.-Col. J. Fane. D.S.O., Commdg. 9th Bn. Gloucestershire Regt. (P)	27/08/1919	27/08/1919
Miscellaneous	Battalion Orders By Lieut.-Col. J. Fane. D.S.O., Commdg. 9th Bn. Gloucestershire Regt. (P)	23/08/1919	23/08/1919
Miscellaneous	Battalion Orders By Lieut.-Col. J. Fane. D.S.O., Commdg. 9th Bn. Gloucestershire Regt. (P)	29/08/1919	29/08/1919
Miscellaneous	Battalion Orders By Lieut.-Col. J. Fane. D.S.O., Commdg. 9th Bn. Gloucestershire Regt. (P)	30/09/1919	30/09/1919

War Diary	Leichlingen	01/09/1919	30/09/1919
Miscellaneous	Battalion Orders By Lt. Col. J. Fane. D.S.O., Cmmg 9th Bn. Gloucester Rgt. (Pioneers)	01/09/1919	01/09/1919
Miscellaneous	Battalion Orders By Lt. Col. J. Fane. D.S.O., Cmmg 9th Bn. Gloucester Rgt. (Pioneers)	02/09/1919	02/09/1919
Miscellaneous	Battalion Orders By Major H.B. Spear Cmmg 9th Bn. Gloucester Rgt. (Pioneers)	03/09/1919	03/09/1919
Miscellaneous	Battalion Orders By Major H.B. Spear Cmmg. 9th Bn. Gloucester Rgt (Pioneers)	04/09/1919	04/09/1919
Miscellaneous	Battalion Orders By Major H.B. Spear Cmmg. 9th Bn. Gloucester Rgt (Pioneers)	03/09/1919	03/09/1919
Miscellaneous	Battalion Orders By Major H.B. Spear Cmmg. 9th Bn. Gloucester Rgt (Pioneers)	06/09/1919	06/09/1919
Miscellaneous	Battalion Orders By Major H.B. Spear Cmmg. 9th Bn. Gloucester Rgt (Pioneers)	08/09/1919	08/09/1919
Miscellaneous	Battalion Orders By Major H.B. Spear Cmmg. 9th Bn. Gloucester Rgt (Pioneers)	09/09/1919	09/09/1919
Miscellaneous	Battalion Orders By Major H.B. Spear Cmmg. 9th Bn. Gloucester Rgt (Pioneers)	10/09/1919	10/09/1919
Miscellaneous	Battalion Orders By Major H.B. Spear Cmmg. 9th Bn. Gloucester Rgt (P)	11/09/1919	11/09/1919
Miscellaneous	Battalion Orders By Major H.B. Spear Cmmg. 9th Bn. Gloucester Rgt. (Pioneers)	12/09/1919	12/09/1919
Miscellaneous	Battalion Orders By Major Spear Cmmg. 9th Bn. Gloucester Rgt. (Pioneers)	13/09/1919	13/09/1919
Miscellaneous	Battalion Orders By Major H.B. Spear Cmmg. 9th Bn. Gloucester Rgt. (Pioneers)	15/09/1919	15/09/1919
Miscellaneous	Battalion Orders By Major H.B. Spear Cmmg. 9th Bn. Gloucester Rgt. (Pioneers)	16/09/1919	16/09/1919
Miscellaneous	Battalion Orders By Major H.B. Spear Cmmg. 9th Bn. Gloucester Rgt. (P)	17/09/1919	17/09/1919
Miscellaneous	Battalion Orders By Major H.B. Spear Cmmg. 9th Bn. Gloucestershire Rgt. (P)	18/09/1919	18/09/1919
Miscellaneous	Battalion Orders By Major H.B. Spear Cmmg. 9th Bn. Gloucestershire Rgt. (P)	19/09/1919	19/09/1919
Miscellaneous	Battalion Orders By Lt. Col. J. Fane D.S.O. Cmmg. 9th Bn. Gloucester Rgt (P)	20/09/1919	20/09/1919
Miscellaneous	Battalion Orders By Lt. Colonel. J. Fane D.S.O. Cmmg. 9th Bn. Gloucester Rgt (P)	22/09/1919	22/09/1919
Miscellaneous	Battalion Orders By Lt. Colonel. J. Fane D.S.O. Cmmg. 9th Bn. Gloucester Rgt (P)	23/09/1919	23/09/1919
Miscellaneous	Battalion Orders By Lt. Col. J. Fane D.S.O. Cmmg. 9th Bn. Gloucester Rgt (P)	24/09/1919	24/09/1919
Miscellaneous	Battalion Orders By Lt. Col. J. Fane D.S.O. Cmmg. 9th Bn. Gloucester Rgt (P)	25/09/1919	25/09/1919
Miscellaneous	Battalion Orders By Lt. Col. J. Fane D.S.O. Cmmg. 9th Bn. Gloucester Rgt (P)	26/09/1919	26/09/1919
Miscellaneous	Battalion Orders By Lt. Col. J. Fane D.S.O. Cmmg. 9th Bn. Gloucester Rgt (P)	27/09/1919	27/09/1919
Miscellaneous	Battalion Orders By Lt. Col. J. Fane D.S.O. Cmmg. 9th Bn. Gloucester Rgt (P)	29/09/1919	29/09/1919
Miscellaneous	Battalion Orders By Lt. Col. J. Fane D.S.O. Cmmg. 9th Bn. Gloucester Rgt (P)	30/09/1919	30/09/1919
War Diary	Leichlingen	03/10/1919	23/10/1919
War Diary	Wiesdorf	24/10/1919	31/10/1919

WO 95/2294
29 Div
9 Bn Gloucestershire Regt (Pioneers) May 1919 – Oct 1919

RHINE ARMY
SOUTHERN DIVISION
LATE 29TH DIVISION

9TH BN GLOSTER REGT
(PIONEER BN)
MAY-OCT 1919

FROM 66 DIV
_____

MISSING

Army Form C. 2118.

WAR DIARY
or
INTELLIGENCE SUMMARY.
(Erase heading not required.)

A.f.O.
9th Gloucesters

Instructions regarding War Diaries and Intelligence Summaries are contained in F. S. Regs., Part II. and the Staff Manual respectively. Title pages will be prepared in manuscript.

1.S
38 sheets

Place	Date	Hour	Summary of Events and Information	Remarks and references to Appendices
Leichtingen Meg	1919		2nd Lt E. A. Johnson proceeded to U.K. for leave	
	2		2nd Lt R. Jones returned from leave	
	3		Lt Col White took over the duties of Transport Officer	
			2nd Lt Middleton A.P. proceeded to U.K. for leave	
			2nd Lt W.E.G. Lehon proceeded to U.K. for demobilization	
			The undermentioned officers were transferred to 2/5th Batt Gloucester Reg't	
			2nd Lt A.B.W. Bell. 2nd Lt C.C. Redden. 2nd Lt R.J. Partridge. 2nd Lt R.P. Angell. 2nd Lt V.G. Williams	
			2nd Lt K.V. Dunn. 2nd Lt A.J. Ogden. 2nd Lt P.E. Rendell. Capt A.D. White.	
	6		Lt B. Le Riche taken off strength - demobilized	
	7		4 O.R's joined the Battalion	
			Lt Col R.J. Rabra left the Battalion	
			Lt Col E. Langley joined this unit for duty	
	10		Battersea-avid returned from leave to U.K.	
	12		2nd Lt R.H. Warren proceeded on leave to U.K.	
	15		2 Platoons of "D" Coy proceeded to Berghakorde for work under C.R.E.	
			1 Platoon of "C" proceeded to Berghakorde for work under C.R.E.	
			Lt R.J. Heward returned from leave to U.K.	
	16		1 on platoon of C. Coy proceeded to London Territorial Race horse at Mucheum	
			Capt L.C. Fu Pennick proceeded to U.K. on leave	
			2nd Lt Stebbings and Lt Howard returned from leave to U.K.	
	17		Lt Col R.J. Roberts proceeded to U.K. for 2 months leave	
			2 Platoons of C. Coy proceeded to London Territorial Race horse at Mucheum	
	19		Lieut Y.C. Smith M.C. proceeded on leave to U.K.	

Army Form C. 2118.

WAR DIARY
or
INTELLIGENCE SUMMARY.
(Erase heading not required.)

Instructions regarding War Diaries and Intelligence Summaries are contained in F. S. Regs., Part II. and the Staff Manual respectively. Title pages will be prepared in manuscript.

Place	Date	Hour	Summary of Events and Information	Remarks and references to Appendices
Luchlingen	May 20		2nd Lt S. Johnson returned from leave to U.K.	
	21		Major L.B.E. Leckhaim M.C. proceeded to U.K. for duty	
	24		2nd Lt. E.E. Turner rejoined Battalion from leave in France	
	25		R.R.C. Pullen rejoined from L.R.E. house at Bladbach	
			2nd Lt. J.W. Everall rejoined from L.R.E. house at Bladbach	
			2nd Lt. N.G. Hicks rejoined from L.R.E. house at Bladbach	
			2nd Lt. W. Stansworthe rejoined from L.R.E. house at Bladbach	
	26		One Platoon of "B" Coy proceeded to join "D" Coy at Buerchied for work under the L.R.E.	
			Major H.B. Spear joined the Battalion	
	28		2nd Lt. R.W. Smiles proceeded on leave to U.K.	
	30		Lt Col. L.P. Knight proceeded on leave to U.K.	
	31		2nd Lt H.A. Hicks proceeded on leave to U.K.	
(No. 3)			The remaining Coys carried on both training and finding guards.	
			Strength of Battalion 39 Offrs 1079 O.Rs.	

H.B. Spear
MAJOR
COMDG. 5TH (S) BN GLOUCESTERSHIRE REGT

Battalion Orders.
by
Lt.Col.R.I.Rawson.
Cmmg.9th.Bn.Gloucester Rgt(Pioneers)
May 1st 1919.

567? **DUTIES.**
Bn.Orderly Officer for To morrow - - - - - 2nd Lt.G.S.Partridge.
Next for Duty - - - - - - - - - - - - - - - - " A.G.Ford.
Bn.Orderly Sgt. for tomorrow - - - - - - - - - Sgt.Johnson.
Next for Duty - - - - - - - - - - - - - - - - - - - Sgt.Shearne.

The Coy for Duty to morrow will be C Coy.

568 **PARADES.**
Coys will parade according to programme.

569. **BACK BADGES.**
The proper place for the back badge is in the centre of the Cap Band centre of the seam Coy Commanders will give this immediate attention.

570. **EDUCATION.**
2nd.Lieut.W.R.Jones will be attached to the Education Department from this date.

571. **PROMOTIONS.**
40415 Cpl.Peat and 10912 Cpl. Andrews J. to be Act/Sgt.(Prov.) from this date.
50711 L/Cpl/ H.Knowles to be acting Corporal and is transferred from A to H.Q.Coy.from this date.
242579 Pte.W.Filer to be acting paid L/Sgt .from the 27/3/19/

572. **REVERSIONS.**
Act.Paid L/Sgt.Filer reverts to private at his own request.

573. **TRANSPORT.**
Lieut.D.H.White will perform the duties of Transport Officer during the absence of 2nd.Lieut S. Johnson on leave.

574. **TRANSPORT.**
31471 Pte. Faulkner A. Coy. will be attached to the transport from this date.

575. **BATTALION ORDERS.**
In future Coy. Commanders will be held responsible that Batt. Orders are read out to their Coy's daily.

576. **PAY;**
In future the unit of Payment of troops in Germany will be 10 marks instead of 5 marks as hitherto.

577. **WATERMEN;**
    A.Coy. will detail one man.
    B.Coy. will detail one man.
    C Coy. will detail two men.
to report to the M.O. as Watermen.

578. **BATHS.**
Reference Batt. Order No.505 dated April 22nd 1919.
There will be no bathing on Fridays The baths however will be open from 1400 to 1600 hours on Monday; Tuesday, Wednesday and Thursday,and from 0830 to 1230 hours on Wednesday for bathing of Individuals or details. A bath is reserved for Sgts.and Cpl

579. **CYCLISTS.**
O.C/Coys will render to this Office by 0900 hours on the 4th. inst;a Nominal Roll of Volunteers for attachment or permanent transfer to the Army Cyclists Corps.

579a. **AMMUNITION.**
In future 3 boxes of reserve S.A.A. for Lewis Guns will be carried in the Lewis Gun Limber by each Coy.

580. **MUSKETRY.**
Attention of all ranks is called to the Rifle Meeting Notice issued to Coys. These meetings will take place on one of the 30 yards ranges during the afternoons from 1400 to 1600 hours and from 1700 to 1900 hours as often as possible and competitions will be varied. A Notice will be put in Batt. orders the day before each meeting.

581.   REVEILLE.
From this date Reveille will sound at 0600 hours.

582.   WORKING HOURS AND CORPS TRAINING ORDER.
The Corps Commander considers that Officers and other ranks
should be fully occupied except as stated in Paragraph 2.
It is most undesirable that Officers and men should have
every afternoon to themselves.
(b) The 8 hours will include
            Cleaning Time
            Stables
            Inspections
            Military Training or Work
            Education
            Recreational Training.
2. Sunday except for Church parades and Stables should be
observed as a holiday. Every opportunity is to be given to
Officers and men of all Denominations to attend their
respective Services.
(b) Saturday after Dinner will be a half Holiday.
(c) It is left to the discretion of Formation and Corps
Troop Units Commanders to have a second weekly half
holiday provided a 44 hours week's occupation is maintained
The new programme will begin from Monday 5th. May
and is to be distributed to those concerned.

583.   R.A.S.C. HORSE TRANSPORT SHORTAGE OF PERSONNEL.
There is a shortage of Horse Transport in the Army
owing to lack of reinforcements.
Nominal roll of volunteers for the above branch of the
Service either for attachment or for permanent transfer
to be submitted to Divisional Headquarters "A" in
quadruplicate by 8th. May 1919.

584.   ORDNANCE STORES.ISSUE TO OFFICERS IN AREA CORPS.
Reference to Divisional Routive Order 647 dated 26/4/19/
Issue of Ordnance Stores to Officers on repayment will be
drawn obtained from Officers Clothing Depot 10
Richarlstrasse Cologne; demands are only to be submitted
to D.A.D.O.S. when depot cannot supply.

                        (signed) G.W.Paul Capt. and Adjt.
                        9th Bn GLOUCESTER REGT.

Battalion Orders
by
Lieut Col. R.I. RAWSON
Cmmg., 9th. BN. Gloucester Rgt.
May 2nd. 1919.

585. **DUTIES.**
Bn. Orderly Officer for Tomorrow- - - - - Lt.K.G.Hxxx. Hicks.
Next for Duty -t - - - - - - - - - - - - - - - - 2nd -Lt.O. Pilcher.
Bn. Orderly Sgt. for to morrow. - - - - - - - Sgt. Shearne.
Next for Duty- - - - - - - - - - - - - - - - - - Sgt.Xxxxx. Andrews.

Coy for Duty to morrow will be A. Coy.

From Sunday next the 4th.inst the Battalion Duties will be carried out by Coy's weekly commencing with A.Coy.

586. **PARADES.**
Coy's will parade as strong as possible on the recreation Ground at 0900 hours to morrow. They will form up in Mass facing South. Dress :- Musketry Order.

587. **PROMOTIONS.**
No.267323 Lance Cpl.Broughton F. to be A/Cpl. (Prov)° from this date.

588. **MUSKETRY ETC.-RETURN.**
O.C.Coy's and Lewis Gun Officer will render a Weekly Return of the number of rounds expended by 0900 hours on Sundays to the Batt. Musketry Officer.
All empty Cases will be returned to the Q/M. Stores at the same time.

589. **RANGE PRACTICE.**
All Coy's will fire a grouping practice next week. A. and B. Coy's on Monday 5/5/19. C.Coy. on Tuesday 6/5/19. on A Coy. range. Coy. Commanders will ensure that every possible man fires this practice. Coy. Commanders will keep a record of results obtained.

(Signed) J. Paul. Capt. and Adjt.
9th.BN .GLOUCESTER RGT.(PIONEERS).

590. **AFTER ORDER.**

WORKING PAY.
No. 50893 Pte. W. Evans, and 53698 Pte. S. Ireland have qualified as efficient Shoeing-smiths (22/4/19) (Board of Officers held by order of the G.O.C. Southern Division, 22/4/19.) entitled to 6d per diem working pay from hat date.

Reference Battn. Order No. 586 (above) Markers will report to the R.S.M. at 0845 hrs. to-morrow.

Battalion Orders
by
Lt.Col.R.I.RAWSON.
Cmmg. 9th BN Gloucester Regt.
May 3rd. 1919.

---

590. DUTIES.

Bn.Orderly Officer for to-morrow - - - - - 2nd Lt. E.O.Pilcher.
Next for Duty - - - - - - - - - - - - - - - " " E.C.Turner.
Bn Orderly Sgt. for To-morrow. - - - - - - Sgt. Andrews
Next for Duty -, - - - - - - - - - - - - - " Green.

Coy. for Duty to morrow will be A Coy.
" " " on Monday " " A Coy.

591. PARADES.

Divine Service.:- The battalion will parade in Drill Order, formed up in line facing West, on the Road leading to the Recreation Ground, at 11,15 hrs. to-morrow, for Church of England Service, which will be held in the Protestant Church, LEICHLINGEN, at 11,30 hrs., followed by Holy Communion for all who wish to attend.
Roman Catholic Service will be held in the R.C Church, LEICHLINGEN, 10,00 hrs.
Non-Conformist Service will be held in the Recreation Room at 11-15 hrs.

592. CASH.

All requisitions for cash, and Officers' Advance of Pay books will be sent to Orderly Room by 09,00 hrs. on Monday 5th. inst.
2/Lieut. R.H.Warren, MC,MM, is detailed to draw same from the Field Cashier.

593. OFFICERS.

The following Officers having proceeded to join the 2/5th. Bn. Gloucestershire Regt. are struck off strength as from 3/5/19.

Capt. C.S.White.   Lieut. A.G.Ford.
2/Lieut. A.E.W.Bolt.   2/Lieut. E.W.Goddard.
2/Lieut. G.S.Partridge.   2/Lieut. N.P.Angell.
2/Lieut. S.E.Williams.   2/Lieut. C.L.Sims.
2/Lieut. A.T.Ogden.   2/Lieut. P.E.Rendell.

OFFICERS contd.
The undermentioned Officer having proceeded to U.K. for demobilisation is struck off strength as from 3/5/19.
    2/Lieut. S.O.A. Collins.

REGIMENTAL STORES. - A.B.TRAILER OF MY OFFICERS AND OTHER RANKS.
A.R.O. No. 861 is Published for Information.
It has been ruled by Higher Authority that permission cannot be given for the retention, on payment, of articles supplied as Regimental Equipment of Units.

                                    (Sgd) C.J. PAUL, Capt. & Adjt.,
                                    8th. Bn. Gloucestershire Regiment.

NOTICE.

The battalion will play No. 3. General Hospital at Football to-morrow the 4th. inst; on the Batth. ground.
Kick-off 14-30 hrs.

BATTN ORDER.

Coy's will parade on Monday under Company arrangements according to programme.

Battalion Orders
by
Lt.Col R.I.RAWSON.
Comg.5th.Bn.Gloucester Rgt.
May 9th.1919.

595. DUTIES.
Batt.Orderly Officer for tomorrow--------------- 2ndLieut T.W.Overall.
Next for Duty--------------------------------- 2ndLieut. W.J.Noah.
Bn.Orderly Sgt.for to morrow------------------ Sgt.Dunn.
Next for Duty--------------------------------- Sgt.Snewyn.

The Coy for duty to morrow will be A Coy.

596. PARADES.
Coy's will parade according to programme.

597. PAY. DRUMMERS.
A DRUMMER'S pay if he is over 18 years of age will only differ from that of an ordinary private when the minimum rate is forfeited under Para.4 of A.C.I.s or A.O.I. of 1918 in which case it should be assessed at 1/1 per diem in lieu of 1/-per diem

598 IRON RATIONS.
The number of iron rations indented for by Coy's will shortly be issued. Any deficiency now discovered will be charged against the Coy.responsible ,who will deal with the individuals concerned.

599. REQUISITIONS. GENERAL PRINCIPALS.
Extract from G.H.Q.3704 dated May 1st.1919.
As a guide to what may,and what may not be requisitioned the following are quoted :-
1. Services and stores which cannot be requisitioned.
(a) All foodstuffs and forage except Greenstuffs.
(b) Railway Material or Railway Premises.
(c) Household furniture,except essentials for messes as laid down in D.of W.Circular 74.
(d) Articles for social Entertainments.
(e) Golf Courses,Polo Courses, Tennis Courts.
2. Services and stores which can be requisitioned.
(a) Billets and accomodation generally .This covers the provision and erection of all necessary Military Buildings and works in connection with RANGES ,and Manoeuvre Grounds;including Roads paths,water supply drainage ,lighting telephone,and telegraph circuits.
(b) Hotels with German Personnel ,when required as offices.
(c) Officers and other messes.
(d) All military stores except as mentioned in Para.II (l) and accommodation for these stores.
(e) Laundries and their German Personnel.
(f) Equipment for messes and cookhouses as laid down in D.of W. Circular 74 and the maintenance of this equipment.
(g) Recreation,including educational grounds,to a reasonable but the approval of G.H.Q. will first be obtained .
Such ground to be equally at the disposal of Officers, N.C.O.s and men. All improvements,repairs and upkeep willbe done with Military labour ,and the necessary tools; labour etc.will be obtained from the M.B.
(h) Land for Agricultural Training up to the maximum of 3 acres per Battalion ,or proportionately,according to strength of Unit. Where possible land not under cultivation may be used .

PROCEDURE OF REQUISITION.
(I) For stores.
A.F.W.3787 ,made out in duplicate ,will be used. Originals will be served on Civil Authority ,stating time and place of delivery duplicates retained.
(bb) On receipt of stores A.F.W.3858 will be made out in triplicate giving particulars of stores,date of receipt,name of supplier; Town or Area;signed by receiving Officer. Original will be given to the Civil Authority in exchange for Stores .
Duplicate with name of Unit to be sent to Branch Requisition Officer G.H.Q. Triplicates to be retained by Receiving officer.

- 2 -

Duplicate with name of Unit to be sent to Branch Requisition Officer, G.H.Q. Triplicate to be retained by Receiving Officer

2. <u>For Land & Buildings</u>.
   (a) To be made through Town Major or Area Commandant.
   (b) To be made out on A.F.W.3856, in triplicate, stating time when required, and particulars of land or building. Original to be retained by German civil authorities. Duplicate and triplicate copies to be retained by Officer demanding.
   (c) Officers demanding will, except for public or government properties, keep a record of the address and period of occupation for all properties; for land; the area occupied; for offices; the average number of rooms occupied; for depots the floor space; for billets, the average number of men and horses accommodated weekly.
   (d) At termination of occupation, a summary of this record, with a note of any damage caused in excess of fair wear and tear, will be endorsed by O.C. Unit on the remaining two copies of A.F.W.3856, and forwarded to B.R.O., G.H.Q.

3. (a) All Requisitions will be made on German civil authorities, and not on individuals, except in cases of failure of civil authorities to supply. On no account will any promises as to payment be made.
   (b) Requisitions should only be made on the civil authorities of the zone in which the unit is stationed; the civil authorities may obtain the goods outside their area, if not available within, by arrangements between authorities concerned.
   (c) The German Military authorities will render monthly, on the 15th. of each month, a return to the Military Governor shewing all requisitions with dates and amounts of payment.
   (d) All Requisitions to bear the Official stamp of the requisitioning authority and to state clearly the name of Unit and address at which delivery is required.

4. (a) Damage caused in excess of fair wear and tear will be payable by the Unit. Anything Requisitioned in contravention of these orders will be charged against the Unit or individual who has made the requisition.

This G.R.O. cancels all A.R.O's and instructions issued by these Headquarters, on the subject of requisitions.

600. <u>RIFLE MEETING</u>.
A Rifle Meeting will take place to-morrow on "A" Coy'. range from 1400 hrs. to 1800 hrs. A & C Coys' on "A" Range; B Coy. on "B" range. The following practice will be fired :-
   5 Rounds Application.
   5 " Snapshooting.
1 Mark for 5 rounds will be charged,- money to be divided amongst the winners.

601. <u>S.A.A. RETURN</u>.
Coys' will render <u>to Musketry Officer</u> by 1800 hrs; on Wednesday, weekly the following returns :-
1. Pouch S.A.A. held on charge.
2. Pistol S.A.A. held on charge.
3. The above will include all S.A.A. for Lewis Guns and reserve.
   Cause for weekly increase or decrease will be stated.
All Returns in connection with S.A.A. or Musketry will be rendered to the Musketry Officer.

<u>ADDITION TO BN. ORDER NO. 596. - PARADES</u>.
In future Tuesdays and Fridays will be devoted to Musketry by the Companies not on duty, and Wednesdays from 1400 hrs. to 1800 hrs. for compulsory training.

(Sgd) G.J.PAUL, Capt. & Adjt.,
9th. Bn. Gloucestershire Regt.

Batt. Orders
by
Lt. Col. R.I. RAWSON.
Cmmg. 9TH. BN. GLOUCESTER RGT.
May 5th. 1919.

602. DUTIES.
Bn. Orderly Officer for tomorrow - - - - - - - - - 2nd Lieut W.J. Noah.
Next for duty - - - - - - - - - - - - - - - - - - - "   " W. Pomment.
Bn. Orderly Sgt. for tomorrow - - - - - - - - Sgt. Shearn
Next for duty - - - - - - - - - - - - - - - - - - Sgt. Wharton.

The Coy. for duty tomorrow will be A Coy.

603. PARADES.
The Battalion will parade tomorrow for C.O.s inspection on the Recreation Ground in Mass facing West at 0900 hours (According to plan issued for G.O.C. Inspection) DRESS:-
Marching Order less Pack and Steel Helmet.
Coy's as strong as possible. Other ranks attached to other Coys will parade with their own Coys.

In future the two coys not on duty will have all employed other ranks at their disposal one day each week.
This week Tuesday is allotted to B. Coy.
   "   "   Friday   "   "   " C. Coy.
Additional Bn. Order 556 5/5/19 is cancelled.

604. RHINE ARMY LETTER (O.A? 69 DATED MAY 5TH.)
The attention of all ranks is drawn to British Army of the Rhine Letter O.A.69 of May 5th. a copy of which is being sent to each Coy. This letter is to be posted conspicuously on every Coy. Notice Board at once.

605. RATIONS FOR LEAVE MEN.
G.R.O. 2713 is published for information::
All leave are now fitted with Truck Kitchens and all arrangements including Halte Repas are in order for feeding personnel during the journey to and from Base Ports. Only sufficient rations for the period between the time of departure from the Unit and the time for boarding the leave train will therefore be issued to personnel proceeding on leave.
G.R.O. (France) 6046 will be amended accordingly.

606. PROMOTIONS.
No.203193 L/Sgt. Beast J. promoted   A/Sgt.   27/3/19.
No.285619 Pte. Thomas B.   "   "   27/3/19.
No.44681 Pte. Inwood C.   "   "   27/3/19.
No.34569 Cpl. Bashford H. appointed A/L/Sgt. 22/3/19.
No.50857 Cpl. Wharton W.   "   "   22/3/19.
No.280174 Pte. Brooker W.   "   "   4/4/19.
No.29881? L/C   Sleeman A.   "   "   27/3/19.
No.50438 L/C. Stagg   H. promoted   A/Cpl.   19/3/19.
No.205750 L/C. Smith   C.   "   "   27/3/19.
No.252550 Pte. Webber F.   "   "   27/3/19.
No.31645 Pte. Baldwin W.   "   "   27/3/19.
No.240455 Sgt. Hardiman G.   "   A/C.Q.M.S. 2/4/19.

The above are provisional until approved.

607. REVERSIONS
No.50823 L/C. Carter G. reverts to private at his own request from this date.

608. TRANSFERS.
No.32683 L/C. Slater G. is transferred from B. to H.Q. Coy.
No.41119 Pte. Pettitt J. "   "   "   H.Q. to C. "

signed R.D. Heppenstall; A/Adjt.

9th. Bn. GLOUCESTER RGT.

Battalion Orders by
Lt-Colonel C. SMYLY,
Commdg. 5th Bn. Gloucestershire Regt.
May 7th. 1919.

---

008. DUTIES.
Bn. Orderly Officer for to-morrow - - - 2/Lieut. W. Ament.
Next for duty- - - - - - - - - - - - - 2/Lieut. W. Watson.

Bn. Orderly Sergeant for to-morrow - - Sgt. Wharton.
Next for duty - - - - - - - - - - - - Sgt. Andrews.

The Coy. for duty to-morrow will be "A" Coy.

010. TRAINING.
Coy's will parade according to programme.

011. TRAINING. - NOT TO BE CARRIED OUT ON RAILWAY LINES.
On a recent occasion a party of Signallers who were carrying out training on a railway line laid a temporary telephone wire which happened to connect together with two railway signal wires and put the electric signal control system out of order.
It is forbidden to use permanent way or railway premises for training purposes.

012. DRESS.
Waterproof sheets, rolled and attached to the back of the waistbelt, will always be worn in Drill Order.

013. LEAVE.
The attention of all ranks is drawn to the instructions regarding leave which were forwarded to companies to-day.
A copy of these instructions should be posted up on Coy. Notice Boards.

014. AMMUNITION. - CARRYING OF S.A.A.
The practice of carrying S.A.A. in canvas bandoliers is to cease forthwith. Men armed with rifles will carry ammunition either in leather bandoliers (in the case of Units issued therewith) or in the pouches provided for this purpose (in the case of Units not issued with bandoliers)

015. PROMOTIONS.
The undermentioned N.C.O.s are appointed Paid Acting Sergeants from 28/4/19, whilst performing the duties of Assistant Educational Instructors.
     28007 L/Cpl. Starkings, C. "C" Coy.
     60385 " Coulson, R. "C" Coy.

016. COY. DUTIES.
No. 30770 L/Cpl. Powell, B. "B" Coy. to be struck off all Coy. duties whilst in charge of Agricultural work.

017. TRANSFERS.
The undermentioned O.R's to be transferred to Coy's as stated, and struck off strength of H.Q. Coy.
202080 Pte Berrington, H. (B) 28850 Pte Burgess, F. (A)
48066 " Brindle, R. (A) 60180 " Dorchester, H. (A)
" Jones, J.L. (C) " Burgess, H. (B)
60351   60779
60455 " Berrett, G. (C) 60839 " Fishman, A. (C)
60208 " Cox, V. (B) 60007 " Clark, F. (A)
60454 " Kimberley, A. (C) 27109 " Lloyd, B. (A)

018. CARDIGAN JACKETS.
Cardigan Jackets will, in future, not be worn outside the trousers.

019. WORSTED SHOULDER TITLES.
All worsted shoulder titles to be returned to the Q.M. Stores at once.

020. **DIVISIONAL COMPETITION.**
It is proposed to hold a Divisional Competition to select the best platoon in the Division for prizes which will be presented by the Divisional Commander.
    The following suggestions have been made.
The events in the competition to be football, cricket, boxing, cross country running, and a musketry ~~xxxxxxxxx~~ event on the lines of the A.R.A. platoon competition.

(Sgd) G.J. PAUL, Capt. & Adjt.,
8th. Bn. Gloucestershire Regiment.

BATTALION ORDERS.
by
Lt.Col. P.F. Smyly.
Commg. 7th. Bn. GLOUCESTER REGT. (PIONEERS).

May 8th. 1919.

631. DUTIES.
Orderly officer for tomorrow. - - - - 2/Lieut. G. Jetson.
Next for Duty - - - - - - - - - - - - " " D.E. Wensman.
Orderly Sgt. for Tomorrow - - - - - - Sgt. _____
Next for Duty - - - - - - - - - - - - Sgt. Bassett

The Coy. for Duty to morrow will be A. Coy.

632. PARADES.
Coy's will parade according to programme.

633. COMMAND.
Lieut.Col. P.F. Smyly, assumed command of the Battalion vice
Lieut.Col. R.I. Gascon from the 7th .inst.

634. STRENGTH DECREASE.
Lieut. A.E.J.M. MINDER having been demobilised in England is
Struck of the strength of this Battalion as from 7/5/19.

635. TRANSFERS.
The following officers and N.C.O.s acting as Educational
Instructors are transferred to H.Q.Coy. as from this date.
    2ndLieut. H.E. Warren transferred to H.Q. Coy.
      "   "   L.G. Holloway   "   "   "   "
      "   "   P.J. Hancox   "   "   "   "
      "   "   H.R. Jones   "   "   "   "

    81673 Sgt. Dunshy A.H.   "   "   "   "
    46681 " Inwood C.   "   "   "   "
    39387 " Starxings C.   "   "   "   "
    28519 " Thomas   "   "   "   "
    60365 " Coulson R.   "   "   "   "

                           Sgd. J.G. PAUL. Capt. and Adjt.
                           7th. Bn. GLOUCESTER REGT. (PIONEERS).

W.D

BATTALION ORDERS
by
Lt.Col.F.P.Smyly
CMMG.9TH.BN.GLOUCESTER RGT.(PIONEERS).   May 9th 1919.

626. **DUTIES.**
Bn.Orderly Officer for to morrow - - - - - - 2/Lt.E.E.Bresman.
Next for duty - - - - - - - - - - - - - - - - "   E.C.Turner.
Bn.Orderly Sgt. for to morrow - - - - - - - Sgt. Bassett.
Next for Duty - - - - - - - - - - - - - - - Sgt. Dymond.

The Coy. for duty to morrow will be A Coy.

627. **PARADES.**
The Battalion will parade for C.O.s inspection on the Recreation Ground in mass facing West at 0900 hours.
Dress:- Full Marching Order,less Packs and Steel Helmets
~~Markers and~~ *on markers parties* H.Q. ~~Coy~~. to report to R.S.M. on parade Ground at 0845 hours.
Officers will wear Sam Browne Belts; Compasses on left side; Revolver and Field Glasses on right,and Box Respirator.

628. **COURSE. FIELD ENGINEERING.**
The undermentioned officers will proceed on the IIth inst to Berg Gladbach where they will report to Capt. J.Robertson R.E. at the Mariensal by 1800 hours, to attend a course of instruction in Field Engineering.
   Lt G.F.Pullen   2/Lieut .H.G.Hicks.
   2/Lt. W.Francombe   2/Lieut. T.W.Everall.
One Batman for two officers will be taken.
Each Officer should be in possession of the following;-
Manual of Field Engineering.   Pencil and Rubber.
Red and Blue Chalk Pencil.   A.B.152
Ruler marked in inches.   S.S.177(instructions on Wiring).
Latest edition of 'Notes on Trench Warfare for Infantry Officers.

629. **SIGNALLERS.**
10 Volunteers are required by the Battalion to be trained as Signallers. O.C. Coy's will submit to this office by noon on the 11th. Inst. Nominal Roll of men of their Coy's who wish to be so trained.

630. **CONDUCT SHEETS.**
In future A.F.B.122 will be entered up in this office immediately after C.O.s orders and checked by the Adjutant.
Minor Offences will be checked on Saturdays at 1100 hours.
Battalion *order* No.542 dated April 28th.is cancelled.

631. **PROMOTIONS.**
No.57051 Cpl.Jones R. C.Coy. is promoted A/Sgt. provisionally from this date.

632. **DRESS.**
In all cases where men are in possession of 2 suits of Service Dress ,Unit Commanders will ensure that one suit is retained for Ceremonial Parades ,inspections and"Walking out" the other being used for drill parades and ordinary wear.
D.R.O.678 published for information.

633. **BONUS UNDER ARMY ORDER 54 (ARMY ORDER XIII DATED 29TH JAN.1919.)**
D.R.O. 682 published for information.
All officers who volunteered for the Army of Occupation and who are subsequently permitted to withdraw their names thereby forfeit their right to receive a bonus under A.O.54 of Feb.1919. Any payments already made such officers in this connection will be recovered by Army Agents who will receive the necessary Notification from the Comm-and PayMaster.
Unit Commanders will inform the Command Paymaster as to the dates on which the Officer became entitled to draw the bonus and the authority under which he has been permitted to withdraw.
The attention of all officers wishing to withdraw their names will be directed to this order and the fact that this has been done will be stated by each Officer in his application.
Authority:-Rhine Army No.A/83/5(O).

634   GUARDS.
D.R.O.673 is published for information.
When Guards turn out to General Officers the Bugler will sound the short Salute only i.e. the salute used when changing Guard.

NOTICE.

A Wet Canteen has been established in H.Q. Coy Dining Room. The draught Beer at present supplied is stated to be double the strength now sold in German Cafés and Hotels.
The Canteen will be open from 6 to 9 p.m. daily as long as the supply of beer lasts.
A quarter of a litre glass costs 20 pfennigs.

sgd. R.D. Heppenstall for Adjt.

9TH. BN. GLOUCESTER RGT. (PIONEERS).

BATTALION ORDERS   May 10th. 1919.

By Lieut-Colonel P.J. SEYLX,
Commdg. 9th. Bn. Gloucestershire Regt.

635. DUTIES.
Battn. Orderly Officer for to-morrow - - - 2/Lieut. E.C. Turner.
" " " " Monday - - - - 2/Lieut. E.O. Pilcher.
Next for duty - - - - - - - - - - - - Lieut. L.F.S. Peacock.

Battn. Orderly Sergeant for to-morrow - - Sgt. Dymond.
" " " " Monday - - - Sgt. Kelly.
Next for duty - - - - - - - - - - - - Sgt. Underwood.

The Coy. for duty next week will be "B" Coy.

636. WORKSHOPS.
The Battalion Workshops will be allotted to "A" Coy. on Monday.

637. PARADES.
Divine Service:- The Battalion will parade in Drill Order, formed up in line facing West, on the Road leading to the Recreation Ground, at 11-15 hrs. to-morrow, for Church of England Service, which will be held in the Protestant Church, LAICHLINGEN, at 11-30 hrs., followed by Holy Communion for all who wish to attend.
Roman Catholic Service will be held in the R.C. Church, LAICHLINGEN, at 10-00 hrs.
Non-Conformist Service will be held in the Recreation Room at 11-00 hrs.

638. PARADES FOR MONDAY.
Coy's will parade according to programme.

639. CASH.
All requisitions for cash, and Officers Advance of Pay books, will be sent to Orderly Room by 0900 hrs. on Monday the 12th. inst.
2/Lieut. X.X. XxxXxxxx. X.X. is detailed to draw same from the Field Cashier. W. Pamment.

640. 1914 & 1915 STAR.
O's C. Coy's will render to the Q.M. by 0900 hrs. on the 14th. inst. a Nominal Roll of Officers and Other Ranks who are entitled to the 1914 or 1915 Star.

641. TRANSFERS.
2/Lieut. H.C. Hicks is transferred from "A" Coy. to "D" Coy. from the 8th. inst.
The undermentioned Signallers, at present attached to "H.Q." Coy. are posted to "H.Q." Coy. from this date, and appointed H.Q. and Coy. signallers:-

25114 Pte. Pillinger R. ("A" Coy)   Appd. H.Q. Signaller.
27765 "   Bishop   A. ("A" ")   "   H.Q.   "
27276 "   Shennon   J. ("B" ")   "   H.Q.   "
24577 "   Pope   G.J ("B" ")   "   "B" Coy.   "
37522 "   Ball   F.J ("C" ")   "   "C" "   "
38515 "   Carter   G.H ("C" ")   "   "C" "   "

642. PROMOTIONS.
50666 L/Cpl. Morton, F; is appointed Paid Act. Cpl. from 8/5/19, vice 67091 Cpl. Jones, R.

643. REGISTERED LETTERS.
In future the Registered Letter book will be examined daily by the Adjutant, and letters not delivered will be handed over to him for safe keeping.

(Sgd) G.J. Paul, Capt. & Adjt.,
9th. Bn. Gloucestershire Regiment.

BATTALION ORDERS
BY
LT. COL. F.P. SMYLY.
Cmng. 9th. Bn. GLOUCESTER RGT. (PIONEERS).

May 12th 1919.

644. DUTIES.
Bn. Orderly Officer for to-morrow - - - - Lieut. E.F.L. Peacock.
Next for duty - - - - - - - - - - - - - - 2/Lieut. W.J. Noah, M.M.

Bn. Orderly Sergeant for to-morrow - - - Sgt. Underwood.
Next for duty - - - - - - - - - - - - - - Sgt. ~~Brooker~~ Sleeman

The Coy. for duty to-morrow will be "B" Coy.

645. PARADES.
Coy's will parade according to programme.

646. BOUNDS.
Until further orders the village of ROTHENBERG is placed out of bounds to all ranks.

647. COLOGNE - PARIS EXPRESS.
G.H.Q. No. 2740 is published for information.
An Express train is now running between COLOGNE & PARIS as follows :-

Cologne	Depart	1408 hrs.	Paris	Depart	2135 hrs.
Duren	"	1505 "	Herbesthal	Arr	1105 "
Aix-le-Chapelle	"	1552 "	Aix-le-Chapelle	arr.	1147 hrs.
Herbesthal	"	1640 "	Duren	"	1230 "
Paris	Arrive	0840 "	Cologne	"	1321 "

The following accommodation is reserved for the British Army of the Rhine :-
    8 First class seats (on some trains this may be 12 seats)
    24 Second " "
    48 Third " "
    8 Sleeping berths at a charge of 48 Francs which is in
      addition to the ordinary fares.
Applications for this accommodation will be made to A.D.R.T. British Army of the Rhine (Telephone address :- Traffic Rhine Army) and the seats and sleeping berths will be allotted by him in the order in which applications are received until all the places are booked. Applicants are therefore recommended to apply in good time, at least 48 hrs. notice is necessary in the case of sleeping berths.
No accommodation in the train will be available unless it has been definitely booked beforehand.

648. LEAVE.
All men proceeding on leave will, in future, proceed to OPLADEN on the day prior to the date of departure from COLOGNE by train.
In future passes will be issued at 1400 hrs from battalion Orderly Room starting from to-morrow, and the men will proceed to OPLADEN by the 1619 hrs. train where they will stay for the night.

649. TEA.
In future tea will be at 1700 hrs.

650. INSPECTION.
All available Sergeants will parade under the R.S.M. at 0915 hrs. to-morrow for inspection by the Adjutant.

651. BATHS.
Battalion orders No. 505 & 578, are cancelled. Baths are allotted to Coy's as under.
    Monday 1400 to 1800 hrs. "A" Coy.
    Tuesday 1400 to 1800 " "B" "
    Wednesday 1400 to 1800 hrs. "C" "
"H.Q." Coy. on Monday, Tuesday, & Wednesday from 1130 hrs; to 1230 hrs.

652. **RIFLE MEETING.**
A Rifle Meeting will be held on "A" Coys' range to-morrow the 13th. inst. from 1400 hrs. to 1600 hrs.
Competitions :-
  10 rounds rapid.   45 Seconds allowed.
  5 rounds Snap shooting.
Later a Company Officers' shoot will also take place.
1 Mark for 5 rounds will be charged, - money to be divided amongst the winners.

653. **PUTTEES**
In future puttees will not be crossed.   O's C. Coy's will ensure that this order is carried out.

(Sgd) G.J. PAUL, Capt. & Adjt.,
5th. Bn. Gloucestershire Regiment.

NOTICE.

=o=o=o=o=o=o=o=o=o=o=o=o=o=o=o=o=

SPORTS SUBSCRIPTION.
+o+o+o+o+o+o+o+o+o+

The above subscription is still being kept open to enable those who have not already had an opportunity of doing so to place their names on the list of subscribers.   The following amounts already received are herewith acknowledged :-

"A" Coy.	Marks.	"B" Coy.	Marks.
No. 1, Platoon	121	No. 5, Platoon	54
2, "	71	6, "	40-50
3, "	200	7, "	33
4, "	90	8, "	61
Coy. H.Q.	25	Coy. H.Q.	18
Officers	120	Officers	100
	625		315-50
"C" Coy.		H.Q. Coy.	
No. 9, Platoon	82)	No. 1, Platoon	36-60
on account	61)		
10, Platoon	340	2, "	38
11, "	125	3, "	29
12, "	115	4, "	17
Coy. H.Q.	36		
Officers	70		
	750		120-60

Grand total up to 12-5-19.   ===   1832-10 Marks.

=o=o=o=o=o=o=o=o=o=o=   =o=o=o=o=o=o=o=o=o=o=o=o=o=

Lt.Col.R.P.SMYLY.
COMMANDING 9TH.BN.GLOUCESTER REGT.   MAY 13th.1919.

654. DUTIES.
Bn.Orderly Officer for to-morrow------------------2/Lt.W.J.Noah.M.M.
Next for duty------------------------------------   "   G.Watson.

Bn.Orderly Sergeant for to-morrow-----------------Sgt. Sleeman.
Next for duty------------------------------------   "   Dymond.

The Coy. for duty to-morrow will be "B" Coy.

655. Parades.
Coy's will parade under Coy. arrangements.

All L/Sgts. and full Cpls. not on duty will parade at 0915 hours
under the R.S.M. for the Adjutants Inspection till 1100hrs. and
all L/Cpls. from 1115hrs. till 1215 hrs.

656. POSTINGS.
Pte.Harris (number to be given later) is posted to "A" Coy.
from the 12th.inst.

657. Signallers.
Batt. Order 641 of May 10th. should read Privates Pope C.J. Ball F.J.
and Carter C.H. appointed H.Q. Coy.
The following men will be attached to H.Q. Coy. from this date to be
trained as signallers:-
    42134 Pte.E.Venables.   "A" Coy. att. H.Q. Coy.
    27169 " P.Lloyd.   "A" "   "   "   "   "
    50597 " P.Banthope.   "B" "   "   "   "   "
    50838 " G.H.Wesley.   "B" "   "   "   "   "

(sgd.)   G.J.PAUL.   Capt. and Adjt.
                            9TH.BN.GLOUCESTER REGT.(PIONEERS)

BATTALION ORDERS.
BY
LT.COL. W.F. BAYLY,
O.C.9TH. BN. GLOUCESTER REGT. (PIONEERS).   MAY 14TH.1919.

658. DUTIES.
Bn.Orderly Officer for To Morrow. - - - - 2nd .Lieut G.Watson.
Next for Duty - - - - - - - - - - - - - - - - " " G.E.Brennan.
Bn.Orderly Sgt. for tomorrow - - - - - - Sgt.Dymond.
Next for Duty - - - - - - - - - - - - - - " Peat.

The Coy. for Duty tomorrow will be "B" Coy.

659 PARADES.
One Platoon of "A" Coy. and B. and C. Coy's will parade according to programme.

660 MOVE.
Two Platoons of "A" Coy with ALL Coy. Transport will report to the C.R.E's Office at BURSCHEID at 1100 hours tomorrow the 15th. inst.   Blankets and the unexpended portion of the Day's rations and rations for the following day to be taken.
This Party will move off at 0820 hours.
One Platoon of "A" Coy will proceed to BERG GLADBACH by train leaving LEICHLINGEN at 1045 hours tomorrow the 15th. inst.
They will report to Lieut. Miller R.E. at the RATHAUS? BERG GLADBACH. with rations as above.
The Remaining platoon will report to the C.R.E.s Office Burscheid at 1200 hours on Saturday the 17th. inst with rations as above .All accomodation will be provided by C.R.E.

661 LECTURES.
A lecture on India ,her peoples,faiths, and industries,illustrated by Lantern Slides and Cinematograph Films will be given by Mr.Pringle of the Y.M.C.A.in the Metropole Cinema Theatre tomorrow the 15th. inst .at 1430 hours.
Coys will attend this lecture as strong as possible.

The Divisional Commander wishes full advantage to be taken of all lectures whether in the morning or afternoon ,these lectures will therefore be attended as strong as possible.
A suitable officer will always be detailed to introduce the lecturer to the Audience.

662 BRITISH EMPIRE LEAVE CLUB.
D.R.O.695 is published for information.
The following will be brought to the notice of all concerned.
THE BRITISH ARMY LEAVE CLUB WAS OPENED ON Monday the 12th. inst. at 5 LANGGASSE, COLOGNE; and the daily entertainments are as follows:-
MONDAYS, Practice Dance in the Club Theatre from 6-30 to 9 p.m.
TUESDAYS. CONCERT AT 7 p.m.
WEDNESDAYS Dance for the men in the Club Theatre from 6-30 to 9;p.m
THURSDAYS. Whist Drive from 6-30 to 9 p.m.
SATURDAYS, Dance for men in the Club Theatre from 6-30 to 9 p.m.
All the above are free entertainments.
Daily from 2-30 to 5-30 p.m. there will be a CINEMA in the CLUB THEATRE ,for which the Tickets are One and Two Marks.

663. PROMOTIONS.
20045 Sgt.A.Thearne promoted to C.S.M. vice Heapkin.
50680 " A.Green   "   " A/C.S.M. " Standen.
202497 Cpl.T.Holbrook "   " A/Sgt.   " Thearne.
23351 L/Sgt L.Sloeman "   " A/Sgt.   " Green.
202254 L/C. Kallimore "   " A/Cpl.   " Holbrook.
33209 " Polton   "   "   "   " Sloeman.
21347 " D.Nutt.   "   " P/L/C.
50899 " L.Bennett   "   "   "   "
50756 " Ronsell   "   " Unp/L/C.
51922 " Lavery   "   "   "

664. ATTACHMENTS.
The following men will be attached to H.Q.Coy.from tomorrow the 15
50392 Pte .Worley H. from C. Coy. 204365 Pte.Bright B. "A" Coy
50506 " Clements T."A. " 25351 " Harley H. "   "
50899 " A.Whittard.

(sgd)C.J.PAUL

BATTALION ORDERS. May 15th, 1919.
by Lieut-Colonel F.P.SMYLY,
Commdg. 9th. Bn. Gloucestershire Regt.

665. **DUTIES.**
Bn. Orderly Officer for to-morrow ------ 2/Lieut. E.E. Bresnen.
Next for duty ---------------------- Lieut. E.F.E. Peacock.
Bn. Orderly Sergeant for to-morrow ----- Sgt. Boast.
Next for duty --------------------- " Bashford.

The Coy. for duty to-morrow will be "B" Coy.

666. **PARADES.**
Remainder of the Battalion will parade to-morrow according to programme.

667. **TRAINING.**
Section and Platoon training will commence on May 17th.
Company training will commence about June 18th.

668. **MOVE.**
Two platoons of "C" Coy., as detailed, will parade to-morrow the 16th. inst. at 0800 hrs. armed and equipped, and will proceed by Motor Lorry to the London Divisional Racecourse at Merheim where they will report at 1200 hrs. to Capt. Mill.
One lorry, with loading party, will proceed to D.A.D.O.S. to pick up 15 tents and will then go on to Merheim.
The unexpended portion of the days rations, together with rations for the 17th. inst., blankets, tools, and cooking utensils will be taken.

669. **ATTACHMENTS.**
No. 50666 Cpl. Horton, F.E. will be attached to H.Q. Coy. from this date for Pay, rations and discipline.

670. **GERMAN AGENTS.**
It is reported that Spartacists and Bolshevist agents are now at work in the area endeavouring to get into touch with British soldiers in cafes and other public places, in order to spread their cause by this means.
All ranks will be instructed that they are to at once arrest and hand over to the nearest British Military Guard any civilian who papagates, in any way, Spartacist or Bolshevistic ideas, or whom they may suspect of attempting, or of having the intention to do so.
All ranks should thoroughly understand that in failing to carry out the above instructions, should the occasion or necessity arise, they are committing a grave breach of duty as a British soldier, and as a representative of Great Britain in a defeated enemy's country.

(sgd) G.J. PAUL, Capt. & Adjt.,
9th. Bn. Gloucestershire Regt.

Battalion Orders by
Lieut.-Colonel F. P. SMYLY,
Commdg 9th Bn. Gloucestershire Regiment (Pioneers)
May 16th 1919.

---

671. **DUTIES.**
Bn. Orderly Officer for tomorrow   -   2/Lt. E. C. Pilcher.
Next for duty   -   Lieut. V. E. Robertson.
Bn. Orderly Sergeant for tomorrow   -   Sgt. Kelly
Next for duty   -   Sgt. Underwood.

The Coy. for duty tomorrow will be "B" Coy.

672. **PARADES.**
B. Coy. will train according to programme.

673. **TRAINING.**
During the hot weather, and at the discretion of the Coy. Commanders, Coys. may carry out their training without tunics.
This applies to Officers as well as to other ranks.

674. **PROMOTIONS.**
All provisional acting ranks are confirmed from date of appointment.

The following A/Cpls are appointed A/Sgts to complete establishment:-

    50844 Cpl Eagles, E.   50739 Cpl. F. Neale.
    50439 " Stagg W.H.   35291 " L. Buchanan.

The following L/Cpls are appointed A/Cpls:-

    32985 L/c Adamson, H.   41132 L/c Blair, M.
    28614 " Bownes, C.   41138 " Smith, W.C.
         50310 L/c Mallett, W.J., Sanitary Corporal.

The following to be A/pd L/Cpls:-

    32363 L/c Slater, G.   36860 L/c Pilkington, M.
    50300 " Birch, C.   35010 " Sparkes, E.W.
         50823 L/c Cheale, G.   12900 L/c Nelson, J.

The following to be unpaid L/Cpls:-
    39208 Pte Gotham, F.   36859 Pte Jones, D.
    50386 " Swarbrick, R.   241788 " Benwell, A.S.

675. **TRANSFERS.**
Sgt. Russon, S., will be returned to duty from Regtl. Police from this date and is transferred from H.Q. to B. Coy.

Cpl. Dallimore will take charge of the Regtl. Police from this date and will report daily to the Adjutant at 09.00 hrs and 21.00 hrs.

50739 Sgt Neale, F., is transferred from B. to A. Coy. from this date

32985 Cpl Adamson, H., is transferred from A to C Coy. from this date.

50827 Cpl Clark is transferred from C to B Coy from this date

53285 Pte Beere   ditto   ditto   ditto
50913 Pte Dixey, A. Coy. to be attached to H.Q. Coy. for pay, rations and discipline from this date.
32975 " Hagart, A. Coy. ditto   ditto   ditto
50812 " Bridgen, B. Coy. to be transferred to A Coy. from this date.
235184 " Lupun W A Coy   "   "   "   B Coy.   "   "

676. **QUARTERLY AUDIT BOARD.**
A board composed as under will assemble on Monday, 19th inst., to audit accounts of Canteen and Sergeants' Mess for quarter ending March 31st. Time & place will be notified by the President.

    President - Major L. S. E. Stockman, D.C.
    Members   - 2/Lt. G. A. Brinkworth, M.M.
               "   L. G. Holloway.

-2-

677. **COMMAND.**
Lieut. E. F. R. Peacock will take over the command of C. Coy while Capt. C. S. Lee is on leave.

678. **JEWISH SERVICE.**
A Special Service for Jewish Officers and O.Rs. will be held on Saturday next, 17th May 1919, at 11.15 hrs at the Synagogue, Glockengasse, COLOGNE.

679. **UNIT TRANSFERS.**
Volunteers are still required for R. E. (Field Coy. & Signals), R.A.S.C. and R.A.M.C.

Coys. will forward to this Office by 09.00 hrs on Tuesday, the 20th inst., nominal rolls of all other ranks who wish to be transferred.

(Sgd) G. J. PAUL,
Capt. & Adjutant,
9th Bn. Gloucestershire Regt. (Pioneers)

BATTALION ORDERS
BY
LT.COL F.PEMYLY.
CMDG. 9TH.BN.GLOUCESTER RGT.(PIONEERS). May 17th. 1919.

680. DUTIES.
Bn.Orderly Officer for tomorrow ----- Lt .V.E.Robertson.
"   "   "   for Monday   ----- Lt B.Kenley.
Next for Duty   ----- 2/Lt.E.R.Bressman.
Bn.Orderly Sgt. for tomorrow   ----- Sgt .Underwood .
"   "   "   for Monday   ----- " Russon.
Next for Duty   ----- " Sleeman.

The Coy. for duty to morrow will be   Coy.

681 PARADES.
Divine Service.:- B.Coy. and two platoons of "C" Coy will parade in drill order, formed up in line facing west, on the road leading to the Recreation Ground at 1115 hrs tomorrow, for Church of England Service, which will be held in the Protestant Church, LEICHLINGEN, at 11-30 hrs., followed by Holy Communion for all who wish to attend.
Roman Catholic Service will be held in the R.C. Church, LEICHLINGEN, at 1000 hrs.
Non-Conformist Service will be held in the Recreation Room at 1100 hrs.
The Commanding Officer will inspect the C. of E. parade before they proceed to Church.
Coy. Commanders will ensure that the men do not reach the parade ground before 11-10 hrs.

682. PARADES FOR MONDAY.
"B" Coy. will parade according to programme.

683. MOVE.
The remainder of "C" Coy. will parade on Monday the 19th. inst. at 0800 hrs. armed and equipped, and will proceed by Motor Lorry to the London Divisional Racecourse at MERHEIM, where they will report at 1200 hrs. to Capt. Hill.
The unexpended portion of the days rations, together with rations for the 20th. inst., and all stores will be taken.

684. FISHING.
It has been brought to notice that some Officers and Other Ranks have been catching large numbers of immature trout, and are in the habit of keeping nearly every fish they land.
The Divisional Commander thinks this is not sporting and is also short sighted, for if the custom is persisted in there will shortly be no fish left, and a healthy sport will cease to exist.
He, therefore, suggests that no fisherman kills more than 12 trout in one days fishing, and that fish under 7 inches be thrown back.

685. BRITISH POSTAL ORDERS.
It is notified that British Postal Orders are not negotiable, and must not, therefore, be accepted by any German shopkeeper, or Civilian, from British Officers or Soldiers in payment for goods purchased or services rendered.   No facilities will be granted for cashing any Postal Order that has been so accepted by German Shopkeepers or Civilians.

686. PROMOTIONS.
12900 A/L/Cpl Nelson to be Act. Cpl. (Paid) from this date.
50745 L/C/ W.Powell "   " "   "   (Paid) "   "   " .
8 0836 L/C.J.Eustace "   " " L/Cpl.(Paid) "   "   " .
50772 A/L/C. S.Powell"   " " Cpl. (Paid) "   "   " .
                        "   " " L/Cpl.(Paid) "   "   " .

687 APPOINTMENTS.
2nd.Lt.R.D.Heppenstall is appointed Asst.Adjt. from the 16th.inst .
50886 A/Cpl.Eustace to be unpaid A/L/Sgt. prov. from this date.

GARDENING CLASS
    See next sheet.

-- 2 --

688. GARDENING CLASS.
O.C."B" Coy. will supply 20 other Ranks to attend this
Class daily during parade hours. They will be available
for Guard Duty.

689. ORDERLY OFFICER.
In future the Orderly Officer will dismount the Chateau
Guard at the H.Q.Guard Room at 0800 hours daily.

690. TRANSFERS.
36889 L/C.Jones is transferred from C. to H.Coy.
36899 Pte.Griffin J.A. " C" Coy.to be attached to H.Q.Coy.
as Medical Orderly for Pay, Rations and Discipline.

691. SIGNAL SECTION.
The following men at present posted to H.Q.Coy. to be
attached to H.Q.Coy. for Pay Rations and Discipline.
No.37529 Pte.Hall. From " C" Coy.
No.36315 " Carter " "C" "
The following men at present attached to H.Q.Coy. to be
posted to H.Q.Coy.
No.33303 Pte.A.Sullivan." A" No.32328 Pte.A.Evans." A" Coy.

692. CASH.
All requisitions for Cash, and Officers advance of Pay
Books will be sent to Orderly Room by 0800 hours on
Monday the 19th.inst. 2ndLieut. P.J.Hancox is
detailed to to draw same from the Field Cashier.

(sgd) O.J.PAUL. Capt. and Adjt.
5TH.BN.GLOUCESTER REGT. (PIONEERS).

BATTALION ORDERS BY
LT.-COL. E. P. SHYLY,
COMMDG. 9TH BN. GLOUCESTERSHIRE REGT. (P)
19th May 1919.

693. **DUTIES.**
Bn. Orderly Officer for tomorrow — 2/Lt. E. A. Brosnan.
Next for duty — 2/Lt. F. J. Stebbings.
Bn. Orderly Sergeant for tomorrow — Sgt. Sloeman
Next for duty — Sgt. Peot

Until further orders "B" Coy. will be on duty.

694. **PARADES.**
"B" Coy. will parade according to programme.
xxxxxxxxxxxxxxxxxxxxxxxxx xxxxxxxxxxxx G.J.P.

695. **REVOLVERS.**
All revolvers held on charge by "B" Coy. will be handed in to
the Armourer's Shop at 09.00 hrs tomorrow for inspection.
O. C. "B" Coy. will detail two fatigue men to assist in cleaning etc.

696. **INOCULATION - OFFICERS.**
O. C. Coys. will render to this Office by 09.00 hrs on Friday next,
23rd inst., a nominal roll of all Officers of their Coys., giving
particulars of the last date of inoculation against Typhoid.
A note will be made of any Officer who does not wish to be inoculated.

697. **SICK PARADE.**
On Sundays in future Sick Parade will be held at 09.00 hrs.

698. **PROMOTIONS.**
41057 Pte W. Bradshaw to be A/Unpaid L/c from this date.

699. **TRANSFERS.**
50351 Pte G. Kirkman is attached to H.Q. Coy. from this date.

700. **GUARD MOUNTING.**
In future the Corporal will fall in on the Left of the front rank
with the Sergeant on the Right.
When ordered to dismiss, the guard will be dismissed by the N.C.O.
in charge from his position in the ranks; he will not step forward.

701. **GAS COURSE.**
The undermentioned N.C.O's who attended the Anti-Gas Course at Berg-
Gladbach are reported on as follows :-
37340 Cpl. Godfrey, D. Practical:- V.Good. Theory:- V. Good.
50625 L/C. Choal, G.E. Practical:- Good.   Theory:- Good.
The C.O. is very pleased with the report of Cpl.Godfrey as this
is the highest standard reached by any Unit.

(Sgd) G.J.PAUL, Capt. & Adjt.,
9th. Bn. Gloucestershire Regt.

BATTALION ORDERS BY
LT.-COL. E.F. SMYLY,
COMMDG. 9TH BN. GLOUCESTERSHIRE REGT. (P)
20th May 1919.

702. **DUTIES.**
    Bn. Orderly Officer for tomorrow - 2/Lt. F. J. Stebbings, M.C.
    Next for duty   - 2/Lt. E. G. Pilcher.
    Bn. Orderly Sergeant for tomorrow - Sgt. Dymond.
    Next for duty   - Sgt. Peet.

703. **PARADES.**
    "B" Coy. will train according to programme.

704. **BOX RESPIRATORS.**
    G.R.O. 3981 (France) of May 10th 1918 is republished for information.
    "Box Respirator Haversacks - Washing of. - It has been brought to notice that in some Units Box Respirator Haversacks are cleaned by scrubbing with water. This treatment diminishes the water resisting power of the fabric and will be discontinued.
    The Haversack should be dried when opportunity offers and the mud can then be readily brushed off."

705. **REGIMENTAL NUMBERS.**
    Coy. Commanders will ensure that all men of their Coys. know their new Regtl. Nos. Several cases have occurred recently when men, on being asked their Regtl. Nos., gave their old ones, and on examination of their pay books it was found that the new Nos. had not been entered.

706. **PROMOTIONS.**
    20383 A/L/c Isherwood,J., to be A/L/c Paid from this date.

707. **REVERSIONS.**
    20735 L/c Heusell reverts to Pte at his own request from this date.

708. **GUARD.**
    In future the H. Q. Guard will parade at 09.30 Hrs on the day previous to that on which they mount, for instruction under the R.S.M.

709. **FRATERNISING.** (Rhine Army Letter No. A.G./81).
    1. The Commander-in-Chief directs that the strictest attention be paid to the bearing of all ranks of the British Army of Occupation in Germany. He feels that he can rely upon all ranks to preserve that careful attention to their deportment, their arms, their accoutrements and their dress, which has always distinguished the British Army, and he is confident that they will in every way maintain the reputation which the British Army has justly earned by its traditions and conduct throughout the war.
    2. Intercourse with the inhabitants will be confined to what is essential, and will be marked by courtesy and restraint. It is not seemly that anything approaching familiarity should be allowed to enter into any relations between British soldiers and men or women of the German nation; but neither is it in accordance with our tradition to do otherwise than respect the persons and property of a beaten foe. The exaction of reparation and compensation from the German people is a matter for the appointed authorities. (Note:- This order must be read out on 3 successive parades, & O.C. Coys. will render a report to Orderly Room when this has been done).

710. **PAYMENT & RATIONING OF TROOPS PROCEEDING ON JOURNEYS (G.R.O. 1892)**
    Several cases have occurred lately of men reporting to R.T.Os. on journeys covering two or three days without having been paid, or having received rations. Steps will be taken to ensure that units pay such men, and ration them for their entire journey.

711. **APPOINTMENT.**
    Lieut. R. H. White is appointed Transport Officer from 3rd inst.

        (Sgd) R. D. HEPPENSTALL, 2/Lt.
                        for Capt. & Adjutant.
                        9th Bn. Gloucestershire Regt. (Pioneers)

BATTALION ORDERS
By Lt-Col. F.F.WHYLY,
Commdg; 9th. Bn. Gloucestershire Regt.
May 21st. 1919.

712. **DUTIES.**
Bn. Orderly Officer for to-morrow ----- 2/Lieut. E.O. Pilcher.
Next for duty ------------------- 2/Lieut. S.Johnson.
Bn. Orderly Sergeant for tomorrow ----- Sgt. Peet.
Next for duty ------------------- Sgt. Kelley.

713. **PARADES.**
"B" Coy. will parade according to programme.

714. **INSPECTION.**
The C.O. is very pleased with the arrangement of "C" Coy's Camp including the Kits, and with the work being done there.
He wishes the attention of all ranks to be drawn to this order.

(Sgd) G. J. PAUL, Capt. & Adjutant.
9th Bn. Gloucestershire Regt. (P)

BATTALION ORDERS BY
LT.-COL. E. P. SMYLY,
COMMDG. 9TH BN. GLOUCESTERSHIRE REGT. (P)
22nd May 1919.

715. DUTIES.
Bn. Orderly Officer for tomorrow — 2/Lt. S. Johnson.
Next for duty — Lieut. V. E. Robertson.
Bn. Orderly Sergeant for tomorrow — Sgt. Kelly.
Next for duty — Sgt. Underwood

716. PARADES.
"B" Coy. will parade according to programme.

717. MEAT RATION.
The Divisional Commander wishes that all ranks should be informed that he is aware of the difficulties experienced by the short meat ration, and that he is taking all possible steps, with higher authority, to remedy the fault with the least possible delay.
A notice to this effect will be placed on all Company Notice Boards.

718. LEAVE (D.R.O. No. 704).
No officers, other than those detailed for duty with leave parties, will report to the British Army of the Rhine Reception Camp, nor will they proceed via Calais.
All officers, other than those detailed for duty, will proceed on leave via BOULOGNE.

719. DISCIPLINE. (G.R.O. 2778, 20/5/19)
It is notified for information of all ranks that the car of the General Officer, Commanding-in-Chief, British Army of the Rhine, now carries the Union Jack. All ranks will therefore salute this car when bearing the Union Jack unfurled.

720. LEAVE (G.R.O. No. 2781, 20/5/19)
Owing to Small Pox, Bury St. Edmunds is placed out of bounds to all troops and members of Q.M.AA.C. proceeding on leave.

(Sgd) G. J. PAUL, Capt. & Adjutant.
9th Bn. Gloucestershire Regt. (Pioneers)

Battalion Orders by
Lt.-Col. E. F. Bayly,
Commdg. 8th Bn. Gloucestershire Regt. (Pioneers)
May 23rd 1919.
----

721. DUTIES.

  Bn. Orderly Officer for tomorrow - Lt. V. E. Robertson.
  Next for duty - 2/Lt. E. Newbury.
  Bn. Orderly Sgt. for tomorrow - Sgt. Underwood
  Next for duty - Sgt. Mason

722. PARADES.
  "B" Coy. will parade according to programme.

723. IRON RATIONS.
  O. C. Coys. will render to the Orderly Room by 10.00 hrs on
  Sunday, 25th inst., a return stating the exact number of Iron
  Rations in possession.

724. LEATHER CLOTHING ETC.
  O. C. Coys. will return to Q. M. Stores not later than 10.00
  hrs Monday, 26th inst., all Leather Jerkins and Gloves (all
  kinds) in their possession.
  Also, all surplus blankets above two per man.

725. MARRIED OFFICERS (Rhine Army Letter No. 1509)
  The following wire has been received from the War Office:-
   "Applications being received from Officers serving with
   "Army of the Rhine to meet their wives in France and
   "Flanders whilst on leave see No objection provided that
   "officers obtain written authority from areas concerned
   "which must be produced by wife to Director of Movements."
  All applications of this nature will be made to General
  Headquarters, British Army of the Rhine, at least 14 clear
  days before the leave commences.

726. BILLETS (B.R.O. No. 710 - AA/B/18).
  Instances have been sixteen reported of officers and troops
  vacating the billets officially allotted to them, and taking
  up others, and also of troops spreading themselves byoccupying
  more billets than allotted to them, without reference to, or
  notifying, either the Sub-Area Commandant or the Civil Authorities concerned. This practice must cease forthwith.

727. PROMOTIONS.
  10511 Pte Margetts, W., to be A/Cpl. (Prov) from this date.

  (Sgd) O. J. PAUL,   Capt. & Adjutant.
            8th Bn. Gloucestershire Regt. (P)

Battalion Orders by
Lt.-Col. E. P. SMYLY,
Commdg. 9th Bn. Gloucestershire Regt.(P)
May 24th 1919.

728. **DUTIES.**
  Bn. Orderly Officer for tomorrow   — 2/Lt. B. Kembrey.
  "   "   "   "   Monday — 2/Lt. N. G. Hicks.
  Next for duty   — 2/Lt. F. J. Stebbing, M.C.

  Bn. Orderly Sgt. for tomorrow   — Sgt. Russen.

729. **DIVINE SERVICE.**
  "B" Coy. will parade in drill order, formed up in line facing West, on the road leading to the Recreation Ground, at 11-15 hrs tomorrow, for Church of England Service, which will be held in the Protestant Church, LEICHLINGEN, at 11-30 hrs., followed by Holy Communion for all who wish to attend.
  Roman Catholic Service will be held in the R. C. Church, LEICHLINGEN, at 10.00 hrs.
  Non-Conformist Service will be held in the Recreation Room at 11-00 hrs.
  The Commanding Officer will inspect the C. of E. Parade before they proceed to Church.
  Coy. Commander will ensure that the men do not reach the parade ground before 11-20 hrs.

730. **PARADES FOR MONDAY.**
  "B" Coy. will parade according to programme.

731. **MOVE.**
  One Officer and 58 O.Rs. of "B" Coy. will move by lorry on Monday to MENNHEIM to be attached to "C" Coy; lorries will be here by 09.00 hrs.

732. **DISCIPLINE.**
  Coy. Commanders will render a report to Orderly Room by 09.00 hrs on Wednesday that all New Regtl. Nos. have been inserted on all documents of O.Rs. in their Companies. This is not at present being done, and is the cause of a great deal of trouble and delay in the Orderly Room. Serious notice will be taken of neglect in this matter in future.

  (Sgd) G. J. PAUL, Capt. & Adjutant.
  9th Bn. Gloucestershire Regt. (Pioneers)

Battalion Orders by
Lt.-Col. E. P. SMYLY,
Commdg 9th Bn. Gloucestershire Regt. (P)
24th May 1919.

AFTER ORDER.

733. CASH.
All requisitions for cash and Officers' advance of Pay Books will be sent to Orderly Room by 09.00 hrs on Monday, 26th inst. Lieut. Allen is detailed to draw same from the Field Cashier.

(sgd) G?J.P Capt. & Adjutant.
9th Bn. Gloucestershire Regt. (P)

Battalion Orders by
Lt.-Col. E. P. SMYLY,
Commdg. 9th Bn. Gloucestershire Regt.(P)
May 26th 1919.

---

733. **DUTIES.**
Bn. Orderly Officer for tomorrow - 2/Lt. F. J. Stebbing, M.C.
Next for duty - 2/Lt. W. Francombe.
Bn. Orderly Sergeant for tomorrow - Sgt. Ellis.
Next for duty - Sgt. Sleeman.

734. **PARADES.**
R. Coy. will parade according to programme.

735. **BATHS.**
In future all bathing will take place in the afternoon, on Tuesday, and Wednesdays, between 14-00 and 16-30 hrs.

736. **SALE OF EGGS TO BRITISH TROOPS.**
Eggs may now be sold to British troops.

737. **REVERSION.**
240358 A/C.Q.M.S. G. H. Hardiman reverts to Sergeant at his own request from this date.

738. **PROMOTIONS.**
27915 Sgt. E. R. Dymond to be A/C.Q.M.S. from this date vice Hardiman.
50365 Pte W. L. Brady appointed Unpd/L/Cpl from 23/5/19.

739. **TRANSFERS.**
240358 Sgt Hardiman will be transferred from "B" Coy. to "C" Coy. from the 27th inst. He will proceed to MEHHEIM tomorrow.
57051 Sgt. Jones, R., is transferred from "C" to "B" Coy.

740. **POSTING.**
242159 Pte Hemming, H., is posted to "B" Coy.

741. **SERGEANTS' MESS CATERER.**
In future no Sergeant on H. Q. Coy. strength will be appointed Sergeants' Mess Caterer.

(Sgd) G. J. PAUL,   Capt. & Adjutant.
9th Bn. Gloucestershire Regt. (Pioneers)

Battalion Orders by
Lt.-Col. E. P. SMYLY,
Commdg. 9th Bn. Gloucestershire Regt. (P)
May 27th 1919.

---

742. **DUTIES.**
Bn. Orderly Officer for tomorrow — 2/Lt. W. Francombe.
Next for duty — 2/Lt. E. E. Bresman
Bn. Orderly Sergeant for tomorrow — Sgt. Sleeman.
Next for duty — Sgt. Brooker.

743. **PARADES.**
"B" Coy. will parade according to programme.

744. **LECTURE.**
A Special Cinema Film will be shown at the Metropole Theatre on Thursday, May 29th, at 11.00 hrs. "B" and "H.Q." Coys. will attend as strong as possible.

745. **STRENGTH.**
Major H. B. Spear reported for duty on the 26th inst. as Second-in-Command, vice Major L. B. L. Beckham.

746. **PROMOTIONS.**
No. 30215 A/Cpl H. Sherratt to be promoted A/L/Sgt. unpd. from this date.
No. 30353 A/L/c W. L. Brady to be A/L/c. Pd. from 23rd inst.
No. 30630 Pte C. Duffin to be A/L/c unpaid from this date.

747. **CERTIFICATE – BOOTS.**
O. C. Coys. will render to this Office daily a certificate stating that all men of their Coys. returning from leave were in possession of Army boots.

748. **POLICE.**
The Police attached to this Battalion, whether Regimental or Brigade, will wear their brassards below the elbow.

(Sgd) G. J. PAUL, Capt. & Adjutant,
9th Bn. Gloucestershire Regt. (P)

War diary

8th. BN. ORDERS.
BY
LT. COL. IREMIN.
COMMANDING 8th. GLOUCESTER REGT.   MAY 28th. 1919.

729. DUTIES.
      Bn. Orderly Officer for tomorrow   ——— 2nd.Lt. R.A. Brooman.
      Next for duty   ——— 2nd.Lt. C. Johnson.
      Bn. Orderly Sgt. for tomorrow   ...... Sgt. Brooker.
      Next for duty.   ——— Sgt. Underwood

730. PARADES.
      "D" Coy. will parade according to programme.

731. DIVISIONAL LIBRARY.
      D.R.O. notice dated May 27th. is published for information:-
      A Divisional is now opened at the Church Army House, NEW SLAUGHTER
      Square.   Books may be borrowed and exchanged by Units of the
      Division daily between 0900 hours and 1930 hours except on Sundays
      or at other times by arrangements with the S.O.F. E.O.C.'s Dept.
      Southern Division.

732. REVERSIONS.
      No.27936. L/C Scull "B" Coy. is deprived of his Lance Stripe from
      this date.

733. ANTI GAS COURSE.
      The undermentioned N.C.O.s who attended the Divisional Gas
      Course on May the 19th. are reported on as follows:-
      No.30527 L/Cpl. Rutt.W.A. Practical :- Fair. Theory :-V. Fair.
      No.203800 "   Donovan H.   "   V. Fair. "   V. Fair.

734. TRANSFER.
      2nd.Lt. J.D. Heaponstall is transferred from "A" to H.Q. Coy. from this
      date.

                                        (sgd) G.J. PAUL. Capt. and Adjt.
                                        8th. BN. GLOUCESTER REGT. (PIONEERS).

BATTALION ORDERS
BY
LT.COL.F.P.SMYLY.
COMMANDING 9TH.BN.GLOUCESTER RGT.

MAY 29TH.1919.

755. DUTIES.
Bn.Orderly Officer for tomorrow ----- 2nd.Lt.S.Johnson.
Next for Duty ----- Lt.V.E.Robertson.
Bn.Orderly Sgt.for tomorrow. ----- Sgt.Underwood.
Next for Duty. ----- Sgt.Peet.

756. PARADES.
"B" Coy. will parade according to programme.

757 MOBILIZATION STORES.
The return regarding Mobilization Stores is not being rendered by all Coy's.
Coy.Commanders will ensure that this return reaches this office every Monday.

758. APPOINTMENTS.
No.203663 A/L/Cpl.Swanzott A. is appointed A/L/Cpl.(Paid) from this date.

sgd.G.G.Paul. Capt.andAdjt.
9TH.BN.GLOUCESTER RGT.(Pioneers).

Battalion Orders by Lt. Col F.P. Smyly.
Commdg 9th Battn Gloucestershire Regt (Pioneers.)
30th May 1919.

759. DUTIES.
Bn Orderly Officer for tomorrow - Lieut V. E. Robertson.
Next for duty.   " 2/Lieut B. Kembrey.
Bn Orderly Sergeant for tomorrow - Sgt Peet.
Next for duty   " Sgt Russon.

760. PARADES.
"B" Coy will parade according to programme.

761 ROUTINE.
Reveille on Sundays in future will be at 05.30 hrs.
Breakfast at 08.00 hrs.

762 OFFICERS COURSE
The undermentioned Officers attended a course of Field Engineering at Berg Gladbach and received very good reports:-
    Lieut G. F. Pullen
    2/Lt   W. Francombe   2/Lt H. G. Hicks
                                       "   T. W. Everall

763 PARADES, LECTURES, ETC.
In future all Officers must attend all parades with their Coys. Officers attached to H.Q. Coy will parade with that Coy.

764 RE-ENLISTMENTS.
There are vacancies for men to re-enlist into the Gloucestershire Regt. O.C. Coys will ensure that all men of their Coys know the favourable terms in regard to Pay, Bonus, Bounty and Furlough.
This information can be obtained on application at Orderly Room.

                    (Signed) G.J.Paul Capt & Adjt.
                    9th Bn Gloucestershire Regt (Pioneers.)

BATTALION ORDERS BY MAJOR H. B. SPEAR,
COMMDG. 9TH BN. GLOUCESTERSHIRE REGT. (P).
31st May 1919.

765. **DUTIES.**
    Bn. Orderly Officer for tomorrow   - 2/Lt. F.J. Stebbings, M.C.
    "   "   "   "   Monday   - 2/Lt. B. Kembrey.
    Next for duty   - 2/Lt. W. Francombe.
    Bn. Orderly Sergeant for tomorrow - Sgt. Russon
    "   "   "   "   Monday   - Sgt. Pakeman.
    Next for duty   - Sgt. Ellis.

766. **DIVINE SERVICE.**
    "B" & H. Q. Coys. will parade in drill order under Capt. Horton, formed up in line facing West, on the road leading to the Recreation Ground, at 11-30 hrs tomorrow, for Church of England Service, which will be held in the Protestant Church, Leichlingen, at 11-45 hrs, followed by Holy Communion for all who wish to attend.
    Roman Catholic Service will be held in the R. C. Church, Leichlingen, at 10-00 hrs.
    Non-Conformist Service will be held in the Recreation Room at 11-00 hrs.

767. **PARADES FOR MONDAY.**
    "B" Coy. will parade according to programme.

768. **MOVE.**
    One Officer and 50 O.Rs. of "B" Coy. will proceed to MANHEIM by motor lorry at 09-00 hrs tomorrow and will be attached to "C" Coy. They will be rationed to the 2nd June inclusive and will take 50 shovels and 50 picks.

769. **COMMAND.**
    Lt.-Col. E. F. Smyly proceeded to England on leave yesterday, the 30th inst., and the command of the Battalion has been assumed by Major H. B. Spear.

770. **CASH.**
    All requisitions for cash and Officers' Advance of Pay Books will be sent to Orderly Room by 09-00 hrs on Monday, 2nd inst., Lieut. V. A. Robertson is detailed to draw same from the Field Cashier.

771. **APPOINTMENT.**
    No. 50369, Pte F. Brockbank, is appointed A/Unpd/L/c from this date.

                  (Sgd) R. M. HEPPENSTALL, 2/Lt. A/Adjt.,
                       for Capt. & Adjutant,
                       9th Bn. Gloucestershire Regt.

Army Form C. 2118.

WAR DIARY
or
INTELLIGENCE SUMMARY.
(Erase heading not required.)

N° Gloster s

Place	Date	Hour	Summary of Events and Information	Remarks and references to Appendices
Leichlingen	1919 June 1		One platoon of 'B' Coy proceeded to join 'L' Coy at Thetheem to both on rise course under R.E.	
	2		'D' Co. with one platoon of 'B' Coy proceeded to join 'L' Coy at Thetheem to work on rise course under R.E.	
	3		Lt. & L.H. Lally proceeded on leave to U.K. Capt. G.J. Lee Warner returned from leave to U.K.	
	5		2nd Lieut R.H. Warren returned from leave to U.K. 2nd Lieut P.J. Hancock proceeded on leave to U.K.	
	6		Capt. J.E. Smith returned from leave to U.K. Lieut & Q.M. Seedon proceeded on leave to U.K.	
	7		Lieut W.H. Palmer proceeded on leave to U.K.	
	8		Lieut R.J. Pullen proceeded on leave to U.K.	
	11		2nd Lieut R. Kembrey proceeded on leave to U.K. Lieut V.E. Robertson proceeded on leave to U.K.	
	12		Lieut W.H. White proceeded on leave to U.K.	
	13		Lieut E.O. Pilcher proceeded on leave to U.K. 'L' Co. returned to Leichlingen from Thetheem	
	17		Capt J.E. Smith proceeded to Southern Division H.Q. to join Education Staff	
	19		'D' Co. moved from Leichlingen to Burscheid, arriving at 19.00 hours. Headquarters and 'L' Co. moved from Leichlingen to Burscheid, arriving at 13.00 hrs. Lieut H. Dalby and Lieut H.L. Hicks returned from leave to U.K. Lieut W. Hancock proceeded on leave to Paris to represent the British Army of the Rhine on the Army Athletic Championships 'B' Coy moved to Burg from Leichlingen at 16.00 hours	
Burscheid	21		Lt. Col. J. Gunn D.S.O reported to take over command of the Battalion & assumed command on this date.	

2. S.
28 sheet

Army Form C. 2118.

WAR DIARY
or
INTELLIGENCE SUMMARY.
(Erase heading not required).

Instructions regarding War Diaries and Intelligence Summaries are contained in F. S. Regs., Part II. and the Staff Manual respectively. Title pages will be prepared in manuscript.

Place	Date	Hour	Summary of Events and Information	Remarks and references to Appendices
Busseboom	1919 June 22		2nd Lieut C.J. Francis returned from leave to U.K.	
	25		2nd Lieut R.N. Hemsley returned from leave to U.K.	
	26		Lieut W.S. Palanch returned from leave to U.K.	
	27		Lieut & Q.M. Lousdon returned from leave to U.K.	
			2nd Lieut A. Watson left Unit for U.K. to report as retiring to W.O. on arrival	
			Lieut W.G. Robertson returned from leave to U.K.	
	28		Lieut M.H. White returned from leave to U.K.	

Strength of Unit :- 36 Offs. 1045 O.Rs.

R. Clare
Lt. COLONEL
COMDG., 8TH (S) BN GLOUCESTERSHIRE REGT

BATTALION ORDERS BY
MAJOR H.B.SPEAR.
COMMANDING 9TH.BN.GLOUCESTER RGT.(PIONEERS).   June 2nd 1919.

772. DUTIES.
   Bn.Orderly Officer for tomorrow   ---------   2nd.Lt.W.Francombe
   Next for Duty   ---------   2nd.Lt.E.O.Pilcher
   Bn.Orderly Sgt.for tomorrow.   ---------   Sgt.Ellis.
   Next for Duty   ---------   Sgt.Peet.

773. PARADES.
   Coy's will parade under Coy arrangements.

774. LEWIS GUNS.
   O.C.Coy's will ensure that all ranks know how to fire a Lewis Gun.

775. DIVISIONAL LIBRARY.
   The Library open daily (except Sundays) from 0900 hours to 1230
   hours and from 1800 to 1930 hours. Books may be exchanged by any
   Officer or other Rank.

776. RATE OF EXCHANGE.
   The Rate of Exchange for June is the same as that for May i.e.
   10 Marks is equal to Three Shillings and Threepence.

777. REVERSIONS.
   L/Cpl.Kershaw has been deprived of his Lance Rank from this date
   for Misconduct.
   Pte.Kershaw is posted to "B" Coy.for Duty from this date.

778. POSTINGS.
   The undermentioned Other Ranks attached 3rd.Bde.H.Q.s are taken on
   Battalion Strength and posted to "C" Coy.
   26624 Pte. Fox C.   41033 Pte.Hart J.   1766 Pte. Mills F.
   3 Obs   " Yates C. 36667 " Balchin.C.

                                    (signed) G.J.Paul. Capt and Adjt.
                                       9TH.BN.GLOUCESTER RGT.(PIONEERS).

N O T I C E.

FEAST OF PENTECOST.
A Special Service for all Jewish Soldiers will be held on
Wednesday June 4th.(Pentecost) at 1115 hours in the Synagogue,
5 Glocken Gasse, Cologne.

BATTALION ORDERS BY MAJOR H. H. SPEAR,
COMMDG. 9TH BN. GLOUCESTERSHIRE REGT. (P).
3rd June 1919.

779. **DUTIES.**
 Bn. Orderly Officer for tomorrow - Lieut. E. O. Pilcher.
 Next for duty - 2/Lt. S. Johnson.
 Bn. Orderly Sergeant for tomorrow - Sgt. Brooker
 Next for duty - Sgt. Underwood

780. **PARADES.**
 Coys. will parade under Coy. arrangements.

781. **POSTAL ORDERS** (G.R.O. No. 2844 of May 30th 1919.)
 1. The amount of postal orders sold to any one person on any one day at Army or Field Post Office will, in future, be limited to a maximum of £10, unless the demand is vouched for by an officer in writing.
 2. Postal orders sent to the troops will be signed by the payees, or the persons to whom they are sent in the cases where the name of the payee has not been inserted in the order, and cashed at the Army Post Office.
 Post Orderlies may cash postal orders on behalf of Officers and men of their own unit, provided the orders are properly filled in and signed by the payees. The Post Orderly will sign his name on the back of all postal orders cashed by him. Postal Orders are not legal tender and do not, like Treasury and Bank of England notes, represent value in themselves. They must not be passed from hand to hand or be offered at canteens, shops, or elsewhere in lieu of money.
 3. With reference to A.R.O. 2679 of April 26th, 1919, only "crossed" postal orders will be cashed by Banks. "Uncrossed" will, as heretofore, be cashed at Army and Field Post Offices.

782. **SPORTS.**
 Officers and O.Rs., when boating, or playing cricket or tennis, may proceed to and from their destination in flannels. Officers will still wear Tunics, Collars, Belts & Revolvers, and O.Rs. Tunics, Belts and Sidearms.

783. **POSTINGS - AMENDMENT.**
 Bn. Order No. 775 of 2/6/19 should read:-
 "26824 Sgt. Fox, C., attached 3rd Bgde. H.Q., is
 "taken on Bn. Strength and posted to "C" Coy."

            G.G.PAUL. Capt. & Adjutant.
         9th Bn. Gloucestershire Regt. (P)

BATTALION ORDERS BY MAJOR H. B. SPEAR,
COMDG. 9TH BN. GLOUCESTERSHIRE REGT. (F),
4th June 1919.

784. **DUTIES.**
Bn. Orderly Officer for tomorrow   -   2/Lt. S. Johnson.
Next for duty   -   2/Lt. R. H. Warren, M.C., M.M.
Bn. Orderly Sergeant for tomorrow   -   Sgt. Underwood.
Next for duty   -   Sgt. Peet.

785. **PARADE.**
Coys. will parade under Company arrangements.

786. **BATHS.**
The Battalion Baths will be open tomorrow, 5th inst., during the usual hours.

787. **SALUTING.**
Several cases have occurred lately where N.C.Os. and men have failed to salute an Officer after Retreat. O. C. Coys. will ensure that all ranks are instructed that an Officer must always be saluted when recognised, whether by day or night.

As the civilians in this area are obliged to raise their hats to Officers it is necessary that other ranks should be extremely punctilious with regard to their salutes. Officers should return all salutes, whether from soldiers or from civilians.

788. **PASSES.**
Until further orders, passes to be away from the billeting area will be limited to ten percent. of ration strength.

789. **APPOINTMENT.**
No. 50923, Pte F. Schofield, is appointed A/Unpaid/L/Cpl. from this date.

            (Sgd)   G. J. PAUL,   Capt. & Adjutant,
                        9th Bn. Gloucestershire Regt. (F).

NOTICE.

A "Lena Ashwell" Concert Party will appear at the

MARIENSAAL, BERG GLADBACH, at 18.00 hrs on Thursday,

5th June 1919.

        Tickets ...   Officers 4 marks.
                       N.C.Os.   2   "
                       O. Rs.   1   "

Doors open at 17-30 hrs.

BATTALION ORDERS BY MAJOR H. B. SPEAR,
COMMDG. 9TH BN. GLOUCESTERSHIRE REGT. (P),
5th June 1919.

790. **DUTIES.**
Bn. Orderly Officer for tomorrow - Lieut. V. E. Robertson.
Next for duty - 2/Lt. B. Kembrey.

Bn. Orderly Sergeant for tomorrow - Sgt. Peet.
Next for duty - Sgt. Russon.

791. **PARADES.**
Coys. will parade under Company arrangements.

792. **CLOTHING.**
In future all clothing will be fitted at the Q. M. Stores under the directions of the Master Tailor; C.Q.M.S's. will always attend.

793. **ORDERLY ROOM.**
On Friday and Saturday of this week Commanding Officer's Orderly Room will be held at 09-45 hours.

(Sgd) G. J. PAUL, Capt. & Adjutant.
9th Bn. Gloucestershire Regt. (Pioneers)

NOTICE.

It is proposed to form classes in folk dancing shortly under the auspices of the Y.M.C.A.

A demonstration of folk dancing will be given (if fine) in the grounds of the Y.M.C.A. at SCHLEBUSCH on 6th June at 18.00 by Miss HANCOCK, assisted by other ladies, and men of the Rhine Army who have already attended classes.

BATTALION ORDERS BY MAJOR H. S. SPEAR,
COMDG. 9TH BN. GLOUCESTERSHIRE REGT. (P),
6th June 1919.

794. **DUTIES.**
Bn. Orderly Officer for tomorrow — 2/Lt. B. Kembrey.
Next for duty — 2/Lt. W. Francombe.
Bn. Orderly Sergeant for tomorrow — Sgt. Russon.
Next for duty — Sgt. Pakeman.

795. **PARADES.**
Coys. will parade under Company arrangements.

796. **LEAVE** — (G.R.O. 2853 dated 2/6/19).
Cases still occur of the combined leave and railway warrant being used for journeys other than those to and from the traveller's destination, when proceeding on or returning from leave.
These warrants are solely for the direct journey to the leave destination and return, and will on no account be used for other journeys.
Each individual will be instructed verbally before proceeding on leave as to the correct and only use of A.Fs. W3741 and W3742.

797. **BOUNDS.** — (G.R.O. 2869 dated 4/6/19).
The Rhine Military Police have orders to take the names of all British Officers and other ranks attempting to leave the British Occupied Zone by river, unless they are individually in possession of a pass signed by the P.M. or are passengers on the trip boats authorised by General Headquarters, Rhine Army.

798. **DEMOBILIZATION - REPATRIATION.** (G.R.O. 2870 dated 4/6/19).
All claims for repatriation overseas by Officers and other ranks must be submitted to Unit Commanders before June 15th 1919.

799. **CAFES.** (G.R.O. No. 2871 dated 4/6/19).
Second Army Routine Order 2254 of January 6th 1919 is cancelled.
Cafes will be open to British and Allied Troops throughout the occupied territory during the following hours:-
11.30 hours to 13.00 hrs.   16.00 hours to 21.00 hours.

800. **OFFICERS' SURPLUS KITS.** (G.R.O. 2872 dated 4/6/19).
Officers Surplus Kits will be accepted for despatch to England by R.T.Os. at Railheads provided they comply with the regulations as under:-
1. The kits should be packed in sacks or boxes.
2. In the case of sacks, the ends of the string securing the mouth of the sacks should be sealed to the backs of the labels, which must bear the Censor's stamp.
3. If kits are packed in boxes, the boxes should be securely fastened, and a stout cord passed round the boxes, the ends of the cord being sealed to the backs of the labels, which must bear the Censor's stamp.
4. All surplus kits should be labelled to the Officers' home address, or to Messrs Cox & Co., 16, Charing Cross, London.
5. Such articles as private typewriters, gramophones, and souvenirs bought in Germany, or France and Belgium cannot be accepted for despatch to England by the M.F. Service.
6. Owing to lack of storage space on Railheads, Officers should send surplus kits to the various railheads on the mornings of the days shown below:-
Mondays and Thursdays ... Ohligs, Bonntor, Berg Gladbach.
Tuesdays and Fridays ... Heumar, Bonn, Siegburg.
Wednesdays and Saturdays ... Wellerswist, Duren, Horrem.

(Sgd) R. D. HEPPENSTALL, 2/Lt., A/Adt.,
for   Capt. & Adjutant,
9th Bn. Gloucestershire Regt. (Pioneers)

BATTALION ORDERS BY MAJOR H. B. SPEAR,
COMMDG. 9TH BN. GLOUCESTERSHIRE REGT. (P).
7th June 1919.
----

801. DUTIES.
    Bn. Orderly Officer for tomorrow - A/Lt. W. Francombe.
    "   "   "   "   Monday - Lieut. E. G. Pilcher.
    Next for duty - 2/Lt. D. Johnson.
    Bn. Orderly Sergeant for tomorrow - Sgt. Ellis
    "   "   "   "   Monday - Sgt. Brooker
    Next for duty - Sgt. Jones.

802. DIVINE SERVICE.
    There will be no Church of England parade tomorrow.
    Roman Catholic Service will be held in the R. C. Church,
    Leichlingen, at 10-00 hours.
    Non-Conformist Service will be held in the Recreation Room
    at 11-00 hours.

803. PARADES FOR MONDAY.
    Coys. will parade under Coy. arrangements.

804. CASH.
    All requisitions for cash and Officers' advance of Pay Books
    will be sent to Orderly Room by 09.00 hours on on Monday, 9th
    inst.
    Lieut. V. L. Robertson is detailed to draw same from the
    Field Cashier.

805. LEATHER EQUIPMENT.
    O. C. Coys. will render to the Orderly Room by 10-00 hours
    on Tuesday next, the 10th inst., a return showing the number
    of sets of Leather Equipment on their charge.

                        (Sgd) R. D. HEPPENSTALL, 2/Lt., A/Adjt.
                                    Capt. & Adjutant.
                            for
                  9th Bn. Gloucestershire Regt. (P)

W.D

BATTALION ORDERS BY

MAJOR H.B.SPEAR.

COMMANDING 9TH.BN.GLOUCESTER RGT.   9/6/19.

806   DUTIES.
       Bn.Orderly Officer for To morrow   ---- 2nd . Lt.S.Johnson.
       Next for Duty   --- 2nd.Lt.J.Noah M?M.
       Bn.Orderly Sgt.for tomorrow.   ---- Sgt .Jones .
       Next for Duty   ---- Sgt.Underwood .

807.   PARADES.
       Coy's will parade under Coy.arrangements.

808.   APPOINTMENTS.
       50328 Pte.J.W.Madeley is appointed Acting Unpaid L/Cpl.
       from ~~this date.~~ 3.6.19

809.   DISCIPLINE.
       G.R.O.2884 is published for information.
       DISCIPLINE ON CALAIS LEAVE TRAIN.
       1. An express Leave train service between Cologne and Calais
       has now been put into force for the benefit of N.C.Os and men
       of the Rhine Army.
       2. The trains running on this service are composed of British
       Ambulance Train Rolling stock, and the attention of all troops
       is called to the necessity od causing no damage to the carriages
       and fittings.
       3. Particular care is to be paid to Windows, doors, Lavatory
       Appointments and fittings, generally, and the troops must be instructed
       to keep the carriages as clean as possible .
       4. The repair of damages is a lengthy matter , and only a limited
       number of suitable coaches are available, so that any considerable
       damage will mean a reduction in the accomodation for Leave Takers.
       ~~4~~5. Any N.C.O. or man convicted of wilful damage of the above nature
       will, if proceeding on leave be returned to his Unit on arrival
       at Calais, and if returning from Leave, will be subject to Disciplinary
       Action on return to his Unit.
       6. A notice calling the attention of troops to the necessity for order
       Conduct will be posted in all carriages .
       7. This order will be repeated in all Unit Routine Orders.
       Ref.A.533/143 P.S.1.

                        (signed) G.J.Paul. CAPT AND ADJUTANT.
                        9TH.BN.GLOUCESTER RGT.(PIONEERS) .

BATTALION ORDERS
BY
MAJOR H.S.SPEAR.

COMMANDING 9TH.BN.GLOUCESTER RGT.(P).   10/6/19.

810.   DUTIES.
       Bn.Orderly Officer for To-morrow   ------ 2nd.Lt.E.O.Pilcher.
       Next for Duty   ------ 2nd.Lt.W.Francombe.
       Bn.Orderly Sgt.for Tomorrow.   ------ Sgt.Underwood.
       Next for Duty.   ------ Sgt.Russon.

811.   PARADES.
       Coy's will parade under Coy.Arrangements.

812.   CASH.
       All requisitions for cash and Officers Advance of Pay Books
       will be sent to Orderly Room by 0900 hours to morrow the
       11 th.inst.
       2/Lt.S.Johnson is detailed to draw same from the Field Cashier.

                              (signed C.J.PAUL. CAPT.AND ADJUTANT.
                              9TH.BN.GLOUCESTER RGT.(PIONEERS).

BATTALION ORDERS BY

MAJOR R.B.CREAR.

11/6/19

COMMANDING 9TH.BN.GLOUCESTER RGT.(PIONEERS).

813. **DUTIES.**
Bn.Orderly Officer for tomorrow. ------ 2nd Lt.W.Francombe.
Next for Duty/ ------ 2nd.Lt.H.R.Jones.
Bn.Orderly Sgt.for tomorrow ------ Sgt.Russon.
Next for Duty. ------ Sgt.Peet.

814. **PARADES.**
Coy's will parade under Coy. arrangements.

815. **DEPARTURE.**
Lt.W.Pamment left the Battalion this day and is attached to Divisional Headquarters for Duty.

816. **DISCIPLINE.**(G.R.O.No.2892 dated 9/6/19.).
Cases have occured of Officers and Other Ranks stopping Civilians and demanding their passes without any authority to do so. This practice will cease forthwith.

817. **CURRENCY.** G.R.O.2894 is published for information.
A.R.O.2641 is republished for information
All payments made to Germans will be made in marks.On no account will English or French Money be used,neither will money of the Allied powers be exchanged for marks,except with Field Cashiers or at other authorized places of exchange, where every facility will be given to all ranks for the purpose. The only authorized places of exchange other than Field Cashiers and Disbursing Officers,are Messrs Cox & Coy. and Messrs Cook & Sons. (A.531/613/ F.S.1.).

818. **RACE MEETING.**
The C.O. wishes the following letter to be brought to the notice of all ranks,-

"I have much pleasure in sending you herewith a cheque
for 1800 marks. for distribution to the N.C.O.s
and men who held official positions on the two
days of the race meeting.
General Reneker and the Committee desires me to
express to you their appreciation of the splendid
work which your Battalion has done in connection
with the whole meeting".
en.
The money will be distributed when "C" Coy. return to Leichling

(signed).G.J.PAUL Capt and Adjutant;
9TH.BN.GLOUCESTER RGT.-(PIONEERS).

BATTALION ORDERS BY MAJOR H. B. SPEAR,
COMDG. 9TH BN. GLOUCESTERSHIRE REGT. (P).

12th June 1919.

319. **DUTIES.**
Bn. Orderly Officer for tomorrow — 2/Lt. H. R. Jones.
Next for duty — 2/Lt. T. W. Everall.

Bn. Orderly Sergeant for tomorrow — Sgt. Peet.
Next for duty — Sgt. Ellis.

320. **PARADES.**
Coys. will parade under Company arrangements.

321. **TRANSFERS.**
No. 10015 Pte Leadbetter, W., is transferred from "B" to H.Q. Coy. from this date.

322. **REVERSIONS.**
No. 70094 L/c Williams, R., ("B" Coy.), reverts to Pte at his own request from this date.

(Sgd) S. J. PAUL,
Capt. & Adjutant.
9th Bn. Gloucestershire Regt. (P)

BATTALION ORDERS BY MAJOR H. B. SPEAR,
COMMDG. 9TH BN. GLOUCESTERSHIRE REGT.(P).
13th June 1919.

---

823. DUTIES.
Bn. Orderly Officer for tomorrow — 2/Lt. T. W. Everall.
Next for duty — 2/Lt. W. J. Noah, M.M.
Bn. Orderly Sergeant for tomorrow — Sgt. Ellis.
Next for duty — Sgt. Hardiman.

Bn. Order No. 693 of 19/5/19 is cancelled.
"B" Coy. will be on duty tomorrow.
From Sunday next, 15th inst., inclusive, "B" and "C" Coys.
will be on duty for one week in turn, commencing with "C" Coy.

824. PARADES.
Coys. will parade under Coy. arrangements.

825. MEDICAL INSPECTION.
In future, all men returning from leave or from courses will parade sick at 08-00 hours the next morning.
A daily report will be rendered to Orderly Room stating that this has been done and also that the men's hair has been cut.

826. DISCIPLINE.
Bn. Order No. 816 is cancelled, and the following substituted:-
Cases have occurred of Officers and other ranks stopping civilians by day and demanding their passes without any authority to do so. This practice will cease forthwith.

G.R.O. No. 2904:-
All Officers below the rank of Lieut.-Colonel will invariably carry their A.B.439 on their persons in order that it may be produced if required as a proof of identity.

827. FOREST FIRES (G.R.O. No. 2907).
Reference G.R.O.2680. The greatest care will be taken by all ranks when smoking in the vicinity of woods, that lighted ashes or matches are not dropped. Several fires have been traced to this cause.

828. BAGGAGE ALLOWANCE. (G.R.O. No. 2912).
An increase in baggage allowance from one and a half hundred weight to three hundredweight is authorized in the case of British Officers of all Arms of the Service, proceeding to or forming part of an Army of Occupation.
Free conveyance of this additional allowance of one and one half hundredweight to and from ports of despatch and arrival, and transport by sea to places abroad, is also authorized for the conveyance of the kit of an Officer already serving with an Army of Occupation.

829. BOULOGNE LEAVE BOATS (G.R.O.No.2012).
Accommodation for Rhine Army leave personnel is reserved on 16-45 boat ex BOULOGNE daily.
It must be clearly understood that the 09-30 boat BOULOGNE-DOVER is for demobilisation personnel only, and Rhine Army Officers may not travel by it, as no arrangements have been made for their onward conveyance to London.

(Sgd) G. J. PAUL, Capt. & Adjutant.
9th Bn. Gloucestershire Regt. (P)

BATTALION ORDERS BY MAJOR M. B. SPEAR,
COMDG. 9TH BN. GLOUCESTERSHIRE REGT.(P).
14th June 1919.

650. **DUTIES.**
Bn. Orderly Officer for tomorrow — 2/Lt. W. J. Nash, M.M.
" " " " Monday — Lieut. E. F. E. Peacock.
Next for duty — 2/Lt. F. J. Stebbing, M.C.

Bn. Orderly Sergeant for tomorrow — Sgt. S. Hardiman.
" " " " Monday — Sgt. L. Buchanan.
Next for duty — Sgt. C. Pixton.

"C" Coy. will be on duty tomorrow and Monday.

651. **DIVINE SERVICE.**
"B", "C" and H.Q. Coys. will parade in drill order formed up in line facing West, on the road leading to the Recreation Ground, at 11-30 hrs tomorrow, for Church of England Service, which will be held in the Protestant Church, Leichlingen, at 11-45 hrs., followed by Holy Communion for all who wish to attend. Roman Catholic Service will be held in the R. C. Church, Leichlingen, at 10-00 hours.
Non-Conformist Service will be held in the Cinema at 11-00 hours.

652. **PARADES FOR MONDAY.**
The Commanding Officer will inspect "C" Coy. in the Football Field at 10-00 hours on Monday.
DRESS:— Fighting order, less steel helmets.

"B" Coy. will parade under Coy. arrangements.

653. **VESTS, WOOLLEN.**
All Vests, Woollen, in possession of O.Rs., will be returned to Q.M. Stores not later than 10-00 hours on Tuesday, 17th inst.

654. **CASH.**
All requisitions for cash and Officers' advance of Pay Books will be sent to Orderly Room by 09-00 hours on Monday, 16th inst. 2/Lt. W. Branscombe is detailed to draw same from the Field Cashier.

655. **POSTING.**
The U/M O.Rs., transferred from 2nd Bn. Oxford & Bucks L.I., are taken on strength of Bn. with effect from 24/6/19 and posted to "C" Coy:—
240807 Pte R. Weaver   Allotted New No. 55969
 23365 " T. Dunslow   "   "   " 55970
240806 " A. Woolford   "   "   " 55971

(Sgd) G. J. PAUL,
Capt. & Adjutant.
9th Bn. Gloucestershire Regt. (P).

BATTALION ORDERS BY MAJOR H. B. SPEAR,
COMMDG. 9TH BN. GLOUCESTERSHIRE REGT. (P).
16th June 1919.

836. **DUTIES.**
Bn. Orderly Officer for tomorrow - 2/Lt. F. J. Stebbings, M.C.
Next for duty - 2/Lt. H. R. Jones.
Bn. Orderly Sergeant for tomorrow - Sgt. C. Pixton.
Next for duty - Sgt. G. Plimsole.
C. Coy. will be on duty tomorrow.

837. **PARADES.**
B. Coy. will parade under Coy. arrangements.
All N.C.Os. will parade under the Adjutant at 09-00 hours tomorrow, the Sergeant Instructors of Musketry & P.T. to attend. (C.S.Ms. and C.Q.M.Ss. will be excused this parade).
The Commanding Officer will inspect "B" Coy. on Wednesday and "C" Coy. on Thursday, at 10-00 hours, in the Football Field. Dress:- Fighting order, less steel helmets.

838. **COMPANY COMMAND.**
Lieut. J. Howard will take over command and payment of "A" Coy. from this date, vice Capt. Smith, attached to Divisional Educational Staff.

839. **REVERSION.**
A/C.S.M. Thorpe reverts to Sergeant at his own request from this date.

840. **PROMOTION.**
26504 Sgt. Ponting, A.S., to be A/C.S.M., vice Thorpe.
28048 L/c Lee to be A/Cpl. vice 11702 Cpl. Herbert.

841. **APPOINTMENTS.**
30357 Sgt. Jones, R., will take over the duties of P.T. Instructor vice Ponting.

842. **TRANSFERS.**
A/C.S.M. Ponting is transferred from H.Q. to B. Coy.
Sgt. Jones, R., is transferred from B. to H.Q. Coy.

843. **CLOTHING.**
Clothing is on no account to be altered unless by the Master Tailor; any infringement of this order will be severely dealt with.
O. C. Coys. will ensure that this order is read out on three successive parades and a report rendered to the Adjutant when this has been done.

844. **FRATERNIZING (C.R.O.No.2018, 14/6/19).**
Cases have occurred in which civilians have been charged before Summary Courts for "Fraternizing with British Soldiers."
This is purely a Military Offence, not civilian, and officers and soldiers only can be charged under this heading.

(Sgd) C. J. PAUL, Capt. & Adjutant.
9th Bn. Gloucestershire Regt. (P).

BATTALION ORDERS BY MAJOR H. B. SPEAR,
COMMDG. 9TH BN. GLOUCESTERSHIRE REGT. (P).
17th June 1919.
----

845. DUTIES.
    Bn. Orderly Officer for tomorrow - 2/Lt. H. R. Jones.
    Next for duty - 2/Lt. T. W. Everall.
    Bn. Orderly Sergeant for tomorrow - Sgt. Boast.
    Next for duty - Sgt. Plimsole.

846. PARADES.
    Coys. will make under parade under Company arrangements.

847. BATHS.
    The Baths will be available tomorrow from 13-30 to 16-30 hours for all who did not bathe yesterday.

848. INOCULATION.
    The undermentioned Officers, who gave their names in for inoculation, are now due for same. Will they please make arrangements with the Medical Officer and report to Orderly Room when this has been done.

        Capt. Paul,
        Capt. Horton.
        2/Lt. Heppenstall.
          "   Watson.
          "   Halward.
          "   Noah.

                (Sgd) G. J. PAUL, Capt. & Adjutant.
                    9th Bn. Gloucestershire Regt. (P).

BATTALION ORDERS BY MAJOR H. B. SPEAR,
COMMDG. 9TH BN. GLOUCESTERSHIRE REGT.(P).
18th June 1919.

---

849. <u>DUTIES.</u>
Bn. Orderly Officer for tomorrow - 2/Lt. T. W. Everall.
Next for duty   - 2/Lt. W. J. Noah, M.M.
Bn. Orderly Sergeant for tomorrow - Sgt. Plimsole.
Next for duty   - Sgt. Boast.

"C" Coy. will be for duty tomorrow.

850. <u>PARADES.</u>
Coys. will parade according to Movement Order.

851. <u>REVERSION.</u>
28043 A/Cpl. Lee, W.G., "B" Coy., reverts to Pte at his own request.

852. <u>LEAVE.</u>
When leave is resumed Officers proceeding on furlough on the COLOGNE-BOULOGNE express may travel on the morning boat from BOULOGNE to DOVER.

(Sgd) G. J. PAUL, Capt. & Adjutant.
9th Bn. Gloucestershire Regt. (P).

9TH BN. GLOUCESTERSHIRE REGT. (PIONEERS).

MOVEMENT ORDER.

18th June 1919.

The Battalion will parade tomorrow in fighting order in accordance with undermentioned instructions:-

(1) "A" and "B" Coys. will move off under Company arrangements.

(2) "C" and H.Q. Coys. will stand by ready to move from 07-00 hours.

(3) Transport will also stand by from 07-00 hours, and when time to move is notified will form up in OPLADENER STRASSE with the head of the column on the West side of the River bridge.

(4) Packs will be stacked in some accessible spot, arranged by Coys., ready to be loaded when lorries arrive.

(5) Lorry for "B" Coy. will arrive at 05-00 hours.
Half of this lorry is for use of "B" Coy. and, when loaded, will proceed to DABRINGHAUSEN to pick up packs of 29th Bn. M.G.C.

(6) Haversack rations will be carried.

(7) Officers' kits will be collected and loaded on Coy. transport under Coy. arrangements.

(8) Instructions regarding destinations etc. etc. have already been issued to Coys.

(Sgd) G. J. PAUL, Capt. & Adjutant.
18/6/19.   9th Bn. Gloucestershire Regt.(P).

BATTALION ORDERS BY MAJOR H. B. SPEAR,
COMMDG. 9TH BN. GLOUCESTERSHIRE REGT.(P).
19th June 1919.

853. **DUTIES.**
Bn. Orderly Officer for tomorrow - 2/Lt. W. J. Noah, M.M.
Bn. Orderly Sergeant for tomorrow - Sgt. Boast.

Guards to be provided under Coy. arrangements.

854. **CHIROPODIST.**
50358 L/c F. Brockbank is appointed Bn. Chiropodist from this date.

(Sgd) G. J. PAUL, Capt. & Adjutant.
9th Bn. Gloucestershire Regt. (P).

BATTALION ORDERS BY MAJOR H. B. SPEAR,
COMMDG. 9TH BN. GLOUCESTERSHIRE REGT. (P).
20th June 1919.

---

853. DUTIES.
Bn. Orderly Officer for tomorrow - Lieut. E. F. E. Peacock.

Bn. Orderly Sergeant for tomorrow - Sgt. Stagg.
Next for duty - Sgt. Hardiman.

Guards will be provided under Coy. arrangements.

854. MARCH DISCIPLINE. (Southern Divisional Letter No. G.S.46/12).
As a result of an inspection of various units on the march on 19th inst. the following remarks are circulated for information:-
1. The Infantry were marching well, properly closed up, and the march discipline was good. That so few fell out, and that the men marched so well on a trying day is very creditable to the discipline and esprit-de-corps of the units inspected. Battalion Headquarters should march in front of Battalions, and Company Headquarters in front of Companies.

X. Four paces distance should be kept between platoons and between Company Headquarters and the leading platoon while on the march.
On seeing the Divisional Commander, or officer senior to him, Companies should be called to attention and "eyes right" or "eyes left" given as the case may be. These compliments should only be given once during the march - the first time the above Commanders are met.

2. Regarding transport, it was noticed that wagons straggled, men rode on wagons, equipment and helmets were taken off and placed on wagons, personnel were badly dressed and turned out.

855. ELSENBORN ARTILLERY RANGE - SAFETY PRECAUTIONS. (G.R.O.2953,18/6/19).
1. It is forbidden for any unauthorised person to enter the danger area on Elsenborn Ranges while practice is in progress.
2. While practice is in progress, the direct road between Kalterherberg and Elsenborn will be closed to all traffic and Signal Baskets will be hoisted on flag poles on all main approaches to the range.
3. During practice the approach to Elsenborn Camp will be via either:-
 (a) The Gemund-Rocherath-Elsenborn-Lager Elsenborn Road.
 (b) The Montjoie-Hofen-Rocherath-Elsenborn Lager Elsenborn Road.
 (c) Along the Western edge of the range via the Kaltenherberg-Am Gruüen Kloster-Munitionsanst-Lager Elsenborn Road. The traffic on this road may be stopped occasionally for short periods only. Reference to the special Elsenborn Training Area Map.

4. Practice will begin on June 15th, and is liable to take place daily commencing at 8-30 a.m. from that date onwards. On the conclusion of the day's practice the barriers will be opened and the Signal Baskets hauled down.

5. It is forbidden for any unauthorized person to handle any unexploded shell or fuze found on or off the Range.

(Sgd) G. J. PAUL, Capt. & Adjutant.
9th Bn. Gloucestershire Regt. (Pioneers).

BATTALION ORDERS by MAJOR H. B. SPEAR,
COMMDG. 9TH BN. GLOUCESTERSHIRE REGT.(P).
21st June 1919.

---

856. **DUTIES.**

Bn. Orderly Officer for tomorrow	- 2/Lt. H. R. Jones.
" " " " Monday	- 2/Lt. T. W. Everall.
Next for duty	- 2/Lt. W. J. Noah, M.M.
Bn. Orderly Sergeant for tomorrow	- Sgt. Hardiman.
" " " " Monday	- Sgt. Ellis.
Next for duty	- Sgt. Pixton.

857. **PARADES.**

Divine Service:- "C" and H.Q. Coys. will parade in drill order outside and facing the Q.M. Stores (H.Q. Coy. on right) at 11-10 hours for Church of England Service in the Cinema at 11-30 hours.

Roman Catholics & Wesleyans will attend voluntarily.

Monday:- Coys. will parade under Coy. arrangements.

858. **CASH.**

All requisitions for cash and Officers' advance of Pay Books will be sent to Orderly Room by 09-00 hours on Monday, 23rd inst.   Lieut. E. F. E. Peacock is detailed to draw same from the Field Cashier.

859. **GERMAN CURRENCY (G.R.O. 2947, 18/6/19).**

Only notes issued by the three undermentioned German banking institutions must be accepted by British troops in Germany.
"Reichskassenscheine."
"Reichsbank."
"Darlegenskassenscheine."

These notes range in value from 1 mark upwards and are all equally guaranteed by the German Government.

Under no circumstances must Rhine Provinces or other notes be accepted.

(Sgd) G. J. PAUL, Capt. & Adjutant.
9th Bn. Gloucestershire Regt. (Pioneers).

BATTALION ORDERS BY LIEUT.-COLONEL J. FANE, D.S.O.,
COMMDG. 9TH BN. GLOUCESTERSHIRE REGT. (PIONEERS).
23rd June 1919.

860. **DUTIES.**
Bn. Orderly Officer for tomorrow — 2/Lt. W. J. Noah, M.M.
Next for duty   — 2/Lt. P. J. Hancox.

Bn. Orderly Sergeant for tomorrow — Sgt. Pixton.
Next for duty   — Sgt. Jones.

861. **PARADES.**
Coys. will parade under Company arrangements.

862. **COMMAND.**
Lt.-Col. J. Fane joined this Battalion on 21/6/19 and took over the Command from Major H. B. Spear, from today.

Major H. B. Spear assumes the duties of 2nd in Command from this date.

863. **OFFICERS' KITS.**
In future, when a move is ordered, Officers' Kits will be brought to either the Q.M. Stores or the Officers' Mess, whichever might be nearer.

864. **POSTING.**
45256, Pte H. T. Keen, is transferred from 2nd Oxford & Bucks. L.I. to Gloucestershire Regt., and posted to 9th Bn. with effect from 22/6/19. He is taken on strength of "C" Coy. and allotted New Regtl. No. 56288.

865. **TRANSFER.**
50730, Pte Matthews, A., (attached H.Q. Coy.), is returned to "C" Coy. for duty from this date.

866. **DISCIPLINE. (G.R.O.2959, 20/6/19).**
Delay to the Tramway Service at Cologne has been caused by troops riding on the buffers, couplings and steps. This practice will cease forthwith.

867. **BOUNDS. (G.R.O.2960, 20/6/19).**
Owing to Smallpox, the Isle of Wight is placed out of bounds to all troops and members of Q.M.A.A.C. proceeding on leave, other than demobilization furlough.

(Sgd) G. J. PAUL, Capt. & Adjutant.
9th Bn. Gloucestershire Regt.(Pioneers).

BATTALION ORDERS BY LIEUT.-COLONEL. J. FANE, D.S.O.,
COMMDG. 9TH BN. GLOUCESTERSHIRE REGT. (P).
24th June 1919.

---

868. DUTIES.
Bn. Orderly Officer for tomorrow — 2/Lt. P. J. Hancox.
Next for duty — 2/Lt. W. J. Noah, M.M.

Bn. Orderly Sergeant for tomorrow — Sgt. Jones.
Next for duty — Sgt. Plimsole.

869. PARADES.
Companies will parade under Company arrangements.

870. NOTES ON MARCH DISCIPLINE (Southern Div. No. C.G.S.69/137).
The following will be substituted for para. 13 of Card "Notes on march discipline" dated May 22nd 1919, which was issued to all Officers:-

13. No compliments are to be paid on the march unless Commanders wish to inspect their Commands when they will notify units that they desire compliments to be paid.

871. VETERINARY COURSE.
The u/m men attended a Brigade Veterinary Course and obtained a "Good" report:-

28347 L/c. Hutt, W. (H.Q. Coy.)

(Sgd) G. J. PAUL, Capt. & Adjutant.
9th Bn. Gloucestershire Regt.(Pioneers).

BATTALION ORDERS BY LIEUT.-COLONEL J. FANE, D.S.O.,
COMMDG. 9TH BN. GLOUCESTERSHIRE REGT. (P).
25th June 1919.

872. **DUTIES.**
Bn. Orderly Officer for tomorrow - 2/Lt. H. R. Jones.
Next for duty   - 2/Lt. T. W. Everall.

Bn. Orderly Sergeant for tomorrow - Sgt. Plimsole.
Next for duty   - Sgt. Boast.

873. **PARADES.**
Companies will parade under Company arrangements.

874. **DRESS (G.R.O. No. 2966 dated 23/6/19).**
All ranks when walking out will be properly dressed.
Relaxation of this order may only be made to officers and men whilst proceeding between billets and recreational grounds for the express purpose of participating in games.
On these occasions military tunics and caps must be worn.

875. **BOUNDS.**
Officers and O.Rs. are not allowed out of billeting area without permission. Officers will obtain permission from the Adjutant and O.Rs. from Company Commanders.

876. **RATES OF EXCHANGE.**
The following rates of exchange will come into force forthwith:-

    Germany   ..... 10 Marks   = 2/9d
    France   ..... 5 Francs (French)   = 3/5d
    Belgium   ..... 5 Francs (Belgian) = 3/4d

877. **REVOLVERS - OFFICERS.**
The carrying of Revolvers by Officers will now be discontinued.

(Sgd) G. J. PAUL, Capt. & Adjutant.
       9th Bn. Gloucestershire Regt. (Pioneers).

BATTALION ORDERS BY LIEUT.-COLONEL J. PARR. D.S.O.,
COMDG. 9TH BN. GLOUCESTERSHIRE REGT. (P).
26th June 1919.

978. DUTIES.
Bn. Orderly Officer for tomorrow — 2/Lt. T. W. Everall.
Next for duty — Lieut. E. F. E. Peacock.

Bn. Orderly Sergeant for tomorrow — Sgt. Boast.
Next for duty — Sgt. Buchanan.

979. PARADES.
Companies will parade under Company arrangements.

980. RHINE TRIPS (D.R.O. No. 766 of 25/6/19).
No troops will land from River Steamers in American Area without permission first being obtained on each occasion from Corps Headquarters.
Applications will be submitted through Divisional Headquarters.

981. EXCHANGE OF MONEY (D.R.O. No.768 of 25/6/19).
No sum over £5 in English, or 150 francs in French or Belgian notes is to be exchanged for marks in any one day by any individual officer with a British Army field cashier, or at Messrs T. COOK & Sons, or Messrs COX & CO.

982. PAY BOOKS, A.B.64.
All completed A.Bs.64 are to be returned to Orderly Room in order that they may be forwarded in bulk to the Regtl. Paymaster.

983. DAMAGE TO RAILWAYS (G.R.O.No.2976 of 25/6/19).
Attention is drawn to Army Routine Order No. 2584 of April 3rd. This order is being deliberately disregarded and wanton destruction of railway installations by soldiers travelling by rail continues. The chief installations which suffer are signal lamps, glass roofs of buildings and switchboards. It appears to be a regular practice to spend halts at stations in stone-throwing at all contrivances which have any glass in them, and the serious danger of accidents occurring, owing, for instance, to the glass of signal lamps being broken in this intolerable manner by thoughtless and ill-disciplined men, cannot be too greatly emphasized. In addition, railway employees have been injured by the throwing of stones and other missiles, and deliberately attacked when politely remonstrating with offenders.

These practices must cease. It is the duty of all Officers and N.C.Os. travelling on trains, whether on duty or not, to assist in putting a stop to these malicious practices which only disarrange the railway service to the disadvantage of the troops themselves, bring discredit on the British Army, and give endless trouble to the railway employees and the British railway staffs who have to rectify them.

It is very desirable that severe disciplinary action should be taken against offenders as soon as possible after they are put under arrest and it is the duty of all Officers and N.C.Os. to assist in this by forwarding charges and statements of evidence without delay to the proper quarter.

984. BOX RESPIRATOR HAVERSACKS - WASHING OF.
The following will be added to Bn. Order No. 704 dated 20/5/19.
Under the present conditions there is no objection to Box Respirator Haversacks being cleaned and treated with Blanco or similar substance, provided the respirator is first removed from the haversack, and the haversack is thoroughly dried before the respirator is replaced.

(Sgd) G. J. PAUL, Capt. & Adjutant.
9th Bn. Gloucestershire Regt.(P).

BATTALION ORDERS BY LIEUT.-COLONEL. J. FANE, D.S.O.,
COMMDG. 9TH BN. GLOUCESTERSHIRE REGT. (P).
27th June 1919.

885. **DUTIES.**
Bn. Orderly Officer for tomorrow   -   Lieut. E. F. E. Peacock.
Next for duty   -   2/Lt. H. R. Jones.

Bn. Orderly Sergeant for tomorrow -   Sgt. Buchanan.
Next for duty   -   Sgt. Ellis.

886. **PARADES.**
Companies will parade under Company arrangements.

887. **PAY & MESS BOOK.**
Until further orders payments by Companies will still be made on acquittance rolls and A.B. 64. The Pay & Mess Book will not be used for the present.

888. **OFFICERS' CASH.**
The attention of all Officers is drawn to the fact that the business hours of Messrs T. Cook & Sons and Messrs Cox & Co. are now from 09-00 hours till 15-00 hours daily, only.

889. **STRENGTH.**
2/Lt. G. Watson (4th Worcs. Regt., attached 9th Glouc. Regt.) proceeded to U.K. 26/6/19 and is struck off the strength of the Battalion accordingly from that date.

890. **TRANSFER.**
Lieut. H. G. Hicks is transferred from "B" Coy. to "A" Coy. from this date.

891. **HAIRCUTTING.**
The charge for Haircutting by Regtl. Barber is 15 pfgs. per man.

(Sgd) G. J. PAUL,   Capt. & Adjutant.
9th Bn. Gloucestershire Regt. (Pioneers).

BATTALION ORDERS BY LIEUT.-COLONEL J. FANE, D.S.O.,
COMMDG. 9TH BN. GLOUCESTERSHIRE REGT. (PIONEERS),
28th June 1919.

892. DUTIES.

Bn. Orderly Officer for tomorrow — Lieut. P. J. Hancox.
" " " " Monday — 2/Lt. H. R. Jones.
Next for duty — 2/Lt. T. W. Everall.

Bn. Orderly Sergeant for tomorrow — Sgt. Ellis.
" " " " Monday — Sgt. Johnson.
Next for duty — Sgt. Pixton.

893. PARADES.

Divine Service:- "Q" and H.Q. Coys. will parade in drill order outside and facing the C.M. Stores (H.Q.Coy. on right) at 11-00 hours for Church of England Service in the Lutherian Church at 11-15, followed by Holy Communion for all who wish to attend.

Roman Catholics & Wesleyans will attend voluntarily.

A voluntary C. of E. Service will also be held at 18-00 hours in GASTHOF (opposite Church).

Monday:- Companies will parade under Company arrangements.

894. CASH.

All requisitions for cash and Officers' advance of Pay Books will be sent to Orderly Room by 09-00 hours on Monday, 30th inst. 2/Lt. R. H. Warren, M.C., M.M., is detailed to draw same from the Field Cashier.

895. SALUTE OF GUNS.

By command of His Majesty the King a salute of 101 guns will be fired on the signing of Peace. Should Peace be signed in the morning the salute will be fired at 12-00 hours, and if in the afternoon at 17-00 hours.

896. OFFICERS' A.Bs. 439.

All Officers will hand their A.Bs. 439 into Orderly Room tomorrow, without fail.

(Sgd) G. J. PAUL, Capt. & Adjutant.
9th Bn. Gloucestershire Regt. (Pioneers).

BATTALION ORDERS BY LIEUT.-COLONEL J. FANE, D.S.O.
COMDG. 9TH BN. GLOUCESTERSHIRE REGT. (PIONEERS),
30th June 1919.

897. DUTIES.
Bn. Orderly Officer for tomorrow - 2/Lt. T. W. Everall.
Next for duty - Lieut. V. E. Robertson.

Bn. Orderly Sergeant for tomorrow - Sgt. Plimsole.
Next for duty - Sgt. Boast.

Reveille tomorrow will be at 04-30 hours.
Breakfast " " " " 05-00 hours.

898. PARADES.
Parades will be according to Memo. No. 2.
On return to Leichlingen Companies will be at the disposal of Company Commanders.

899. GUARDS (S.D.No.G.S.24/57).
Re Southern Division Instructions for Guard Mounting, etc.
On page 3. JOIN YOUR GUARD. QUICK MARCH.
In future sentries will turn about on the move at the end of their beat, and will not halt and make deliberate turns.

900. FRATERNIZATION.
Bn. Orders Nos. 313, 709 & 844 are cancelled.
The Commander-in-Chief leave is to the good sense of all ranks as to their behaviour to and relations with the civil population, bearing in mind that they still form part of an Army of Occupation.

901. CAFES.
From tomorrow, 1st July, Cafes in the Leichlingen area will be open to troops until 21-30 hours. This privelege will be withdrawn if there is any trouble in O.Rs. answering their names at Roll Call.

902. TRANSFER.
265178 Sgt. J. Jones is transferred to the R.E. Signal Service from the 20th ult. as a Sapper.

903. PAYMASTER.
In future, all communications to any Paymaster regarding the a/cs. of O.Rs. will be made through Orderly Room.

904. TRANSPORT.
Companies will render to Orderly Room nominal rolls of any volunteers who wish to be transferred to the Transport of this Battalion.

905. AUDIT BOARD.
A Quarterly Audit Board, composed as under, will assemble at the Officers' Mess 10-00 hours on Monday, 7th inst., to audit the Regtl. A/cs. (i.e., Officers' Mess, Sergeants' Mess, Canteen, Sports, Band). All Bank Pass Books will be produced.
Capt. C. S. Lee - President.
Lieut. V. E. Robertson)
2/Lt. S. Johnson) Members.

(Sgd) G. J. PAUL, Capt. & Adjutant.
9th Bn. Gloucestershire Regt. (Pioneers).

NOTICE:-

A SMOKING CONCERT will be held in the Recreation Room at LEICHLINGEN at 18-30 hours tomorrow. All ranks are invited. This Concert is in lieu of the one which was intended to be held on 19th inst.

WAR DIARY or INTELLIGENCE SUMMARY

Army Form C. 2118.

(Erase heading not required.)

Instructions regarding War Diaries and Intelligence Summaries are contained in F.S. Regs., Part II. and the Staff Manual respectively. Title pages will be prepared in manuscript.

Place	Date 1918	Hour	Summary of Events and Information	Remarks and references to Appendices
Burscheid	1 July		H.Qs and "C" Company proceeded to Leichlingen from Burscheid	
Leichlingen	2 "		"B" Company returned to Leichlingen from Burg	
	6 "		Lieut F.J. Pullen returned from leave to U.K.	
	9 "		2nd Lieut W. Chancourt returned from Paris having attended the Inter-Allied Games.	
	13 "		Lieut E.T.C. Peacock proceeded on leave to U.K.	
	14 "		2nd Lieut R.S. Hippenstall proceeded on leave to U.K.	
	15 "		Lt. Col. A.J. Rawson and Capt E.T. Amato taken off strength.	
			Two platoons of "B" Company proceeded to the Racecourse at Halk to 17th under the L.R.B.	
	16 "		2nd Lt L.F. Waddell joined Battalion from U.K. and taken on strength.	
	17 "		2nd Lt. Chancourt W. proceeded on leave to U.K.	
	19 "		Battalion Sports.	
	25 "		The remainder of "B" Company proceeded to the Racecourse at Halk to 4th under the L.R.B.	
	28 "		13th Platoon returned to Leichlingen from Burscheid	
	30 "		2nd Lieut R.S. Hippenstall returned from leave to U.K.	
	31 "		No. 11 Platoon proceeded to Racecourse at Halk to 14th under the L.R.B.	
			During the month "C" Company carried on with training, also "B" Company when possible.	

Strength of Battalion Off. 38. O.Rs 944.

J Pace
Lt. Colonel.

BATTALION ORDERS BY LIEUT.-COLONEL J. FANE, D.S.O.,
COMDG. 9TH BN. GLOUCESTERSHIRE REGT. (PIONEERS),
1st July 1919.

906. DUTIES.
Bn. Orderly Officer for tomorrow – Lieut. V. E. Robertson
Next for duty – 2/Lt. B. Kembrey.

Bn. Orderly Sergeant for tomorrow – Sgt. Bogs Kembrey.
Next for duty – Sgt. Buchanan.

907. PARADES.
H.Q. & "C" Companies will parade under Company arrangements.
"B" Company will parade for Commanding Officer's inspection on football field, facing West, at 11-00 hours.
Formation – as for G.O.C's. inspection.
Dress – Drill Order.

908. INSPECTION.
The Commanding Officer will inspect all the stores and equipment of C. Company at Co. H.Q. on Thursday, the 3rd inst. at 11-00 hours. The Company administrative staff will be present.

(Sgd G. J. PAUL,   Capt. & Adjutant.
9th Bn. Gloucestershire Regt. (Pioneers)

BATTALION ORDERS BY LT.COL.J.FANE D.S.O.
COMMANDING 9TH.BN.GLOUCESTER RGT.(PIONEERS). July 2nd.1919.

909. DUTIES.
Bn.Orderly Officer for Tomorrow .... 2/Lt.B.Kembery.
Next for Duty. .... Lieut.R.H.F.Warren.
Bn.Orderly Sgt.for Tomorrow. .... Sgt.Buchanan.
Next for Duty. .... Sgt.Ellis.

910. PARADES.
Companies will parade under Company Arrangements.

911 DENTAL MECHANIC.
A dental Mechanic is required as instructor at the Southern Division Dental College. Acting Rank and extra pay will be granted to the selected Instructor.
O/C Companies will forward to this Office by 0900 hours 5th.inst. nominal rolls of any dental mechanics under their command, giving Statement of their Qualifications. Nil returns are required.

912 RIFLES.
The Rifles of "B" Co., by platoons, will be overhauled by the Armourer Sergeant. O/C "B" Co. will make arrangements direct with the Armourer Sgt.so that the Inspection will not interfere with Bn.Order No.913.

913 MUSKETRY.
"B" and "C" Companies will commence training on the 30 Ranges tomorrow the 3rd.inst.
Practices. 5 rounds, deliberate, standing, Fixed Bayonets.
          10   "   Rapid (One Minute allowed).
Steel Helmets to be worn for each practice.
Average results by platoon to be rendered to Orderly Room.

914 BATHS.
The Baths are allotted to "B" Company at 13.30 hours tomorrow.

915 APPOINTMENTS.
Lieut.W.F.Palmer is appointed Band President from this date.
2nd.Lieut.D.E.Bresman is to assume Civil Duties from this date. vice Lieut.R.H.F.Allen.

916 PROMOTION.
50636 L/Sgt.J.Eustace is promoted A/Sgt.paid from 20/5/19.and to be Assistant instructor in Signalling from same date.

917 INSPECTION.
Reference Bn.Order No.998 1st.Inst.
The Commanding Officer will inspect Stores etc.of "B" Coy.at 1130 hours on same date.

918 PEACE CELEBRATIONS.
The Commander in Chief wishes the signing of Peace to be commemorated by a holiday for the troops. This Holiday will be observed on on Friday the 4th.inst.
The attention of all ranks is called to the notices at the end of B/Orders.

919 x LEAVE..CALAIS SERVICE.
No Officers, other than those selcted to conduct Leave Parties, may proceed by the Calais Leave Services.

(signed)G.J.PAUL Capt.and Adjutant,

9TH.BN.GLOUCESTER RGT.(PIONEERS).

SPORTS COMMITTEE MEETING.

A Sports Committee Meeting will be held in the Officers Mess at 1400 hours on Thursday the 3rd.inst.
Representatives as detailed are requested to attend.

SPORTS ETC.

On Friday and Saturday 4th.and 5th.inst. two 2-day Cricket Matches will take place.

   "B" Coy. v "C" Coy.
   HQ. Coy. v Officers.

Play will commence on Friday at 1100 hours, adjourn for Lunch at 1245 hours and re-commence at 1400 hours.
On Saturday Play will commence at 1400 hours.
On Sunday the Winners of these Two matches will play one another.

A Concert will also be held on Friday, at 1900 hours, in the recreat Room.

BATTALION ORDERS BY LIEUT.-COLONEL J. FANE, D.S.O.,
COMDG. 9TH BN. GLOUCESTERSHIRE REGT. (PIONEERS),
3rd July 1919.

920. **DUTIES.**
Bn. Orderly Officer for tomorrow — Lieut. R. H. F. Allen.
" " " " Saturday — Lieut. G. F. Pullen.
Next for duty — 2/Lt. F. J. Stebbings, M.C.

Bn. Orderly Sergeant for tomorrow — Sgt. Ellis.
" " " " Saturday — Sgt. Johnson.
Next for duty — Sgt. Pixton.

921. **PARADES.**
There will be no parades tomorrow.

Saturday:— Companies will parade under Company arrangements.

922. **RATES OF EXCHANGE (G.R.O. 776 of 1/7/19).**
The following rates of exchange are fixed for July:—

      France — 5 Francs = 3/5d
      Belgium — 5 Francs = 3/3d
      Germany — 10 Marks = 2/9d

923. **FIELD CASHIER (G.R.O. 778 of 2/7/19).**
The Field Cashier will visit Units as follows, until further notice:—
    Berg Gladbach 10.00 — 11.30 Every Tuesday
    Burscheid 12.00 — 13.00 " "
    Wermelskirchen 14.30 — 15.30 " "

924. **LEWIS GUN COURSE.**
Os. C. "B" & "C" Cos. will each detail 3 N.C.Os. to attend a Regtl. Lewis Gun Course, commencing at 09-30 hours on Monday next, the 7th inst.
The duration of the course will be 12 working days.
Nominal Rolls of N.C.Os. selected will be forwarded to the Lewis Gun Officer not later than 12-00 hours on Saturday, the 5th inst.

925. **GERMAN FACTORIES.**
Arrangements have been made by the Army of the Rhine for certain factories to be visited by Officers & O.Rs. with a view to studying the German methods of manufacture in comparison with our own. Company Commanders will forward to Orderly Room by 12-00 hours on the 6th inst. lists of Officers & O.Rs. wishing to avail themselves of this opportunity, stating in each case which type of factory it is desired to examine.

926. **APPOINTMENT.**
Lieut. S. Johnson is appointed Messing Officer to the Battalion.

G. Paul
Capt. & Adjutant.
9th Bn. Gloucestershire Regt. (Pioneers).

NOTICE.

Ref. Notice in Bn. Orders of 2nd inst. regarding cricket for Friday.

For "13-45 hours" read "12-45 hours."

BATTALION ORDERS BY LIEUT.-COLONEL J. FANE, D.S.O.,
COMMDG. 9TH BN. GLOUCESTERSHIRE REGT. (PIONEERS),
5th July 1919.

927. **DUTIES.**
Bn. Orderly Officer for tomorrow — 2/Lt. F. J. Stebbing, M.C.
"   "   "   "   Monday   — Lieut. V. E. Robertson.
Next for duty   — Lieut. E. F. E. Peacock.

Bn. Orderly Sergeant for tomorrow   — Sgt. Russon.
"   "   "   "   Monday   — Sgt. Sleeman.
Next for duty   — Sgt. Brooker.

928. **DIVINE SERVICE.**
"B", "C" and H.Q. Cos. will parade in drill order formed up in line facing West, on the road leading to the Recreation Ground, at 11-30 hours tomorrow, for Church of England Service, which will be held in the Protestant Church, Leichlingen, at 11-45 hours, followed by Holy Communion for all who wish to attend.
Roman Catholic Service will be held in the R.C. Church, Leichlingen, at 10-00 hours.
Non-Conformist Service will be held in the Cinema at 11-00 hours.

PARADES FOR MONDAY.
Companies will parade under Company arrangements.

929. **ADVANCES TO OFFICERS IN GERMAN TERRITORY ON A.F.W.3421 (G.R.O.3116)**
In future Officers will not draw from an Army Field Cashier more than three times in any one month up to a maximum, monthly, of the nearest equivalent in marks of
£15 for Subalterns.   £20 for Captains.
£25 for Field Officers and above.

930. **BARRIERS AT RAILWAY LEVEL CROSSINGS - IMPROPER RAISING OF.** (G.R.O.
It has been reported that on several occasions when barriers (3127) at level crossings have been closed to allow the passage of a train, they have been forcibly raised by British Troops to allow transport to go through.
Such action not only holds up railway traffic but involves serious risk of accident.
All drivers of motor lorries, motor cars, and horse transport are to be informed that this practice must cease forthwith, and that no attempt is to be made to pass over level crossings until the barriers have been raised by the German Railway Officials.

931. **INSPECTION OF BOX RESPIRATORS.**
Box Respirators, by platoons, will be inspected as follows:-
"B" Co.,   Monday.
"C" Co.,   Tuesday.
H.Q.Co.,   Wednesday.
The Bn. Gas N.C.O. will make the necessary arrangements direct with Os. C. Companies.

932 **MUSKETRY.**

Ref. Bn. Order No. 913 dated 2nd inst.
Firing will take place on Monday, 7th inst.

R D Hepkinstall 2/Lt for Capt. & Adjutant.
9th Bn. Gloucestershire Regt. (Pioneers).

BATTALION ORDERS BY LIEUT.-COLONEL. S. PAUL, D.S.O.,
COMDG. 9TH BN. GLOUCESTERSHIRE REGT. (PIONEERS).
7th July 1919.
==

932. **DUTIES.**
Bn. Orderly Officer for tomorrow - Lieut. R. F. E. Pocock.
Next for duty - Lieut. R. H. F. Allen.

Bn. Orderly Sergeant for tomorrow - Sgt. Brooker.
Next for duty - Sgt. Foot.

934. **PARADES.**
Companies will parade under Company arrangements.

935. **BUGLES.**
In future, the First Post will be sounded at 21-40 hours and the Last Post at 22-00 hours.

936. **OFFICERS' MESS.**
An Officers' Mess Meeting will take place at 19-30 hours on Wednesday, 9th inst., in the Ante Room.
All Officers not on duty will attend.

937. **WAR SAVINGS ASSOCIATION.**
A War Savings Association will be started in the Battalion from today, with objects as stated in pamphlets issued to all Companies.

Committee:-
Président   ...   Commanding Officer.
Treasurer   ...   Lieut. V. H. Robertson.
Secretary   ...   R. S. M.
Members   ...   All ranks.

Sub-Committee:-
O.C. 's Companies.
C.S.M.'s. of Companies.

The amounts subscribed by Companies will be published in Bn. Orders weekly, on Saturdays.

In connection with this, the Battalion, less "A" Company, will attend a lecture in the Cinema at 17-00 hours tomorrow, 8th inst.

938. **TRANSPORT.**
The Commanding Officer will inspect the personnel of the transport at the Transport Lines at 10-00 hours tomorrow.

939. **CASH.**
All requisitions for cash and Officers' advance of pay books will be sent to Orderly Room by 09-00 hours tomorrow, 8th inst.
2/Lt. R. A. Brown is detailed to draw cash from the Field Cashier at DORTMUND at 10-00 hours.

940. **CALAIS-COLOGNE EXPRESS (D.R.O.785 of 1/7/19).**
From the 1st July the CALAIS-COLOGNE express will leave CALAIS at the following times:-
10-15, 12-45, 13-45, 14-15 hours.
Departure from COLOGNE will remain unaltered.

(Sgd) G. S. PAUL,
Capt. & Adjutant.
9th Bn. Gloucestershire Regt. (Pioneers).

BATTALION ORDERS BY LIEUT.-COLONEL J. PAUL, D.S.O.,
COMDG. 9TH BN. GLOUCESTERSHIRE REGT. (PIONEERS).
8th July 1919.

==

941. DUTIES.
  Bn. Orderly Officer for tomorrow   - Lieut. R. E. P. Allen.
  Next for duty   - 2/Lt. F. J. Stebbing, M.C.
  Bn. Orderly Sergeant for tomorrow - Sgt. Post.
  Next for duty   - Sgt. Runson.

942. PARADES.
  Companies will parade under Company arrangements.

943. INLYING PIQUET & BILLET GUARDS.
  An Inlying Piquet consisting of two platoons will be detailed daily.
  The Piquet must not leave the vicinity of its billets and must be ready to turn out at any hour during the day or night at short notice.
  "B" and "C" Companies will each detail one platoon daily, which will parade at 19-00 hours for inspection by the Bn. Orderly Officer.
  Companies will detail the necessary billet guards to ensure that arms, equipment and ammunition are not removed from the billets whilst the men are absent on duty or for recreational purposes.

944. AUDIT BOARD.
  (Ref. Bn. Order No. 906, dated 30/6/19).
  This Audit Board will reassemble at 10-00 hours tomorrow, the 9th inst.
  The following Officers & O.Rs. will attend:-

  P.M.C., Band President, Sports Officer, President Sgts.' Mess.

945. TIMES OF TRAINS (D.R.O. No.786 of 7/7/19).
  From the 17th July inclusive the train running at 21-45 hours from COLOGNE to OPLADEN is cancelled. The train running at 22-45 from COLOGNE to OPLADEN will be substituted.
  Passengers for DUNSCHEID and WERMELSKIRCHEN must, therefore, leave COLOGNE by the 20-40 train, as the 22-45 train is too late for the connection at OPLADEN for DUNSCHEID & WERMELSKIRCHEN.

946. ATTACHMENTS.
  Capt. H. Adamson ("C" Co.) is attached to transport for duty from today.

  60394 Pte A. Clinch ("D" Co.) is attached to H.Q. Co. for duty as Bn. Runner.
  61980 Pte A. Cole ("C" Co.) is attached to H.Q. Co. for duty as Bn. Runner.

947. BATHS.
  In future, the Bn. Baths will be open on Wednesdays & Thursdays during the following hours:-
    09-30 till 12-30 ... 13-30 - 16-00 hours.
  It is essential that all unemployed men attend during these hours.

                              (Sgd) G. S. PAUL, Capt. & Adjutant.
                              9th Bn. Gloucestershire Regt. (Pioneers).

BATTALION ORDERS BY LIEUT.-COLONEL J. FANE, D.S.O.,
COMDG. 9TH BN. GLOUCESTERSHIRE REGT. (PIONEERS),
9th July 1919.

948. **DUTIES.**
Bn. Orderly Officer for tomorrow — 2/Lt. F. J. Stebbing, M.C.
Next for duty — 2/Lt. W. Francombe.

Bn. Orderly Sergeant for tomorrow — Sgt. Russon.
Next for duty — Sgt. Sleeman.

949. **PARADES.**
Companies will parade under Company arrangements.

950. **INLYING PICQUET.**
Ref. Bn. Order No. 943 dated 8/7/19.
The Inlying Picquet will be inspected daily at 18-00 hours by the Company Orderly Officer, who will report to the Adjutant that everything is correct or otherwise.

951. **1914 STAR.** (G.R.O.3137 dated 7/7/19.)
The wearing of a silver rosette or other emblem on the ribbon of 1914 Star is unauthorized.
Any such emblems now being worn are to be removed forthwith.

952. **IMPORTATION OF PRIVATELY-OWNED MOTOR CARS & MOTOR BICYCLES INTO FRANCE, FLANDERS & TERRITORY OCCUPIED BY ARMY OF THE RHINE.**
G.R.O. No. 3146 of 7/7/19 is re-published for information.
1. Officers serving with the British Troops in France and Flanders, and the British Army of the Rhine, may import into those countries their private motor cars, or motor bicycles, under the following conditions:-
   (a) Rail and sea transport must be arranged for, and the expense borne by owners.
   (b) The maintenance of such vehicles must be carried out under local arrangements to be made by owners. In no case may British Military labour or British Military Workshops be used for repairs.
   (c) Petrol, lubricants and such tyres and spare parts as may be available and can be spared from local Army stocks, may be issued on repayment. On no account, however, are stocks to be increased to meet these demands.
2. Petrol will be issued at list price, cans also being charged for at list price on issue, and allowed for at the same rate when returned.
3. The price to be charged for lubricants, tyres and spare parts, will include an addition of 17 per cent. to the vocabulary rate to cover freight and departmental expenses.

953. **LECTURE.**
A Lecture on "China", illustrated by films, will be held in the Metropole Theatre at 11-15 hours on Friday next, 11th inst.
150 men from each of "B" and "C" Companies, and as many of H.Q. Co. as can be spared, will attend.

954. **PROMOTIONS.**
50655 C.Q.M.S. A. Green to be A/C.S.M. vice Shearne, to U.K. 2/7/19.
50380 Sgt. Bassett to be A/C.Q.M.S. vice Green, promoted.
32988 A/Cpl. D. Adamson to be A/Sergt. vice Bassett, promoted.
50353 A/pd/L/c. W. Brady to be A/Cpl vice Adamson, promoted.
50328 A/Unpd/L/c. J. Madeley to be A/pd/L/c. vice Brady, promoted.

955. **APPOINTMENT.**
32988 A/Cpl. D. Adamson to be Transport Sergeant, vice Harris, to duty.

(Sgd) G. J. PAUL, Capt. & Adjutant.
9th Bn. Gloucestershire Regt.

BATTALION ORDERS BY LIEUT.-COLONEL J. FANE, D.S.O.,
COMDG. 9TH BN. GLOUCESTERSHIRE REGT. (PNRS),
10th July 1919.

956. DUTIES.
Bn. Orderly Officer for tomorrow   - 2/Lt. W. Francombe.
Next for duty   - Lieut. V. E. Robertson.

Bn. Orderly Sergeant for tomorrow   - Sgt. Sleeman.
Next for duty   - Sgt. Thorpe.

957. PARADES.
Companies will parade under Company arrangements.

958. TRAIN SERVICE.
Ref. Bn. Order No. 945 dated 8th July.
For "17th July" read "7th July."

959. WIVES IN OCCUPIED TERRITORY (D.R.O. No. 791, 8/7/19).
No orders have yet been received from the War Office as to whether wives will be permitted to come out officially, and partly or wholly at Government expense.
The Commander-in-Chief, however, is prepared to grant a limited number of passes for officers' wives to visit their husbands in occupied territory on the distinct understanding that this is entirely at the expense of the latter.
All requests of this nature will be made to Bn. Orderly Room.

960. COURT OF ENQUIRY.
A Court of Enquiry, composed of the u/m Officers, will assemble at the Q. M. Stores tomorrow, 11th inst., at 10-00 hours, to investigate the loss of new clothing and the state of old clothing returned from I.C.S. at MULHEIM.
    President ... Capt. Horton.
    Members ... 2/Lt. E. A. Bresman.
            2/Lt. W. Francombe.

961. REGIMENTAL ACCOUNTS.
All Regimental Accounts will in future be submitted monthly, on 7th of the month, for the Commanding Officer's approval.

962. ADVANCES TO OFFICERS. (C.R.O. No. 2036, 8/7/19).
Ref. Bn. Order No. 929 of 5/7/19.
At the present rate of exchange the following maximum advances can now be paid three times in any one month:-
  Field Officers and above - Marks 600.
  Captains   - " 480.
  Subalterns   - " 360.

G. Paul
Capt. & Adjutant.
9th Bn. Gloucestershire Regt. (Pioneers).

S P O R T S.

The 51st Bn. The Hampshire Regiment invite entries for the following events to be held at their Regimental Sports on the 24th July.
 100 yards. Open to 3rd Southern Infantry Brigade.
 1 mile. Open to 3rd Southern Infantry Brigade.
 3 miles Flat. Open to Southern Division.
 Not more than three entries per Unit.
 Entries for these events should reach the battalion Sports Officer, 51st Battalion The Hampshire Regiment, by July 11th.

BATTALION ORDERS BY LIEUT.COL.J.FANE D.S.O.

COMMANDING 9TH.BN.GLOUCESTER RGT.(PIONEERS).

11/7/19.

963 DUTIES.
Bn.Orderly Officer for to morrow .... Lt.V.E.Robertson.
Next for Duty.   .... 2ndLt. T.W.Everall.
Bn.Orderly Sgt.for to morrow.   .... Sgt.Thorpe.
Next for Duty.   .... Sgt.Brooker.

964. PARADES.
Companies will parade under Company arrangements.

965. POSTINGS.
No.50725 Pte.E.Meecham.is posted to H.Q.Coy.

966 BOX RESPIRATORS. (G.R.O.3151 dated 9/7/19.).
In future Box Respirators will not form part of the Equipment taken to Dispersal Stations by Soldiers for disposal.
A.F.Z.10 Dispersal Certificate will be amended by the deletion of the words "Box Respirators.

967 REGIMENTAL ACCOUNTS.
Officers in charge of Regimental Accounts are not to hand over their funds when going on leave or courses. The Officer to take over accounts will be detailed by the Commanding Officer.

(Signed)G.J.PAUL.   Capt.and Adjt.

9RH. N.GLOUCESTER RGT.(PIONEERS).

BATTALION ORDERS BY LIEUT.-COLONEL. J. FANE, D.S.O.,
COMDG. 9TH BN. GLOUCESTERSHIRE REGT. (PIONEERS),
12th July 1919.

968. DUTIES.
Bn. Orderly Officer for tomorrow - Lieut. G. F. Pullen.
"   "   "   "   Monday   - 2/Lt. W. J. Nosh, M.M.
Next for duty   - 2/Lt. F. J. Stebbing, M.C.

Bn. Orderly Sergeant for tomorrow - Sgt. Plimsole.
"   "   "   "   Monday   - Sgt. Hardiman.
Next for duty   - Sgt. Boast.

969. DIVINE SERVICE.
"B", "C" and H.Q. Coys. will parade in drill order formed up in line, facing West, on the road leading to the Recreation Ground, at 11-30 hours tomorrow, for Church of England Service, which will be held in the Protestant Church, Leichlingen, at 11-45 hours, followed by Holy Communion for all who wish to attend.
Roman Catholic Service will be held in the R.C. Church, Leichlingen, at 10-00 hours.
 Note:- The Roman Catholic clergyman will be at the R.C. Church on Saturdays from 14-00 to 16-00 hours, for the purpose of interviewing any R.Cs. who wish to see him.
Non-Conformist Service will be held in the Schutzenhaus, Leichlingen, at 11-00 hours.

PARADES FOR MONDAY.
Companies will parade under Company arrangements.

970. DEFINITION OF THE PHRASE "TERMINATION OF THE WAR."(C.R.O.2057).
The "Termination of the War" has been defined by Parliament in the "Termination of the Present War" Definition Act of 1918, as the date of the exchange or deposits or ratifications of the Treaty or Treaties of Peace, which date will subsequently be promulgated by order in council. The phrase "Termination of Hostilities" has exactly the same meaning as "Termination of the War." An armistice is merely a suspension of hostilities which may or may not be resumed. The period of the "Duration of the War" does not end with the armistice of November 11th 1918, but with the "Termination of the War" as above defined. Apart from the above definitions all men are liable under the Naval, Military and Air Force Service Act 1919 to be retained with the Colours beyond the expiration of their original engagements up to April 30th 1920. In addition to the above, those men (not being soldiers of the regular forces serving on a pre-war attestation) who are serving in imperial units, the Depots of which are situated in the United Kingdom of Great Britain and Ireland, who are, at the termination of the present War, in actual service, are also liable to be retained with the Colours up to 30th April 1920.

971. MOVE.
O. C., "B" Coy. will detail two platoons to report to Lieut. Garbutt, R.E., Racecourse, KALK, on 15th inst. Details regarding transport, rations, accommodation etc. will be issued direct to this Company.

972. TELEPHONES - USE OF. (S.D. Letter No. C.G.S.51/133).
With reference to the various orders which have been issued (since the Division arrived in the Bridgehead) regarding the closing of offices and telephone exchanges between 22-00 and 08-00 hours, the G.O.C. directs that, whilst those orders will be fully complied with as they now stand, arrangements must exist in all exchanges whereby "Urgent Priority Operation" calls and wires can be got through at all times during "closed" hours. Such calls and wires will be the only ones that will be accepted and then only when originated by an Officer duly authorised to do so. If a tendency arises in any area to use lines during the closed hours for "illegal" messages report of the fact will be made to Divisional H.Q., the names of the offenders (subscribers) being stated.

(Sgd) G. J. PAUL, Capt. & Adjutant.
9th Bn. Gloucestershire Regt.(p)

BATTALION ORDERS BY LIEUT.-COL. J. FANE, D.S.O.,
COMMDG. 9TH BN. GLOUCESTERSHIRE REGT. (PIONEERS),
14TH JULY 1919.

---

973. DUTIES.
Bn. Orderly Officer for tomorrow — 2/Lt. W. J. Noah, M.M.
Next for duty — 2/Lt. T. W. Everall.

Bn. Orderly Sergeant for tomorrow — Sgt. Boast.
Next for duty — Sgt. Buchanan.

974. PARADES.
Companies will parade under Company arrangements.

975. BATHS.
In future, baths will be available as follows:-

Thursdays	...	13-30 to 16-00 hours.
Fridays	...	09-30 to 12-30 hours.
		13-30 to 16-00 hours.
Saturdays	...	09-30 to 11-00 hours.

976. CASH.
All requisitions for cash and Officers' advance of pay books will be sent to Orderly Room by 09-00 hours tomorrow, 15th inst. 2/Lt. F. J. Stebbing, M.C., is detailed to draw cash from the Field Cashier at BURSCHEID at 12-00 hours.

977. RHINE TRIP.
In future, parties detailed for the Rhine Trip will always take overcoats, unless otherwise detailed.

978. OFFICERS.
Officers desiring to leave the billeting area before 12-30 hours must obtain permission from the Commanding Officer.

979. OFFICERS' SERVANTS.
Officers' servants are to report to their Company Sergeant-Major for duty when their Officers go on leave.

980. MUSKETRY.
H.Q. Co. and Transport will commence firing on Tuesday on "B" Co's. range.
Practices:- 5 Rounds, deliberate, standing, fixed bayonet.
10 Rounds, rapid, lying (1 min. allowed).
Steel Helmets to be worn for each practice.
Average results by platoons to be rendered to Orderly Room.

(Sgd) G. J. PAUL,
Capt. & Adjutant.
9th Bn. Gloucestershire Regt. (Pioneers).

BATTALION ORDERS BY LIEUT.-COL. J. FANE, D.S.O.,
COMDG. 9TH BN. GLOUCESTERSHIRE REGT. (PIONEERS),
15th July 1919.

981. DUTIES.

Bn. Orderly Officer for tomorrow — Lieut. V. E. Robertson.
Next for duty — Lieut. G. F. Pullen.

Bn. Orderly Sergeant for tomorrow — Sgt. Buchanan.
Next for duty — Sgt. Ellis.

982. PARADES.
Companies will parade under Company arrangements.

983. DISCIPLINE – AMENDMENTS TO THE ARMY ACT. (D.R.O. 808, 14/7/19).
1. Attention is drawn to the additions and amendments to the Army Act contained in the Army (Annual) Act, 1919, and published in Army Council Instructions No. 305 of 1919, which come into force in the Army of the Rhine on July 31st 1919.
All copies of the manual of Military Law will be brought up to date accordingly.
2. The amendments to King's Regulations contained in Army Order 105 of 1919 should be read in connection with Sections 46 and 46a of the Army Act.
(Authority G.H.Q. 3157).

(Sgd) G. J. PAUL, Capt. & Adjutant.
9th Bn. Gloucestershire Regt. (Pioneers).

BATTALION ORDERS BY LIEUT.-COL. J. FANE, D.S.O.,
COMDG. 9TH BN. GLOUCESTERSHIRE REGT. (PIONEERS),
16TH JULY 1919.

984. **DUTIES.**
Bn. Orderly Officer for tomorrow — 2/Lt. L. J. Waddell.
Next for duty — 2/Lt. T. W. Everall.

Bn. Orderly Sergeant for tomorrow — Sgt. Ellis.
Next for duty — Sgt. Johnson.

985. **PARADES.**
Companies will parade under Company arrangements.

986. **BOUNDS.** (G.R.Os. 3180 & 3181, 14/7/19).
Owing to an outbreak of measles the town of Newtownards, County Down, is placed out of bounds to all troops and Q.M.A.A.C. proceeding on leave other than demobilization furlough.

Owing to the outbreak of typhoid fever, Altenahr and all places on the river Ahr east of it to Remagen (exclusive) are out of bounds to British troops until further orders.

987. **WEARING OF SWORDS - OFFICERS.** (G.R.O. 3188, 14/7/19).
1. Until further orders, Field Marshals, General Officers and Colonels will, when dismounted, wear swords with the "Sam Browne" belt on all ceremonial parades, at inspections, presentation of colours and at official ceremonies. When mounted the sword will be carried on the saddle.

2. Swords will not be worn by Regimental Officers when parading with Units under inspection, except in those Services where the sword is the arm carried in the field.

988. **STRENGTH.**
2/Lt. L. J. Waddell joined the Bn. for duty on 15/7/19 and was posted to "B" Co.

Lt.-Col. R. I. Rawson and Capt. E. T. Smith, M.C., are struck off the strength of this Bn. from 14/7/19.

(Sgd) G. J. PAUL, Capt. & Adjutant.
9th Bn. Gloucestershire Regt. (Pioneers).

DIVISIONAL TOURNAMENT.

Entries for Mounted & Dismounted Events in Southern Division Tournament must reach Hon. Secretary at Div. H.Q. on or before July 28th.

BATTALION ORDERS BY LIEUT.-COL. J. FANE, D.S.O.,
COMDG. 9TH BN. GLOUCESTERSHIRE REGT. (PIONEERS),
17th JULY 1919.

989. **DUTIES.**
Bn. Orderly Officer for tomorrow — 2/Lt. T. W. Everall.
Next for duty — 2/Lt. W. J. Noah, M.M.

Bn. Orderly Sergeant for tomorrow — Sgt. Johnson.
Next for duty — Sgt. Plimsole.

990. **PARADES.**
Companies will parade under Company arrangements.

991. **DEMOBILIZATION.**
Attention of Os. C. Companies is drawn to G.R.O. 502 dated 31/12/18, concerning return of ammunition, ground sheets etc.

992. **BOOTS.**
Blacking used by men is ruining uppers; dubbin must be used at least once weekly.

993. **ANIMALS – EXCHANGE OR TRANSFER OF. (D.R.O.806, 14/7/19).**
No exchange or transfer of any animals between Units or Formations (other than exchanges or transfers already ordered by H.Q. or Corps or Divisions) is under any circumstances to be made after this date without the consent of D.Q.M.G., or D.D.R., G.H.Q. Os. C. Units will be held responsible that this order is strictly complied with. (Authority G.H.Q. 5165 dated 11/7/1919).

994. **NEW SYSTEM OF PAY AND MESS BOOKS (D.R.O. No. 815, 16/7/19).**
Command Paymaster will lecture at 2nd Southern Infantry Brigade Headquarters at 11.00 hours on the 18th July on the new pay and mess book accounting. At least one Officer and one Clerk from each Infantry Company and Battery, and each imprest holder, will be present.

Ref. above each Company Commander and one Clerk from each Co. will attend, together with the imprest holder.

995. **MOVEMENT.**
It is proposed that the following movements will take place on 22nd inst.

A. Co. — "A" Co., less 1 strong platoon (which will remain at BURSCHEID) will move to Leichlingen.
B. Co. — The remainder of "B" Co. and Co. H.Q. will move to BURSCHEID.
C. Co. — 1 Officer, 4 N.C.Os. & 56 O.Rs. of "C" Co. will proceed to BERG GLADBACH for duty with the 455 Field Co. R.E.

Further particulars will be issued later.

(Sgd) G. J. PAUL, Capt. & Adjutant.
9th Bn. Gloucestershire Regt. (Pioneers).

NOTICES.

A Divisional Boxing Tournament will be held towards the end of August. Date will be notified later.

BATTALION SPORTS.

Os.C., B. C. & H.Q. Cos. will arrange to send one SOYER stove each to sports ground by 10-00 hours on Saturday next, to report to Lieut. Johnson or Lieut. & Q.M. Creedon.
O. C. C. Co. will detail a fatigue party of 1 N.C.O. & 20 men to report to Lieut. Johnson at 10-00 hours on Friday, 18th inst., at the Concert Room.

AFTER ORDER.

996. **DEMOBILIZATION.**
Ref. Bn. Order No. 991.
Reference to G.R.O. No. 502 (quoted in this Bn. Order)
may be obtained on application to the Q.M.

997. **NEW SYSTEM OF PAY AND MESS BOOKS (D.R.O.No.815, 16/7/19).**
Ref. Bn. Order No. 994.
The "clerk" referred to in this Bn. Order must be the C.Q.M.S.

BATTALION ORDERS BY LIEUT.-COL. J. PAUL, D.S.O.,
COMDG. 9th Bn. GLOUCESTERSHIRE REGT. (PIONEERS),
19th JULY 1919.

998. HQ DUTIES.

Bn. Orderly Officer for tomorrow — 2/Lt. W. J. Roch, M.M.
"   "   "   " Sunday   — Lieut. J. F. Pullen.
"   "   "   " Monday   — 2/Lt. L. J. Waddell.
Next for duty   — Lieut. W. K. Robertson.

Bn. Orderly Sergeant for tomorrow — Sgt. Pinnock.
"   "   "   " Sunday   — Sgt. Hastings.
"   "   "   " Monday.   — Sgt. Rossi.
Next for duty   — Sgt. Dickenson.

999. PARADES.

Tomorrow, having been reserved for Regimental Sports, will be observed as a holiday after 09-00 hours.

Sunday:— "B", "C" and H.Q. Coys. will parade in drill order formed up in line, facing West, on the road leading to the Recreation Ground, at 11-00 hours, for Church of England Service, which will be held in the Protestant Church, Leichlingen, at 11-45 hours, followed by Holy Communion for all who wish to attend.

Roman Catholic Services:— The following R.C. Services will be held in the R.C. Church, Leichlingen.

    Holy Communion   ...   07-30 hours.
    Morning Service   ...   10-30   "
    Benediction   ...   15-00   "

The Roman Catholic clergyman will be at the R.C. Church on Saturdays from 16-00 to 18-00 hours, for the purpose of interviewing any R.Cs. who wish.

Non-Conformist Service will be held in the Cinema at 11-00 hours.

On Monday, Companies will parade under Company arrangements.

1000. KHAKI DRILL SHORTS — ISSUE ON PAYMENT (D.R.O.817, 17/7/19).

Units requiring Khaki Drill Shorts for recreational purposes may obtain them from Ordnance on re-payment (credit being secured on priced vouchers in the usual manner) at the reduced price of 1/4 per pair. Supplies from this source and at this price are limited, and no guarantee can be given that all demands are met. Indents for these shorts should not yet be submitted but a return rendered to D.A.D.O.S. by 19th inst. showing estimated requirements. Attention is drawn to G.R.O. 1090, 2828 and 4187. The cutting down of Service Dress Trousers into shorts is strictly forbidden.

1001. RELEASE ON COMPASSIONATE GROUNDS.

Numerous applications are being submitted by Companies for the release of O.Rs. on compassionate grounds. The majority of these applications do not conform with the procedure as laid down in Army Council Instructions No. 207 of 1919 (extracts from which were sent to all Company Commanders under this office No. L.22, dated 20/6/19). O.C. Companies will ensure that all future applications are submitted strictly in accordance with the above-quoted A.C.I.

(Sgd) C. J. PAUL, Capt. & Adjutant.
9th Bn. Gloucestershire Regt. (Pioneers).

NOTICE.

Competitors in the Regtl. Sports are notified that the heats will commence promptly at 10-00 hours tomorrow.

BATTALION ORDERS BY LIEUT.-COL. J. FANE, D.S.O.,
COMMDG. 9TH BN. GLOUCESTERSHIRE REGT. (P),
21st JULY 1919.

1002. **DUTIES.**
Bn. Orderly Officer for tomorrow   -   2/Lt. T. W. Everall.
Next for duty   -   2/Lt. W. J. Noah, M.M.

Bn. Orderly Sergeant for tomorrow   -   Sgt. Buchanan.
Next for duty   -   Sgt. Pixton.

1003. **PARADES.**
Companies will parade under Company arrangements.

Bn. Order No. 463 is re-published.
"In future rifles and ammunition will be carried by
"all men when on parade, including bathing parade.
"When not on parade there will always be an orderly
"man at each billet left in charge of all rifles and
"equipment."
O. C. Companies will ensure that this order is carried out.

1004. **MOVEMENT.**
Bn. Order No. 995 of 17th July is suspended.

1005. **BRITISH WAR MEDAL.** (D.R.O.No.820, 19/7/19).
The British War Medal Riband is authorized to be worn by
all entitled to the medal.
A preliminary issue of the riband will be made by D.A.D.O.S.
on receipt of indents.
(Authority - Rhine Army No. Q/851, dated 18-7-1919).

1006. **MUSKETRY.**
"B" & "C" Coys. will fire the following practices:-
            Grouping   ...   5 rounds.
            Application ...   5 rounds.
            Snap-shooting   5 rounds.
As for practices 1, 2 and 12 in new Musketry Course.

1007. **BOX RESPIRATORS.** (Southern Division No. C.G.S.60/148, 19/7/19).
Cases are occurring frequently of wilful damage to Box
Respirators. The satchels are often used as receptacles for a
variety of unauthorised articles, which inevitably do damage
to the respirator; furthermore, the number of unofficial tests
by the wearers of the unbreakable quality of the eye pieces has
resulted in scarred and dented glass in a great many cases.
All ranks must take this matter up personally and ensure that
the respirators are maintained in an efficient condition.

1008. **ANTI-GAS COURSE.**
The u/m N.C.Os. attended the Anti-Gas Course at BERG GLADBACH
on July 9th 1919, and are reported on as stated:-
        50910 L/c Mobbs,   C.   Very Good.) Practical
        201227 " Blackwell, C.   Good.   )

        50910 L/c Mobbs,   C.   Excellent) Theory
        201227 " Blackwell, C.   Very Good.)

1009. **CASH.**
All requisitions for cash and Officers' advance of pay books
will be sent to Orderly Room by 09-00 hours tomorrow, 22nd inst.
2/Lt. T. W. Everall is detailed to draw cash from the Field
Cashier at BURSCHEID at 12-00 hours.

(Continued

1010. **PROMOTIONS & APPOINTMENTS.**
The under-mentioned are promoted to Temp. ranks as stated for duration of war, i.e., up to 30th April 1920:-

    50666 Cpl. F. Horton to be paid Sergeant, vice Butler, and to be Orderly Room Sergeant.
    50594 L/c. L. Bennett to be paid Corporal, vice Horton.
    50328 " J. Madeley " " " " " Shewring
    50745 " W. Powell " " " " " Lewis

The under-mentioned are appointed paid Lance-Corporals:-

    50803 Pte F. Steel, vice Bennett.
    50331 " G. Kirkman, " Madeley.

The under-mentioned is appointed unpaid Lance-Corporal:-

    53286 Pte E. Price.

1011. **ATTACHMENT.**
53286 L/c. E. Price ("C" Co.) to be attached to H.Q.Co. from 22nd inst.

        (Sgd) G. J. PAUL,
                                  Capt. & Adjutant.
        9th Bn. Gloucestershire Regt. (Pioneers).

N O T I C E S.

CONCERT.-
A Concert will be given by Madame Sara Silvers in the Concert Hall (behind Recreation Room) at 18-00 hours on 22nd inst.

DIVISIONAL TOURNAMENT.
All entries for Divnl. Tournament to be in to Bn. Sports Officer by 09-00 hours on 24th inst.

BATTALION ORDERS BY LIEUT.-COL. J. FANE, D.S.O.,
COMMDG. 9TH BN. GLOUCESTERSHIRE REGT. (P).
22nd JULY 1919.
****

1012. **DUTIES.**
Bn. Orderly Officer for tomorrow - 2/Lt. W. J. Noah, M.M.
Next for duty   - 2/Lt. L. J. Waddell.

Bn. Orderly Sergeant for tomorrow - Sgt. Pixton.
Next for duty   - Sgt. Johnson.

1013. **PARADES.**
Companies will parade under Company arrangements.

1014. **INDENTS FOR CLOTHING NECESSARIES ETC.**
Company Commanders will indent once monthly to the Quartermaster for all requirements for the following month, stating whether the article is for exchange or on payment. These indents will be rendered on the 24th of each month.
Indents for detailed stores, tools, etc., will be rendered weekly, on Saturdays.

1015. **ATTACHMENTS.**
50602 Pte M. Bond, ceases to be attached to H.Q. Co. as Signaller and is returned to "B" Co. for duty, commencing 23rd inst.

1016. **TRANSFERS.**
50666 Sgt. F. Horton is transferred from "A" Co. to H.Q. Co. from this date.
12488 L/c. E. Townsend is transferred from "B" Co. to H.Q.Co. from this date.

(sgd) G. J. PAUL, Capt. & Adjutant.
9th Bn. Gloucestershire Regt. (Pioneers).

NOTICE.

The Cinema will not be shewing tonight.

BATTALION ORDERS BY LIEUT.-COL. J. FANE, D.S.O.,
COMMDG. 9TH BN. GLOUCESTERSHIRE REGT. (P).
23RD JULY 1919.

1017. DUTIES.
Bn. Orderly Officer for tomorrow — 2/Lt. L. J. Waddell.
Next for duty — Lieut. E. O. Pilcher.

Bn. Orderly Sergeant for tomorrow — Sgt. Johnson.
Next for duty — Sgt. Stagg.

1018. PARADES.
Companies will parade under Company arrangements.

1019. VICTORY LOAN — INVESTMENT OF OFFICERS' GRATUITIES IN. (D.R.O.821).
It may be possible to meet a limited number of applications of Officers to invest their gratuities in the Victory Loan provided that such applications are received by Army Agents by 15/8/1919. So far as possible they will be dealt with in order of receipt. All applications must be sufficiently clear to enable Agents to identify the Officer submitting the application and must state the precise amount to be invested.
(Authority II Corps No. D.874 dated 20-7-19).

1020. PROMOTIONS AND APPOINTMENTS.
The undermentioned W.Os. and N.C.Os. are promoted to Temporary Ranks, as stated, for the period of the Army of Occupation, i.e., up to 30th April 1920, with effect from 20/6/1919.
Auth:- 91/Gen No. 2573 (A.G.4D). A.C.I.386/19. A/4073 (O3).

No.	Acting Rank	Name		Promoted
7777	A/R.S.M.	W. Stenner	Promoted	R.S.M.
50952	A/R.Q.M.S.	T. Portman	"	R.Q.M.S.
26509	A/C.S.M.	A. Ponting	"	C.S.M.
27195	A/C.Q.M.S.	S. Dymond	"	C.Q.M.S.
27538	A/Sgt.	H. Holland	"	Sgt.
51040	"	H. Peet	"	"
10912	"	J. Andrews	"	"
50357	"	R. Jones	"	"
50739	"	F. Neale	"	"
50644	"	E. Eagles	"	"
32291	"	L. Buchanan	"	"
50439	"	E. Stagg	"	"
50656	"	J. Eustace	"	"
31645	A/Cpl.	W. Baldwyn	"	Cpl.
50444	"	T. Ringrose	"	"
27349	"	D. Godfrey	"	"
50802	"	J. Sherwood	"	"
30426	"	W. Jones	"	"
28552	"	H. Palmer	"	"
28351	"	N. Pearce	"	"
50613	"	W. Clarke	"	"
32201	"	G. Clarke	"	"
50813	"	H. Sherratt	"	" & appointed unpd. Lance-Sergeant.
50711	"	G. Knowles	"	"
50408	"	F. Broughton	"	"
33209	"	H. Boulton	"	"
41132	"	H. Blair	"	"
41138	"	W. Smith	"	"
28614	"	C. Bownes	"	"
50640	"	W. Mallett	"	"
12900	"	J. Nelson	"	"
288062	A/C.Q.M.S.	H. Prestridge	"	C.Q.M.S.
203693	A/Sgt.	J. Boast	"	Sgt.
203161	"	A. Mills	"	"
260073	"	J. Starling	"	"
202497	"	T. Holbrook	"	"

-2-

1020. **PROMOTIONS AND APPOINTMENTS** (Continued).
266811 A/Sgt. A. Sleeman   Promoted Sgt.
260174 A/Cpl. J. Brooker   " Cpl. & appointed paid
                                         Lance-Sgt.

203750   "   C. Smith   "   "
242530   "   F. Webber   "   "
202554   "   H. Dallimore   "   "

The undermentioned A/W.Os. and A/N.C.Os. are promoted to Temporary Ranks as stated for the period of the Army of Occupation, i.e., up to 30/4/1920, with effect from dates shewn:-
Auth:- 91/Gen No. 2373 (A.G.4D). A.C.I.386/19. A/4073.(03).
50655 A/C.S.M.   A. Green   Promoted C.S.M.   2/7/19.
50380 A/C.Q.M.S. P. Bassett   "   C.Q.M.S. 2/7/19.
32998 A/Sgt.   D. Adamson   "   Sgt.   2/7/19.
50553 A/Cpl.   W. Brady   "   Cpl.   2/7/19.

The undermentioned are promoted to Temporary Ranks as stated with effect from this date (23/7/1919):-
50741 Cpl. Neale, J. Promoted Sgt. vice Harris, to U.K. 17/7/19.
201821 L/c. W. Cook   "   Cpl. "   Eustace, prom. 20/6/19.
36666 "   H. Clarke   "   "   "   Neale,   "   23/7/19.
28547 "   W. Hutt   "   "   "   Bradney, to U.K.10/7/19.
50910 Unpaid L/c C. Mobbs promoted pd.L/c. vice Cook,   prom.23/7/19.
50431   "   " W. Brackley "   "   "   Sparkes,off strength.
50598   "   " H. Burgess   "   "   "   Trevor, to U.K.17/7/19
50875   "   " B. Jenkins   "   "   "   Clarke, prom. 23/7/19.
50620   "   " H. Timms   "   "   "   Hutt   "   "

The undermentioned are appointed unpaid Lance-Cpls. from this date:-
28819 Pte C. Page
52293 "   H. Harwood   50894 Pte F. Howard
50472 "   W. Shayler   50905 " A. Watson
50705 "   A. Fursden   50606 " J. Bye
40170 "   W. Currie   50667 " G. Hands.

1021. **ANTI-GAS COURSE.**
Ref. Bn. Order No. 1008 dated 21/7/1919.
The Divisional Commander wishes to congratulate 50910 L/c. C. Mobbs on the results attained by him.

1022. **PAY AND MESS BOOKS.**
Attention is directed to "Circular letter to all Units and "formations in the Army of the Rhine", a copy of which has been sent round for the information of all Companies.

1023. **IMPREST ACCOUNTS.** (D.R.O. 823, 22/7/1919).
All Imprest Holders will render their accounts to the Command Paymaster, G.H.Q., British Army of the Rhine, twice monthly, to take effect after August 1st 1919. The first account will be closed on the 15th, and the second on the last day of the month. The accounts will include all transactions to those dates.
(Authority - G.R.O.3195 dated 18-7-1919).

(Sgd) G. J. PAUL, Capt. & Adjutant.
9th Bn. Gloucestershire Regt. (Pioneers).

NOTICES.

DIVNL. TOURNAMENT.
As a result of the draw for the Tugs of War in 2nd Southern Inf. Brigade Group, this Bn. will pull the 1/5th Devons at Leichlingen on 26th inst.

CONCERT. The "Darts" Concert Party will appear at Leichlingen on Aug. 2nd.

BATTALION ORDERS BY LIEUT.-COL. J. FANE, D.S.O.,
COMMDG. 9TH BN. GLOUCESTERSHIRE REGT. (P).
24TH JULY 1919.

1024. DUTIES.
Bn. Orderly Officer for tomorrow   - Lieut. E. O. Pilcher.
Next for duty   - Lieut. G. F. Pullen.

Bn. Orderly Sergeant for tomorrow - Sgt. Johnson.
Next for duty   - Sgt. Pakeman.

1025. PARADES.
"C" and H.Q.Cos. will parade under Company arrangements.

1026. MOVE.
The remainder of "B" Co. will proceed to KALK Racecourse tomorrow under instructions issued to Company Commander.

1027. ATTACHMENT.
50749 Pte A. Payne ("B" Co.) to be attached to H.Q. Co. while acting as Cinema Operator.

1028. TRANSFER.
50353 Cpl. W. Brady ("B" Co.) is transferred to H.Q. Co. from this date.

1029. AUTOMOBILE ASSOCIATION ROAD SCOUTS. (S.D.No.E.O.29/1, 23/7/19).
It is understood that there are likely to be a considerable number of vacancies in the near future for road scouts employed by the Automobile Association. The chief qualifications required are:-
    (i) A first aid certificate.
    (ii) Good knowledge of tyre repairing.
    (iii) Capacity to write short concise reports.
    (iv) Capacity to read a road map intelligently.
The men must be intelligent, smart in appearance, tactful, cheerful, and of good conduct.
Names of N.C.Os. and Men wishing to be trained as Road Scouts must be in in ord submitted to Orderly Room by 09-00 hours on Aug. 1st 1919.

1030. WAR SAVINGS, - VICTORY BONDS AND FUNDING LOAN. (A.O.IX, 25/6/19).
Investments in these securities may be made by soldiers by means of Army Form W.3275 (amended as may be necessary).
The amount to be invested must be £4/5/0 or a multiple thereof for Victory Bonds and £4 or a multiple thereof for the Funding Loan. Officers who wish to invest in these securities will make their own arrangements with their agents or bankers.

1031. HORSES (C.R.O. No. 2045 dated 22/7/19).
Horses of the Army of the Rhine are not to be ridden except by Officers and other ranks.
(Auth:- British Army of the Rhine No. 55 QAZ.)

1032. BRITISH WAR MEDAL. (C.R.O. No. 2044 dated 22/7/19).
British War Medal authorised by Army Order of 16th.
Preliminary issue of ribbon may proceed and ribbon may be worn by all entitled to the medal.
(Authority Rhine Army No. Q/581 of the 18th July 1919).

1033. DAMAGE TO CROPS, CULTIVATED FIELDS, ETC.
The inhabitants of LEICHLINGEN are continually complaining that men of the British Army are damaging the fields & orchards everywhere; the fruit, not yet ripe, is knocked from the trees, vegetables and garden-fruits are stolen, potato-plants pulled out, etc. Most of these fruits are not yet fit to be eaten, and the stealing of them is therefore only a question of mischief. Also, in a good many places, pathways are being made through cultivated fields (for

instance, by the Convalescent Depot at RODERBIRKEN).

    The field and garden-fruits are not only very expensive but they are very difficult to get at present.

    The Commanding Officer wishes it to be impressed upon all ranks of the Battalion that conduct such as that complained of must cease.

    Any infringement of this order will be severely dealt with.

(Sgd) G. J. PAUL,
Capt. & Adjutant.
9th Bn. Gloucestershire Regt. (Pioneers).

BATTALION ORDERS BY LIEUT.-COL. J. FANE, D.S.O.,
COMMDG. 9TH BN. GLOUCESTERSHIRE REGT. (P).
25TH JULY 1919.

1034. DUTIES.
Bn. Orderly Officer for tomorrow   - Lieut. G. F. Pullen.
Next for duty   - Lieut. V. E. Robertson.

Bn. Orderly Sergeant for tomorrow - Sgt. Pakeman.
Next for duty   - Sgt. Plimsole.

1035. PARADES.
"C" and H.Q. Cos. will parade under Company arrangements.

1036. REVERSION.
36859 A/Unpd/L/c. Jones, D., ("B" Co.), is deprived of lance-stripe for absence in U.K. without leave, reversion to date from to-day.

1037. P. & R. T. COURSE.
The following is the report from 2nd Army School of P. & R. T. on 50439, Sgt. E. Stagg, as a result of the Course which he attended there:-
    Leadership   -   Good.
    Technical Ability   -   Good.
    Application   -   Very Good.
    Keenness at Work   -   Very Keen.

1038. TRANSFER.
The undermentioned O.Rs. are transferred to H.Q. Co. from Cos. as stated, from this date:-

    50982 Pte Lewington, H.   "B" Co.
    50345 " Easton,   T.   "
    37824 " Beavis,   H.   "
    58315 " Carter,   C.   "C" Co.
    36899 " Griffin,   J.   "
    34591 " Smith,   P.   "
    37962 " Amos,   G.   "A" Co.
    204265 " Bright,   B.   "
    50586 " Clements, T.   "
    50496 " Scott,   W.   "B" Co.

(Sgd)   G. J. PAUL, Capt. & Adjutant.
9th Bn. Gloucestershire Regt. (P).

BATTALION ORDERS BY LIEUT.-COL. J. FANE, D.S.O.,
COMMDG. 9TH BN. GLOUCESTERSHIRE REGT. (P).
26TH JULY 1919.

1039. DUTIES.
Bn. Orderly Officer for tomorrow   - Lieut. V. E. Robertson.
 "   "   "   "   Monday   - 2/Lt. T. W. Everall.
Next for duty   - 2/Lt. W. J. Noah, M.M.

Bn. Orderly Sergeant for tomorrow   - Sgt. Plimsole.
 "   "   "   "   Monday   - "   Boast.
Next for duty   - "   Buchanan.

1040. PARADES.

Divine Service:-
"C" and H.Q. Cos. will parade in drill order formed up in line, facing West, on the road leading to the Recreation Ground, at 11-30 hours tomorrow, for Church of England Service, which will be held in the Protestant Church, Leichlingen, at 11-45 hours, followed by Holy Communion for all who wish to attend.

Roman Catholic Services will be held in the R.C. Church, Leichlingen, as follows:-
  Holy Communion   ...   07-30 hours.
  Morning Service   ...   10-30   "
  Benediction   ...   15-00   "
The Roman Catholic clergyman will be at the R.C. Church on Saturday from 14-00 to 16-00 hours, for the purpose of interviewing any R.Cs. who wish.

Non-Conformist Service will be held in the Cinema at 10-30 hours.

Monday.
"C" and H.Q. Cos. will parade under Co. arrangements.

1041. LEAVE.
Companies will render to Orderly Room every Saturday morning a roll of O.Rs. who have not had leave to U.K. for more than five months.

1042. BICYCLES.
Bicycles in possession of Companies are to be used only by runners & orderlies. Great inconvenience is caused by bicycles continually arriving at Bn. workshops in a damaged condition.
Co. Commanders will be held responsible for bicycles in their possession, and will be charged for any damage beyond that caused by fair wear and tear.

1043. BRITISH WAR MEDAL.
This medal will be awarded to all Officers & O.Rs. who have served outside the U.K. between Aug. 5th 1914 and Nov. 11th 1918. Co. Commanders are held responsible that the riband is worn as soon as possible by all entitled to it, and will render a report to Orderly Room when this has been done.

            (Sgd)   G. J. PAUL,
                                   Capt. & Adjutant.
               9th Bn. Gloucestershire Regt. (Pioneers).

BATTALION ORDERS BY LIEUT.-COL. J. FANE, D.S.O.,
COMMDG. 9TH BN. GLOUCESTERSHIRE REGT. (P).
28TH JULY 1919.

1044. **DUTIES.**
Bn. Orderly Officer for tomorrow - 2/Lt. W. J. Noah, M.M.
Next for duty - Lieut. G. F. Pullen.
Bn. Orderly Sergeant for tomorrow - Sgt. Buchanan.
Next for duty - Sgt. Stagg.

1045. **PARADES.**
"C" and H.Q. Cos. will parade under Company arrangements.
All available N.C.Os. will parade under the R.S.M. on the
Recreation Ground at 09-30 hours. The Gas, P.T. & Musketry
N.C.Os. will attend.

1046. **APPOINTMENT.**
37202 Pte F. Pitman (H.Q. Co.) is appointed A/Unpaid /L/c. from
this date.

1047. **DISPATCHES.**
The following Officers received Mention in Sir Douglas Haig's
Dispatch.-
    Q.M. & T/Lieut. A. P. Creedon.
    T/Lieut.   C. S. Lee.
Dated War Office July 8th 1919.

1048. **HIGHER RATES OF PAY FOR MILITARY POLICE.** (G.R.O. 3225, 25/7/19).
1. Volunteers for the Military Foot Police are now urgently
   required and can be accepted, if they agree to serve with the
   Military Police until April 30th 1920, up to a maximum No. of
   160 from each Corps of the Rhine Army. All volunteers must
   be serving on a Duration of War engagement, or else to be time-
   expired Regulars or T.F. Soldiers.
2. The War Office have decided to grant for the limited period
   only, starting from August 1st 1919 and terminating April 30th
   1920, the following rates of additional pay as an inducement to
   W.Os., N.C.Os. and men to remain with or volunteer for duty
   with the Military Police.-
       For Sergeants & upwards   - 1/6d extra per diem
       For ranks below that of Sergeant - 2/- per diem.
   This pay will be in addition to the rates of pay that may be
   in force for the Military Police during that period.
3. The following personnel serving with this Army will be eligible
   for this additional pay:-
   (a) Permanent members of the Corps of Military Police.
   (b) Men from other arms and branches of the service at present
       temporarily transferred or attached to the Corps of Military
       Police.
   (c) Any men belonging to the arms mentioned in para. 1 who
       volunteer and are finally accepted for transfer to the Corps
       of Military Police during the period mentioned in para. 2.
4. All volunteers from this Army who are accepted will be
   temporarily transferred to the Military Police in accordance
   with A.C.I. 1733 of 1916. After transfer they will cease to
   draw their former rates of pay (including Proficiency Pay or
   Service Pay) and will come on to the normal rates of pay for
   privates of the Military Foot Police as provided in Article
   854 of the Royal Warrant for Pay, plus the additional pay authorised in this G.R.O. for the limited period stated in para. 2.
   Thus, a private in the Military Foot Police will draw from Aug.
   1st 1919:-

s.	d.	
2	3	per diem pay.
1	6	Army of Occupation bonus.
2	0	Additional pay authorised in this G.R.O.
Total 5	9	per diem.

   Plus 1d per diem war pay for each completed year of service, and
   also the usual separation and dependants' allowances. Men promoted afterwards to higher rank will draw correspondingly higher
   pay as laid down in Article 854 of the Royal Warrant for Pay.

5. The necessary qualifications for candidates for transfer are:-
   (a) Men must be of good phisyque, fair education, able to write, and of character not less than "Good."
   (b) Men must not be less than 5 feet 7 inches in height.
   (c) N.C.Os. who are candidates for transfer must be prepared to sign a certificate that they are willing to revert to the rank of private on first joining the Military Police.
6. Corps will arrange that all volunteers considered fit for transfer by the Commanding Officers are interviewed by the A.P.Ms. of Divisions, who will immediately reject any men whom they consider unsuitable.
7. Men passed by A.P.Ms. of Divisions as suitable candidates will be despatched under Divisional arrangements to report to the Commandant, Provost School, Gannymed, 10 Jakhordenstrasse, Cologne.
7. Candidates will be medically examined under arrangements made between the P.M. and D.M.S., Rhine Army, after reporting to the Provost School. Men who are accepted as candidates by the P.M., G.H.Q., will be attached to the school for three weeks' probationary period and any who do not appear likely to become efficient Military Police may be returned to their Units by the P.M., G.H.Q., at any time during that period. The final veto as regards the acceptance or rejection of all candidates will rest with the P.M., G.H.Q. The particulars of men accepted as suitable for transfer by the P.M., G.H.Q., at the end of the three weeks' probationary period will be reported to the D.A.G., G.H.Q. (Branch A.G3). Candidates who have been accepted will be eligible for drawing the rates of pay mentioned in para. 4 from the day following their three weeks' probationary attachment.
8. The attention of all W.Os., N.C.Os. and men should be drawn to the fact that men who have served in the Military Police are eligible for recommendation for appointments in the Metropolitan Police. In this connection attention should be drawn to the higher rates of pay for civil police suggested by Lord Desborough's Committee on the conditions of pay, pensions and allowances of the Police, which was issued to the press on July 14th.
The conditions suggested by this Committee are stated to be in brief-
   Pay for Sergeants:- 100s. per week rising by five annual increments to 112s per week.
   Pay for Constables:- 70s per week, rising by yearly advances of 2s. to 90/- per week, with two long service advances of 2/6d per week after 17 and 22 years' service. Also eligibility for good conduct and special proficiency pay after five years' service.
   Houses and quarters rent free for all (except constables on probation) or allowances in lieu.
   Eight hours day, with either time off for extended hours of duty, or pay for overtime.
   After 25 years' service, half the annual pay as a pension on retirement.
   After 30 years' service, two-thirds of the annual pay as a pension.
   Between 25 and 30 years' service, proportional rates.
Company Commanders will submit names of volunteers for above to Orderly Room as soon as possible.

1049. **CASH.**
All requisitions for cash and officers' advance of pay books will be sent to Orderly Room by 09-00 hours tomorrow, 29th inst. 2/Lt. W. J. Noah, (M.M.) is detailed to draw cash from the Field Cashier at Burscheid at 12-00 hours.

1050. **DAMAGE TO RAILWAYS.**
Attention is drawn to Bn. Order No. 883 dated 26th June 1919. This Order is not being complied with. Company Commanders will read same out to their Companies on three successive morning parades, and will render a certificate to Orderly Room when this has been done.

(Continued

1051. **AGRICULTURE.** (Southern Division No. 22/24 G.S.36/93, 26/7/19.)
The Agricultural Wing of the Divisional School is now in full working order. It affords opportunities for those interested in all branches of farm work to gain really valuable experience. The Course is thoroughly practical and includes dairy work of all kinds, looking after live stock, and work on the land, including tilling the soil, sowing and gathering of crops.
The men going through the course are expected to work the hours required on a farm; in fact they are for the time being the farmers who are actually working for a living.
From recent experience it has been found that many men who present themselves for this course, and who call themselves farm hands, know only one small item of the whole affair. It is the intention to help these men to know a great deal more and to enable them to take up farming seriously.
Any men who would like to avail themselves of this excellent opportunity are requested to give their names to Co. Commanders, who will pass same on to the Orderly Room.
It is doubtful if the majority will ever have such an opportunity again.

1052. **EMIGRATION.** (Southern Division No. 63/24 of 26/7/19).
It is thought that there may be in the Rhine Army many Officers and men who, on returning to civil live, intend to emigrate to some part of the British Empire.
The Director of Native Industries, Rhodesia, is now in Cologne for a short period, under the War Office Education Scheme, and will attend in the Conference Room, G.H.Q. (Ground Floor, Excelsior Hotel) COLOGNE, between the hours of 14-00 and 16-00 on 30th July for the purpose of giving any information he can regarding prospects of settlement in Southern Rhodesia.
Company Commanders will submit to Orderly Room by 09-00 hours tomorrow, 29th inst., the names of any Officers or O.Rs. wishing to meet the Director of Native Industries on the 30th at G.H.Q.

1053. **MOVE.**
No. 4 Platoon, "A" Co., rejoined H.Q. today from BURSCHEID.

(Sgd) G. J. PAUL, Capt. & Adjutant.
9th Bn. Gloucestershire Regt. (Pioneers).

BATTALION ORDERS BY LIEUT.-COL. J. FANE, D.S.O.,
COMMDG. 9TH BN. GLOUCESTERSHIRE REGT. (P).
29TH JULY 1919.

1054. **DUTIES.**
Bn. Orderly Officer for tomorrow — Lieut. G. F. Pullen.
Next for duty — Lieut. V. E. Robertson.
Bn. Orderly Sergeant for tomorrow — Sgt. Pakeman.
Next for duty — Sgt. Plimsole.

No. 9 Platoon ("C" Co.) will provide the Guard tomorrow.

1055. **PARADES.**
No. 4 Platoon, "A" Co., will fire on the range tomorrow.
Lewis Gun Teams of "C" Co. will practise firing.
H.Q. Co. and the remainder of "C" Co. will parade under arrangements of O.C. Company.

1056. **PROMOTIONS & APPOINTMENTS.**
50353 T/Cpl. W. Brady is prom. T/Sgt. vice Horton and appd. Orderly Room Sergeant from this date.
50910 T/L/c. C. Mobbs is prom. T/Cpl. vice Brady from this date.
50923 Unpd.L/c. F. Schofield is appd. T/Pd/L/c. vice Mobbs, from today
50393 Pte J. Morris (H.Q.Co.) is appd. Unpd.L/c. from today.

50910 T/Cpl. C. Mobbs is appd. Battalion Gas N.C.O. vice Sgt. Ellis, to duty.

1057. **TRANSFERS.**
27470 Sgt. F. Ellis is transferred from H.Q.Co. to "A" Co. from today
50910 T/Cpl.C. Mobbs " " " "C" " " H.Q. " " "

1058. **DEPRIVATION.**
36852 L/c. T. Miller ("A" Co.) is deprived of lance-stripe 28/7/19 for overstaying leave to U.K.

1059. **BILLETS.** (D.R.O.No.840, 28/7/19).
It has been brought to notice that troops billeted in parts of factories are demanding access to the entire premises. Workshops and storerooms are frequented. The attention of the personnel is engaged with the result that the smooth running of the concern is interfered with.
All factory premises excepting those portions which are actually allotted as billets are "Out of Bounds."
This order is to be brought to the notice of all Officers, N.C.Os. and men at once, and they are to be warned that disciplinary action will be taken in all cases of infringement of this order.

1060. **WIRES IN CAPS.**
It has been brought to the notice of the Commanding Officer that men, on receiving new caps which are freshly wired, remove the new wires and replace old ones.
In future charges will be brought against men committing this offence, and the charges will be dealt with by the Commanding Officer, not by Company Commanders.

(Sgd) G. J. PAUL, Capt. & Adjutant,
9th Bn. Gloucestershire Regt. (P).

N O T I C E S.

3rd Southern Inf. Bgde. Sports. Brig.-Gen. D. E. CAYLEY, C.B., C.M.G., Officers & O.Rs. of 3rd S. Inf. Bgde. request the pleasure of the company of all Officers & O.Rs. of the Southern Division at the 3rd S. Inf. Bgde. Sports to be held at No. 1 Football Field, WERMELSKIRCHEN, on 1st August, MINDEN DAY. Sports commence at 14-30 hours.
There will be a half Mile Race open to the Southern Division, to take place at 16-00 hours on Friday, August 1st. Entries should reach 3rd S. Inf. Bgde. by 16-00 hours Thursday July 31st.

N O T I C E S. (Continued).

ROYAL AIR FORCE ATHLETIC CHAMPIONSHIP to be held on the POLLER WEISEN Sports Ground, COLOGNE, on Aug. 9th 1919, commencing at 14-00 hrs. The following events are open to all ranks of the Imperial & Allied Forces:-

    1.   100 yards.
    2.   440 yards.
    3.   One Mile Inter-Regiment or Unit Relay Race - 220, 440, 880, 220 yards.

Entrance Fees.

Individual Entries ... 3 Marks. Team Events - 15 Marks per Team. Entries to be made to the R.A.F. Athletic Association, Rhine Headquarters, Royal Air Force, not later than August 2nd 1919.

N.B.- THE POLLER WEISEN GROUND is opposite the BISMARCK statue on the DEUTZ side of the Rhine.

CONCERTS:- The "New Bing Boys" Concert Party will give a concert in the Concert Hall (behind Recreation Room) tomorrow evening, 30th inst., at 18-00 hours.

The "Darts" Concert Party will appear on Saturday, 2nd prox.

BATTALION ORDERS BY LIEUT.-COL. J. FANE, D.S.O.,
COMMDG. 9TH BN. GLOUCESTERSHIRE REGT. (P).
30TH JULY 1919.

1061. **DUTIES.**
Bn. Orderly Officer for tomorrow - Lieut. V. E. Robertson.
Next for duty   - 2/Lt. T. W. Everall.

Bn. Orderly Sergeant for tomorrow - Sgt. Plimsole.
Next for duty   - Sgt. Neale.

No. 10 Platoon will provide the Guards tomorrow.

1062. **PARADES.**
No. 4 Platoon "A" Co. will fire on the range tomorrow.
Lewis Gun Teams of "C" Co. will practise firing.
H.Q. Co. and the remainder of "C" Co. will parade under arrangements of O.C. Companies.
All available N.C.Os. will parade under the R.S.M. on the Recreation Ground from 09-30 to 11-45 hours.

1063. **BLUE BOOKS - OFFICERS.**
All Officers' Blue Books will be sent to the Adjutant by the 4th August. Officers will pay particular attention that books are filled in correctly and up to date before handing in.

1064. **GAS TRAINING.** (Extract from Rhine Army Letter No. G.T./54/7).
As regards the general policy of gas training; although details have not yet been worked out, it has been decided that the box respirator shall remain part of the soldier's equipment, and that anti-gas training shall be maintained at a high level.
Training will be carried out under regimental arrangements by regimental officers, but certain schools will probably be maintained at which regimental officers will be given the necessary training as Instructors.

(Sgd)   G. J. PAUL, Capt. & Adjutant.
          9th Bn. Gloucestershire Regt. (P).

NOTICE.

The visit of the "Darts" Concert Party to this Bn. on 2nd August is cancelled.

BATTALION ORDERS BY LIEUT.-COL. J. FANE, D.S.O.,
COMMDG. 9TH BN. GLOUCESTERSHIRE REGT. (P).
31st JULY 1919.

1065. **DUTIES.**
Bn. Orderly Officer for tomorrow — 2/Lt. R. H. Warren, M.C.M.M.
Next for duty — 2/Lt. E. C. Turner.

Bn. Orderly Sergeant for tomorrow — Sgt. Neale.
Next for duty — Sgt. Boast.

No. 12 Platoon will provide the Guards tomorrow.

1066. **PARADES.**
No. 4 Platoon "A" Co. will fire on the range tomorrow.
Lewis Gun Teams of "C" Co. will practise firing.
H.Q. Co. and the remainder of "C" Co. will parade under arrangements of O.C. Companies.

1067. **BRITISH WAR MEDAL, 1914-1919.** (G.R.O. 3234 of July 28th 1919).
1. His Majesty the King has been graciously pleased to signify his pleasure that a medal be granted to record the bringing of the war to a successful conclusion, and the arduous services rendered by His Majesty's Forces.
2. The medal in silver will, provided the claims are approved bb the competent military authorities, be granted to the undermentioned who either entered a theatre of war on duty, or who left their places of residence and rendered approved service overseas, other than the waters dividing the different parts of the United Kingdom; between August 5th 1914 and November 11th 1918, both dates inclusive—

Officers, warrant officers, attested non-commissioned officers and men of the British, Dominion, Colonial and Indian Military Forces.

1068. **BRITISH EMPIRE LEAVE CLUB.** (G.R.O. 3237 of July 28th 1919).
Complaints have been received that soldiers are arriving at the Leave Club in a verminous condition. Soldiers proceeding to the Club will be given a certificate that they are free from vermin before they leave their Unit.

1069. **LEAVE.** (G.R.O. 3238 of July 28th 1919).
Subject to the exigencies of the Service, Officers and Other Ranks may be granted leave after they have completed a period of at least three months out of the United Kingdom without leave.

2. A leave roster will be kept in all Units, and after allowing for special cases, leave will be given first to those who have been longest out of the United Kingdom.
3. Leave will not be granted to Other Ranks who are eligible for demobilization under A.O.55 of 1919, unless they have taken on for a short period under G.R.O. 2970, or on urgent compassionate grounds.

  4. (a) The period of leave will not exceed 14 days; this can be spent either in the United Kingdom or on the Continent.
    (b) Short leave on the Continent, not exceeding four days, may also be granted.
    (c) All other leave willbe "special."

5. Leave to the United Kingdom will count from the date of embarkation at a Continental port to the date of embarkation at the Home port. Leave on the Continent will count from the date of leaving Unit until date of rejoining Unit.

6. Corps and Divisional Commanders may stop leave in any Unit for any reason they think necessary.

1070. COLLECTION OF PHOTOGRAPHS BY THE IMPERIAL WAR MUSEUM. (G.R.O.NOTE)

1. The Committee of the Imperial War Museum are anxious to ~~complex~~ complete their collection of photographs of the war, both for inclusion in the permanent Museum which will shortly be opened and for sale and publication from the Bureau now open at 10 Coventry St., London W.1.

2. Owing to the limited number of official photographers in the various areas of war, many scenes of great historical interest are not represented in the collection, while no records were made previous to the appointment of the first photographers in 1916. It is known, hozever, that many unofficial photographs are in existence whose inclusion in the Museum would be in the interests of the Service.

3. Officers and Other Ranks in possession of such photographs are asked to communicate with the Keeper of Photographs, Imperial War Museum, 10 Coventry Street, W.1; forwarding prints with description titles for his inspection. He is prepared to acquire from them the rights in these photographs on conditions which can be obtained from Orderly Room.

(Sgd) G. J. PAUL, Capt. & Adjutant.
9th Bn. Gloucestershire Regiment. (P).

Army Form C. 2118.

WAR DIARY
or
INTELLIGENCE SUMMARY.
(Erase heading not required.)

Instructions regarding War Diaries and Intelligence Summaries are contained in F.S. Regs., Part II. and the Staff Manual respectively. Title pages will be prepared in manuscript.

H.S.
3rd sheet

Place	Date 1919	Hour	Summary of Events and Information	Remarks and references to Appendices
Tuckhingen	1st Aug		1 Platoon of H.Qs. proceeded to Kalk for duty under R.E.	
	2nd "		H.Qs. of "C" Co. returned to Tuchhingen from Bensdorf	
	3rd "		2nd Lieut. W. Hancock returned from leave to U.K.	
	5th "		Lieut. J. Howard proceeded to Hunner Labour Batt. for duty and taken off strength	
	9th "		2nd Lieut. R.W. Smith proceeded to hospital	
			Capt. W.H. Horton M.C. proceeded on leave to U.K.	
	9th "		2nd Lieut. W.J. Nash M.M. proceeded on leave to U.K.	
	12th "		1 Platoon of "C" Co. returned from Bensdorf	
	13th "		Lieut. W.F. Palmer proceeded to U.K. to report to Reserve Batt. Taken off strength	
			2nd Lieut. A.O. Brinkworth proceeded on leave or leave to U.K.	
	15th "		2nd Lieut. C.C. Brennan proceeded to U.K. on leave	
	16th "		2nd Lieut. R.W. Smith returned from hospital	
			2nd Platoon of "B" Co. returned from Kalk	
			No. 11 Platoon returned from Bensdorf	
	17th "		Lieut. R.M.F. Allen proceeded on leave to U.K.	
	19th "		Capt. A.J. Paul proceeded on leave to U.K.	
			Capt. A.J. Paul relinquished the appointment of Adjutant and is as posted to H.C. to take command	
	20th "		Lieut. J.C. Pluter appointed Adjutant	
	23rd "		2nd Lieut. J.W. Birtall proceeded on leave to U.K.	
			2nd Lieut. C.C. Turner reported from leave to U.K.	
	24th "		2nd Lieut. H.J. Halworth proceeded on leave to U.K.	
			Lieut. H.E. Hicks proceeded to U.K. for demobilization	
	25th "		Capt. C.B. Bingham M.C. taken off strength to H.K. sick	

Army Form C. 2118.

WAR DIARY
or
INTELLIGENCE SUMMARY.
(Erase heading not required.)

Instructions regarding War Diaries and Intelligence Summaries are contained in F. S. Regs., Part II. and the Staff Manual respectively. Title pages will be prepared in manuscript.

Place	Date	Hour	Summary of Events and Information	Remarks and references to Appendices
Quedlinburg	25th Aug		2nd Lieut J Stebbings proceeded on leave to U.K. Lieut L Johnson proceeded on leave to U.K.	
	26th "		Remainder of O.R.s returned from Buschied. Capt R.S.Lee proceeded on leave to U.K. on demobilization. Lieut J Ashby proceeded to U.K. for demobilization	
	28th "		2nd Lt R Pethanc.... from leave to U.K.	
	29th "		2nd Lt J.A.Brooks-Otte returned from leave to U.K.	
	30th "		Capt W.H.Hollow returned from leave to U.K.	
			Strength of Unit 33 Officers 861 O.Rs.	

J. Farr Lt. Colonel,
COMDG. 8TH (S) BN GLOUCESTERSHIRE REGT

BATTALION ORDERS BY LIEUT.-COL. J. FANE, D.S.O.,
COMMDG. 9TH BN. GLOUCESTERSHIRE REGT. (P).

1st August 1919.

1071. DUTIES.
Bn. Orderly Officer for tomorrow — 2/Lt. E. C. Turner.
Next for duty — 2/Lt. W. J. Noah, M?M.
Bn. Orderly Sergeant for tomorrow — Sgt. Boast.
Next for duty — Sgt. Pakeman.

No. 4 Platoon, "A" Co., will provide Guards tomorrow.

1072. PARADES.
No. 4 Platoon, "A" Co., will fire on "A" Co.'s range tomorrow at 09-30 hours.
Lewis Gun Teams of "C" Co. will practise firing.
H.Q. Co. and the remainder of "C" Co. will parade under arrangements of O. C. Companies.

1073. REGIMENTAL ACCOUNTS.
All Regtl. A/cs. will be submitted on 7th of the month for the Commanding Officer's inspection.
Receipts must be attached for monies expended; a balance sheet will not required.
Officers in charge of A/cs. need not attend.
Books will be placed in the Commanding Officer's Office by 09-00 hrs.

1074. CANTEEN ACCOUNT.
Outstanding accounts due to P.R.I. must be settled weekly. Fresh stocks will not be sent to Companies until the previous account is settled.

1075. BANK HOLIDAY (D.R.O.No.850 dated 31st July 1919).
On Monday, August 4th, military training will be suspended.

1076. WIVES OF OFFICERS & O.RS. VISITING GERMANY (D.R.O.852, 31/7/19).
All applications for authority for Rations on repayment for wives of British Officers & O.Rs. will quote the number on the white pass issued to the lady by Home Authorities.
Attention is directed to G.R.O. 3185 dated 14th July 1919.

1077. RATES OF EXCHANGE (D.R.O.853, 31/7/19).
The following rates of exchange are fixed for the month of Aug. 1919 —
France   Five Francs equals   3/3d
Belgium   Five   "   "   3/1d.
Germany   Ten Marks   "   2/10d
Greece   Five Drachmai "   4/-
Holland and Italian Rates are unchanged.

1078. CONFESSIONS.
The Roman Catholic Chaplain will attend at the R.C. Church, Leichlingen, every Saturday from 14-00 to 16-00 hours for the purpose of interviewing any R.Cs. who wish.

(Sgd) R. D. HEPPENSTALL, 2/Lt., A/Adjt.,
9th Bn. Gloucestershire Regt. (P).

NOTICE.

Cricket — "A" Co. v. "C" Co. on Saturday.
Arrangements regarding sports etc. for Monday next will be notified in Bn. Orders tomorrow.

BATTALION ORDERS BY LIEUT.-COL. J. FANE, D.S.O.,
COMMDG. 9TH BN. GLOUCESTERSHIRE REGT. (P).
2nd August 1919.

1079. DUTIES.

Bn. Orderly Officer for tomorrow — 2/Lt. W. J. Noah, M?M.
" " " " Monday — " B. Kembery.
" " " " Tuesday — Lieut. H. G. Hicks.
Next for duty — " P. J. Hancox.

Bn. Orderly Sergeant for tomorrow — Sgt. Eagles.
" " " " Monday — " Dunn.
" " " " Tuesday — " Andrews.
Next for duty — " Neale, J.

Guards will be provided as follows:—
    Tomorrow — By No. 9 Platoon, "C" Co.
    Monday — " " 10 " " "
    Tuesday — " " 12 " " "

1080. PARADES.

Tomorrow.— "A", "C" and H.Q. Cos. will parade in drill order formed up in line, facing West, on the road leading to the Recreation Ground, at 11-30 hours for Church of England Service, which will be held in the Protestant Church, Leichlingen, at 11-45 hours, followed by Holy Communion for all who wish to attend.
    Roman Catholic Services will be held in the R.C. Church, Leichlingen, as follows:—
        Holy Communion ... 07-30 hours.
        Morning Service ... 10-30 "
        Benediction ... 15-00 "
    Non-Conformist Service will be held in the Cinema at 10-30 hours.

Monday.— Training will be suspended.

Tuesday.— "A" Co. will fire on their own range.
    Lewis Gun Teams of "C" Co. will practise firing.
    H.Q. and remainder of "C" Co. will parade under arrangements of O.C. Companies.

1081. CASH.
All requisitions for cash and Officers' advance of pay books will be sent to Orderly Room by 09-00 hours on Tuesday, 5th inst. Lieut. H. G. Hicks is detailed to draw cash on that day from the Field Cashier at 12-00 hours.

1082. CANTEEN ACCOUNTS.
O. C. Companies are responsible that their Company Canteen A/cs. are in order, although they may delegate that duty to an Officer of their Company.

1083. CASHING OF CHEQUES (S.D. Wire No. A.836 of 1st inst.)
From Aug. 1st 1919 cheques of Officers and other ranks may be cashed by any bank willing to do so but at commercial rates of exchange. The official rate will no longer apply to these transactions. This also will apply to the changing of any currency notes. Field advances up to the amounts allowed by G.R.O. 3116 will be converted into sterling at the official rate which will be fixed periodically.

1083. DIVISIONAL SIGN (D.R.O. No. 844 dated 30/7/19).
The Divisional Sign will be painted on the near side coal box in the case of travelling kitchens, and on the spare part box in the case of watercarts.

        (Sgd) G. J. PAUL, Capt. & Adjutant.
        9th Bn. Gloucestershire Regt. (P).

BATTALION ORDERS BY LIEUT.-COL. J. FANE, D.S.O.,
COMMDG. 9TH BN. GLOUCESTERSHIRE REGT. (P).
5th August 1919.

1085. **DUTIES.**
Bn. Orderly Officer for tomorrow - Lieut. G. F. Pullen.
Next for duty   - Lieut. P. J. Hancox.

Bn. Orderly Sergeant for tomorrow - Sgt. Neale, J.
Next for duty   - Sgt. Boast.

No. 2 Platoon ("A" Co.) will provide the Guards tomorrow.

1086. **PARADES.**
One Platoon each of "A" & "C" Cos. will fire on range tomorrow, at 09-00 hours.

H.Q. & remainder of "A" & "C" Cos. will parade under arrangements of O.Cs. Companies.

1087. **BONUS - OFFICERS** (D.R.O.854 - 2/8/19).
A ruling has been received that Officers will only forfeit their Army of Occupation Bonus if they withdraw during the period 1st February to 30th April 1919. In all cases they will receive Bonus from 1st May until demobilized, if they have not been disposed of before that date.

1088. **POSTAL CENSORSHIP** (C.R.O.No.2048 - 31/7/19).
Cases have occurred of letters being handed in for stamping with the censor stamp which do not shew the rank of the writer. This practice, which is contrary to G.R.O.5941, dated 29th December 1918, which must cease forthwith.
All letters and postcards must bear in the left hand bottom corner of the address side the name and rank, if any, of the writer.

1089. **WEBBING EQUIPMENT.**
In future, all men proceeding on demobilisation will take leather equipment.
Os. C. Companies will be held responsible that no Webbing equipment leaves their Company.

1090. **ROUTINE.**
Sick Parade tomorrow will be held at 07-15 hours.

1091. **STRENGTH.**
Lt. J. Howard, M.M., having proceeded to join the Chinese Labour Corps Depôt, NOYELLES, is struck off the strength of this Bn. as from 3rd inst.
(Sgd) H. P. HEFFERNAN,
2/Lt., A/Adjt.,
9th Bn. Gloucestershire Regt. (P).

NOTICE.

The Bn. Band will play by the Guard Room from 17-30 to 18-30 hours tomorrow, 6th inst.

The "New Bing Boys" Concert Party will appear at Leichlingen on Wednesday, 13th inst.

BATTALION ORDERS BY LIEUT.-COL. J. FANE, D.S.O.,
COMMDG. 9TH BN. GLOUCESTERSHIRE REGT. (P).
6th August 1919.

1092k. DUTIES.
Bn. Orderly Officer for tomorrow — Lieut. P. J. Hancox.
Next for duty — ~~2/Lt. R. J. Hancox.~~
2/Lt. R. H. Warren; M.C.,M.M.

Bn. Orderly Sergeant for tomorrow — Sgt. Boast.
Next for duty — Sgt. Eagles.
No. 4 Platoon, "A" Co., will provide Guards tomorrow.

1093. PARADES.
One Platoon each of "A" & "C" Cos. will fire on the range tomorrow at 09-00 hours.
H.Q. Co. and the remainder of "A" & "C" Cos. will parade under arrangements of Os. C. Companies.

1094. DEPRIVATION.
50431 L/c. W. Brackley is deprived of lance-stripe for misconduct, from 5th inst.

1095. PAY BOOKS, A.B. 64.
All Soldiers' Pay Books will be completed, collected and forwarded by Cos. to Bn. Orderly Room.

1096. OFFICERS.
All Officers will attend Orderly Room as soon as possible to initial a confidential document.

1097. DRESS - TRANSPORT.

1. On the Person, Drill Order.
   Cap, F.S. Ankle Boots & Puttees.
   Haversack & Water-bottle (if ordered).
   Clasp Knife & Lanyard. Spurs.
   Web Belt & Side Arms.

2. On the Person, Marching Order
   In addition to Drill Order:-
   Steel Helmet (slung on the left shoulder).
   Pouches & Braces (60 rounds S.A.A.)
   Haversack (carried on the back), waterbottle.
   Box Respirator (slung over the left shoulder)
   Pack & Rifle carried in the wagon (Mess Tin in Pack), Ground Sheet (folded under flap of haversack). Hold-all carried in haversack.

3. On the Person, Fighting Order
   As for Marching Order, except that Box Respirator will be carried in "Alert" position, and Steel Helmet worn in place of Cap, F.S.

4. Horse Furniture.
   (a) Drill Order
       Nose Bag (if ordered).
       Head Chain.
       Saddle Blanket on or near animal.

   (b) Marching Order
       In addition to Drill Order:-
       Hay net - carried as follows -
       (a) Limbered G.S. Wagon. On the tail board of the forward portion of wagon.
       (b) Cooker   ) On front portion.
       (c) Water Cart)   ditto
       (d) Maltese Cart) Inside.
       (e) Mess Cart)   "
       (f) G.S. Wagons of Pioneer Bns., slung on the back of the driver's seat.
       Surcingle Pad - <u>Near Animal</u>, - On the surcingle underneath the horse's belly.
            <u>Off Animal</u>. On the surcingle in the middle of the horse's back.
       Nose Bag - As for Hay Nets.
       Grooming Kit - In the Wagon.
       Picketing Gear - ditto.

   (c) Fighting Order, as for Marching Order.

1098. **FIELD DRESSINGS - WITHDRAWAL OF.** (G.R.O.3269, 4/8/19).
Field Dressings will be withdrawn from all troops forthwith and stored under Regimental arrangements so as to be available for re-issue within 48 hours if required.
O.C. Cos. will arrange direct with Q.M. who will report completion to this Office.

1099. **BILLETING IN COLOGNE.** (G.R.O. 3266, 4/8/19).
It has been brought to notice that troops, more especially officers, are being billeted and billetting themselves in Cologne without reference to the proper authorities. This practice must cease forthwith, and no billets will be occupied unless allotted by Town Major or Camp Commandant's Office.

1100. **ISSUE OF RATIONS ON PREPAYMENT TO WIVES & FAMILIES** (G.R.O.3263, 4/8/19).
The following instructions as to the mode of payment, issue and accounting for rations issued on prepayment to wives and families of all ranks are published for guidance.
The system of issue by coupons will be adopted (A.F.W.3887). Sheets of coupons will be obtainable on production of A.F.W.3887a duly signed by O.C. Unit, Camp Commandant or Town Major, and bearing office stamp, from all Cashiers, the price of a sheet of ten coupons being £1/3/4d? Subject to any variation in price or composition which may be published from time to time in G.R.Os., the ration will be as laid down in Ration Pamphlet; the price 2/4d (two shillings and fourpence). Coupons not used will be returned and money refunded.
Commanding Officers, Camp Commandants and Town Majors will be responsible that the coupons are only issued by them to Officers and other ranks whose wives and families are authorised to reside in the territory occupied by the Rhine Army.

1101. **DEMOBILIZATION - SERVICE IN MERCANTILE MARINE** (D.R.O.856,4/8/19)
Service with the Mercantile Marine prior to 1-1-1916 counts as service towards eligibility for demobilization, provided it can be substantiated that the service claimed was on a ship chartered by the Government as a transport ship, hospital ship, etc.
Claims should be submitted to this Office in the usual manner.

         (Sgd) G. J. PAUL, Capt. & Adjutant.
         9th Bn. Gloucestershire Regt. (P).

AFTER ORDER.

1102. **CAP BADGES.**
Os. C. Companies will indent on Q.M. immediately for cap badges.

BATTALION ORDERS BY LIEUT.-COL. J. FANE, D.S.O.,
COMMDG. 9TH BN. GLOUCESTERSHIRE REGT. (P).
7TH AUGUST 1919.

1103. **DUTIES.**
Bn. Orderly Officer for tomorrow - 2/Lt. R. H. Warren, M.C., M.M.
Next for duty   - 2/Lt. H. R. Jones.

Bn. Orderly Sergeant for tomorrow - Sgt. Eagles.
Next for duty   - Sgt. Dunn.

No. 9 Platoon, "C" Co., will provide Guards tomorrow.

1104. **PARADES.**
Companies will parade under Company arrangements.

1105. **DUTIES - OFFICERS.**
Lieut. W. F. Palmer will take over the duties of D.A.P.M. from 2/Lt. Brinkworth, while the latter is on leave, from 11th inst.

Lieut. V. E. Robertson will take over Civil Duties from 2/Lt. E. A. Bresnan, while the latter is on leave, from 15th inst.

1106. **CAFES.**
In future; cafés will be open to British troops throughout British Occupied Territory during the following hours:-

12-00 to 14-00 hours and 16-00 to 21-30 hours.

1107. **COMPANY COMMAND.**
Lieut. E. O. Pilcher will take over the command and payment of "B" Co/ during the absence on leave to U.K. of Capt. Horton.

1108. **RHINE TRIP.**
The Rhine Trip for Monday, 11th inst., is cancelled.

(Sgd) G. J. PAUL, Capt. & Adjutant.
9th Bn. Gloucestershire Regt. (P).

NOTICE.

The Army Horse Show will be held on 12th, 13th & 14th inst.

Os. C. Companies will render to Orderly Room by 16-00 hours on 9th inst. a return shewing the number of men in their Company who would like to go; this return is required for the purpose of Divisional arrangements for catering at the Horse Show.

BATTALION ORDERS BY LIEUT.-COL. J. FANE, D.S.O.,
COMDG. 9TH BN. GLOUCESTERSHIRE REGT. (P).
8TH AUGUST 1919.

1109. **DUTIES.**
Bn. Orderly Officer for tomorrow - 2/Lt. H. R. Jones.
Next for duty - 2/Lt. B. Kembery.

Bn. Orderly Sergeant for tomorrow - Sgt. Dunn.
Next for duty - Sgt. Ellis.

No. 10 Platoon, "C" Co., will provide Guards tomorrow.

1110. **PARADES.**
Parades will be held under Company arrangements.

1111. **UNDERCLOTHING.**
All underclothing in excess of one set per man will be returned to the Quartermaster by 09-00 hours on Tuesday, 12th inst.

1112. **BONUS UNDER ARMY ORDER 54 (ARMY ORDER XIII dated Jan.29/19).**
G.R.O. 3272 of 6/8/19 is re-published for information:-
Under War Office instructions now received; G.R.O. 2733 will not apply to Officers who applied to withdraw their names from the list of volunteers for the Army of Occupation after April 30th 1919. Only those Officers should forfeit their Army of Occupation Bonus who withdrew during the period of February 1st to April 30th 1919, and in such cases they will receive bonus from May 1st until demobilization if they have not been disposed of before that date; e.g., an Officer who applies to withdraw his name from the list of volunteers on April 20th 1919, and who is not released till May 15th, will forfeit his bonus for the period February 1st to April 30th, but will draw bonus for the period May 1st - May 15th.
This decision should be communicated to officers affected who have already been demobilised, in order that they may cause the necessary adjustments to be made in their accounts.

1113. **CENSORSHIP OF MAILS** (G.R.O.3279, of 6/8/19).
A large number of parcels are now being despatched containing Government property, especially Government issues of articles of of clothing, the sending home of which is strictly forbidden to all ranks. The contents of such parcels are frequently falsely declared and then passed by officers without proper investigation. All parcels must be legally franked by an Officer and censor-stamped before despatch. Any Government property found in parcels will be confiscated, and disciplinary action will be taken against the sender and the franking officer.

1114. **COURT MARTIAL.**
50615 Pte J. Cutler, a soldier of the Regular Forces, has been sentenced by a F.G.C.M. to 61 days F.P. No. 1 for absenting himself without leave.

(Sgd) G. J. PAUL, Capt. & Adjutant.
9th Bn. Gloucestershire Regt. (P).

BATTALION ORDERS BY LIEUT.-COL. J. FANE, D.S.O.,
COMMDG. 9TH BN. GLOUCESTERSHIRE REGT. (P).

9TH AUGUST 1919.

1115. DUTIES.
Bn. Orderly Officer for tomorrow — 2/Lt. B. Kembery.
"   "   "   "   Monday   — Lieut. G. F. Pullen.
Next for duty   — Lieut. V. E. Robertson.

Bn. Orderly Sergeant for tomorrow — Sgt. Ellis.
"   "   "   "   Monday   — " Andrews.
Next for duty   — " Neale, J.

No. 12 Platoon, "C" Co., will provide Guards tomorrow.
No. 2   "   "A" Co.,   "   "   "   Monday.

1116. PARADES.
Tomorrow:- "A", "C" and H.Q. Cos. will parade in drill order formed up in line, facing West, on the road leading to the Recreation Ground, at 11-30 hours; for Church of England Service, which will be held in the Protestant Church, Leichlingen, at 11-45 hours, followed by Holy Communion for all who wish to attend.
Roman Catholic Services will be held in the R.C. Church, Leichlingen, as follows:-
    Holy Communion   ... 07-30 hours.
    Morning Service   ... 10-30   "
    Benediction   ... 15-00   "
Non-Conformist Service will be held in the Cinema at 10-30 hrs.

Monday:-   Parades will be held under Company arrangements.

1117. DUTIES.
Lieut. G. F. Pullen will take over the duties of Band President and Signal Officer from Lieut. Palmer on the 11th inst.

Ref. Bn. Order No. 1105 dated 7th inst.- 2/Lt. Brinkworth will be relieved by Lieut. Pullen.

1118. CONTINENTAL LEAVE (C.R.O. 2051 of 6th inst.)
Ref. Bn. Order No. 1069 of 31/7/19.
All leave granted on the Continent of over 4 days duration, including the railway journey, will count against the next leave to U.K.

(Sgd) R. D. HEPPENSTALL, 2/Lt., A/Adjt.,
       9th Bn. Gloucestershire Regt. (P).

BATTALION ORDERS BY LIEUT.-COL. J. FANE, D.S.O.,
COMDG. 9TH BN. GLOUCESTERSHIRE REGT. (P).
11TH AUGUST 1919.

1119. DUTIES.
Bn. Orderly Officer for tomorrow - Lieut. E. F. E. Peacock.
Next for duty - 2/Lt. R. H. Warren, M.C., M.M.
Bn. Orderly Sergeant for tomorrow - Sgt. Johnson.
Next for duty - Sgt. Hardiman.
No. 9 Platoon, "C" Co., will provide the Guards tomorrow.

1120. PARADES.
H.Q. Co. and "C" Co. will parade under Company arrangements.

1121. INSPECTION.
The Commanding Officer will inspect "A" Co. on the Recreation Ground at 10-45 hours tomorrow, 12th inst.
Dress - Drill Order.   Formation - As for G.O.C's inspection.
All ranks at present with the Battalion, with the exception of cooks, will attend.
At 11-15 hours the Commanding Officer will inspect all stores and equipment of "A" Co. at Co. H.Q., when the Company administrative staff will be present.

1122. LECTURE.
A lecture will be given in the Bn. Recreation Room on Wednesday, 13th inst., at 11-30 hours, by Miss M. G. Williamson, M.A., entitled "Paris & Vienna." All available Officers and O.Rs. will attend.

1123. CASH.
In future, all Companies will make their own arrangements for drawing cash. The following is a programme of the Field Cashier's visits:-

    Monday:-   Corps H.Q., Leverkusen   09-30-12-30 & 14.00-16.00
    Tuesday   Berg Gladbach   10.00-11.30
                  Burscheid   12.00-13.00
                  Wermelskirchen   14.30-15.30
    Wednesday:-   Corps H.Q., Leverkusen   09.30-12.30 & 14.00-16.00
    Thursday:-   Light Division - Benrath   10.00-11.00
                                   Ohligs   11.30-12.30
                                   Solingen 14.30-15.30
    Friday:-   Corps H.Q., Leverkusen   09.30-12.30 & 14.00-16.00
    Saturday   "   "   "   09.30-12.30

1124. MUSKETRY.
All O.Rs. of H.Q. Co. will fire the following practices during the ensuing week:-

    Application   ... 5 Rounds, as in Practice 5.
    Grouping   ... 5   "   " "   "   1.
    Rapid   ... 10   "   " "   "   10.
    Snapshooting ... 5   "   " "   "   12.

O.C. H.Q. Co. will attend and will submit to Orderly Room by 10-00 hrs., 17th inst., a return stating No. of men who have fired.

1125. BATHING.
Os.C. Cos. will ensure that every N.C.O. and man will be in possession of a bathing card as issued today. These cards will always be produced at the baths, handed in to the M.O., and handed back to the owners on their departure from the baths.
They will always be shewn on kit inspections.
Baths will be open daily at 14-00 hours on Monday, Tuesday & Wednesday for voluntary bathing, but this does not excuse men from the bathing parade on Thursday, Friday & Saturday.

(Continued:-

-2-

1125. PROMOTIONS & APPOINTMENTS.
50627 Cpl. Clarke, A.,   appd T/pd.L/Sgt. to complete establishment.
28401 " Workman, T., appd.   "   "   "   "   "
50813 " Sherratt, H.,   "   "   "   "   "   "
50445 " Odell,   H.,   "   "   "   "   "   "
50906 L/c. Tinson,   A., promoted T/Cpl. vice Barnes.
50616 Unpd.L/c. Caddick, A., appd. T/Pd/L/c. "   Tinson.
50763   "   " Picken, J.,   "   "   "   Brackley.
50459   "   " Leaver, H.,   "   "   to complete establishment.

50436. Pte. Hollis. W. appd. unpd. L/c. from 9th inst.

                (Sgd)   G. J. PAUL,
                              Capt. & Adjutant.
                    9th Bn. Gloucestershire Regiment (P).

NOTICE.

The "PRONGS" Concert Party will give a concert at LEICHLINGEN
on Saturday, 16th inst.   Details will be given later.

BATTALION ORDERS BY LIEUT.-COL. J. FANE, D.S.O.,
COMMDG. 9TH BN. GLOUCESTERSHIRE REGT. (P).
12TH AUGUST 1919.

1127. DUTIES.
Bn. Orderly Officer for tomorrow   -   2/Lt. R. H. Warren, M.C., M.M.
Next for duty   -   Lieut. H. G. Hicks.

Bn. Orderly Sergeant for tomorrow -   Sgt. Hardiman.
Next for duty   -   Sgt. Neale, J.

No. 4 Platoon ("A" Co.) will provide the Guards tomorrow.

1128. PARADES.
Parades will be held under Company arrangements.

1129. POSTAL ORDERS.
Until the 16th inst. the sale of Postal Orders at all Army Post Offices will be restricted to one Pound Postal Order per Officer or O.R. per day, and the purchase must be covered by a written statement from the Commanding Officer certifying its immediate necessity.

1130. STRENGTH.
50944 Pte Pullen, S., is taken on the Bn. strength today and posted to "C" Co.

1131. TRANSFERS & ATTACHMENTS.
50354 Pte Meade,   H., is transferred from "C" Co. to H.Q. Co.
26092 " Stephens, F.,   "   "   "   "   " "   "
27970 " Mitchell, C.,   "   "   "   "   " "B" "   "   "
203240 " Hall,   R.,   "   "   "   "   " H.Q. "   " "C" "
50657 L/c Griffiths,B.,   "   "   "   "   "   "   "   "   "
38367 Pte Eveleigh, F., ceases to be attached to H.Q. Co. and is returned to "A" Co. for duty.

1132. COURT MARTIAL.
260405 L/c. Wellock, H., a soldier of the regular forces, has been sentenced by a F.G.C.M. to 40 days F.P. No. 1 for absenting himself without leave.

(Sgd) G. J. PAUL, Capt. & Adjutant,
9th Bn. Gloucestershire Regt. (P).

BATTALION ORDERS BY LIEUT-COL. J. FANE, D.S.O.
COMMDG. 9th. BN. GLOUCESTERSHIRE REGT.(P).
AUGUST 13th. 1919.

1133. DUTIES.
Bn. Orderly Officer for to-morrow --------- Lieut. H.G. Hicks.
Next for duty ------------------------------- 2LLieut. H.R. Jones.

Bn. Orderly Sergeant for to-morrow -------- Sergeant Neale, J.
Next for duty ------------------------------- Sergeant Pixton.

1134. PARADES.
Parades will be held under Company arrangements.

1135. WASTE PAPER.
O's C. Companies and Specialists Officers will arrange that all waste paper be kept, and not destroyed.
It will be stored in sacks and will be collected weekly by the Q.M.

1136. BANDOLIERS.
Reference Battalion Order 1097, dated Aug. 6th. 1919. All Bandoliers with the exception of those in the possession of Officers' grooms will be returned to the Q.M. by 10,00 hrs. Friday the 15th. inst.

(Sgd) G.J. PAUL, Capt. & Adjt.,
9th. Bn. Gloucestershire Regt.

BATTALION ORDERS BY LIEUT-COL. J. FANE, D.S.O.
COMDG. 9th. BN. GLOUCESTERSHIRE REGT: (F).
AUGUST 14TH. 1919.

1137. **DUTIES.**
Bn. Orderly Officer for to-morrow - - - 2/Lieut. H.R. Jones.
Next for duty - - - - - - - - - - - - - 2/Lieut. B. Kembery.

Bn. Orderly Sergeant for to-morrow - - Sgt. Pixton.
Next for duty - - - - - - - - - - - - - Sgt. Boast.

1138. **PARADES.**
Parades will be held under Company arrangements.

1139. **DIVISIONAL TOURNAMENT.**
The following letter from the General Officer Commanding the Division, concerning "B" Co. and No. 11. platoon "C" Co. is published for the information of all ranks:-

" I wish to thank you for the trouble you took in the construction and laying out of the Tournament ground.
 Would you please convey my thanks to all Officers, N.C.O's and men who worked under you."

(Sgd) W. Henneker, Major-General
Commdg. Southern Division.

1140. **PROMOTIONS.**
No. 50856; L/Cpl. H. Cutler is promoted T/Cpl from the 11-8-19.

1141. **TRANSFERS.**
No. 50856, Cpl. H. Cutler is transferred from "A" Co. to "C" Co.
No. 50906, Cpl. A. Tinson   "   "   "   "A" " to "C" "

1142. **BATHS.**
Battalion Order No. 975, dated July 14th. 1919 is re-published for information. The attention of all ranks should be drawn thereto:

" In future the baths will be available as follows:-

Thursdays - - - - - - 13-30 to 16-00 hrs.
Fridays - - - - - - - 09-30 to 12-30 "
   "   13-30 to 16-00 "
Saturdays - - - - - - 09-30 to 11-00 "   "

1143. **MOTOR CARS AND MOTOR CYCLES.**
Any Officer who wishes to bring to Germany either a motor car or a motor cycle should apply to this office for full particulars.

(Sgd) G.J. PAUL, Capt. & Adjt.,
9th. Bn. Gloucestershire Regt.

BATTALION ORDERS BY LIEUT-COL. J. FANE, D.S.O.
COMMDG. 9th. BN. GLOUCESTERSHIRE REGT. (P).
AUGUST 15th. 1919.

1144. DUTIES.
Bn. Orderly Officer for to-morrow — — — — — 2/Lieut. B. Kembery.
Next for duty — — — — — — — — — — — — — Lieut. P. J. Hancox.

Bn. Orderly Sergeant for to-morrow — — — — Sgt. Boast.
Next for duty — — — — — — — — — — — — — Sgt. Eagles.

1145. PARADES.
Parades will be held under Company arrangements.

1146. STRENGTH.
Lieut. W.F. Palmer having proceeded to England on the 13th. inst, is struck off the strength of the Battalion from that date.

1147. ATTACHMENTS.
No. 41132, Cpl. Blair, "C" Co. will be attached to "H.Q." Co. from this date.

1148. DEMOBILIZATION - SHORT PERIOD ENGAGEMENTS.
All W.O's, N.C.O's and men who enlisted for immediate service prior to July 1st. 1916 under Lord Derby's scheme are now eligible for demobilization and will proceed in order of priority of date.
It has been brought to notice that a number of these soldiers are anxious to defer their demobilization for a short period.
To meet this contingency it has been decided that such soldiers may be permitted to remain in the Service for one or more consecutive periods of three months on signing to this effect.
All Other Ranks who are now eligible for demobilization but who desire to remain for three months or longer in the Service will give in their names to their respective Companies before 09-00 hrs. on Sunday next the 17th. inst.
Company Commanders will render to Orderly Room by 12-00 hrs. on the 17th. inst; Nominal Rolls of all men desirous of remaining.

(Sgd) G.J. PAUL, Capt. & Adjt.,
9th. Bn. Gloucestershire Regt.

BATTALION ORDERS BY LIEUT-COL. J. FANE, D.S.O.
COMMDG. 5th. Bn. GLOUCESTERSHIRE REGT.(T):
AUGUST 16th. 1919.

1149. DUTIES.
Bn. Orderly Officer for to-morrow — — — — Lieut. F.J. Hancox.
Bn. Orderly Officer for Monday — — — — 2/Lieut. T.W. Everall.
Next for duty — — — — — — — — — — 2/Lieut. L.G. Holloway.

Bn. Orderly Sergeant for to-morrow — — — Sgt. Wharton.
Bn. Orderly Sergeant for Monday — — — — Sgt. Eagles.
Next for duty — — — — — — — — — — Sgt. Dunn.

1150. No. 3. Platoon "A" Co. will provide the Guards to-morrow.

1150. DIVINE SERVICE.
To-morrow the Battalion, less the two detached platoons of "B" Co. will parade in Drill Order, formed up in line facing west, on the road leading to the Recreation Ground, at 11-30 hrs. for Church of England Service. This will be held in the Protestant Church, Leichlingen at 11-45 hrs., followed by Holy Communion for all who wish to attend. Roman Catholic Service will be held in the R.C. Church, Leichlingen as follows:-
    Holy Communion — — — 07-30 hrs.
    Morning Service — — — 10-30 hrs.
    Benediction — — — — 18-00 hrs.
NON-CONFORMIST Service will be held in the Cinema at 10-30 hrs.

1151. PARADES.
On Monday parades will be held under Company arrangements.

1152. MUSKETRY.
All Other Ranks of "A", "B" and "C" Companies will fire the following practices during the ensuing week :-
    5 rounds Grouping as in Practice 1.
    5 " Application " " 5
    5 " Snapshooting " " 12.
    10 " Rapid as in " 10.
O's C; Companies will submit to Orderly Room by 10-00 hrs. 25th. inst. a return shewing the number of men who have fired.

1153. RHINE TRIP.
The following Officers and Other Ranks are detailed for a Rhine Trip on Monday the 18th. inst.:-
    "A" Co. — — — Lieut. R.G. Hicks, and 20 Other Ranks.
    "B" " — — — 2/Lt. F.J. Stebbings,M.C. and 10 Other Ranks.
    "C" " — — — Lieut. R.F.R. Peacock, and 20 Other Ranks.
    "H.Q." — — — — — — — — 10 Other Ranks.
These parties will be marched off to reach the station at 07-30 hrs. Waterproof sheets will be taken strapped on the back of the belt. Rations for the day will also be taken.
Lieut. R.F.R. Peacock will be in charge of the party.

1154. DEMOBILIZATION.
Those Companies having employed men who are likely to be demobilised under Army Order 292 should forthwith train understudies.
This applies especially to Headquarter Co.
Lieut. Johnson should warn Officers who are responsible for all employed men under the above Army Order.
Specialists Officers will make the necessary application to the Adjutant for men to maintain their strength, i.e., Signallers, Lewis Gunners, Pioneers etc.

4.

1195. **BOOTS.**
Boots of men not for demobilization requiring exchange will be exchanged at the Q.M. Stores on Monday the 18th. inst. commencing:-

"H.Q." Co. - - - - 09-00 hrs.
"A"   " - - - - 09-30 "
"B"   " - - - - 10-15 "
"C"   " - - - - 10-45 "

An Officer and the C.Q.M.Sgt. of each company will be present to superintend the fitting, and signing of Clothing Ledger.
In future clothing, boots, necessaries etc. will only be issued to an Officer representing a Company.

(Sgd) G.J. PAUL, Capt. & Adjt.,
9th. Bn. Gloucestershire Regnt.

BATTALION ORDERS BY LIEUT-COL. J. FANE, D.S.O.
COMMDG 9TH BN. GLOUCESTERSHIRE REGIMENT (P).
AUGUST 18TH. 1919.

1155. DUTIES.
Bn. Orderly Officer for tomorrow - - - - - 2/Lieut. L.G. Holloway.
Next for duty - - - - - - - - - - - - - - 2/Lieut. F.J. Stebbings, M.C.

Bn. Orderly Sergeant for to-morrow - - - - Sergt Dunn.
Next for duty - - - - - - - - - - - - - - Sergt Ellis.

No. 9 Platoon "C" Co. will provide the Guards for to-morrow.

1156 PARADES.
Parades will be held under Company arrangements.

1157 COURSES, ETC.
In future no man who is eligible for demobilization will be sent on a course or detached from the Battalion.

1158. APPOINTMENTS ETC.
2nd Lieut. R.H. Warren, M.C., M.M. having at his own request relinquished the appointment of Battalion E.O. is posted to "A" Co. for duty from this date.
Lieut. P.J. Hancox takes over the duties of Senior E.O. of the Battalion from this date. He will also take over the cinema a/c and act as Entertainment Officer.

1158a. LEAVE - DENTAL TREATMENT.
It has been brought to notice that frequent applications have been made to War Office, by officers on leave in the United Kingdom, for extension of leave to undergo dental treatment.
As facilities exist in the Rhine Army for dental treatment of all kinds, this practice must cease.

1159 LEAVE - PAYMENT OF SOLDIERS.
Consequent on the withdrawal of pay books the following will be the proceedure for the payment of soldiers granted leave to the U.K.
All men will take A.F. W. 3448B duly completed.
If proceeding via London the soldier will receive an advance from his Company Commander to meet his requirements on the journey to London. He will receive a further £2 at Furlough Pay Office, Victoria or Waterloo and will hand his A.F. W.3448B there for transmission to the Regimental Paymaster.
A Soldier not passing through London will be given an advance of £2.10.0 by his Company Commander and will be instructed to dispatch A.F. W.3448B to his Regimental Paymaster immediately on arrival in England.
On receipt of A.F. W. 3448B the Regimental Paymaster will make further cash advance as necessary having regard to the state of the account.

1160 PAY & MESS BOOKS.
The Pay and Mess Book will always be rendered in duplicate twice monthly, the first for the period 1st to 15th and the second for the period 16th to the last day of the month. O.C. Cos. will arrange direct with the Second-in-Command for the checking of their A.F. No. 1504A.

1161 RATE OF EXCHANGE.
The Official rate of exchange from 16th inst. to the end of August is as follows:-
        10 Mks = 2/7d
        £1 = 77m.40pfs.

1162. **EXCHANGE OF EQUIPMENT.**
All leather equipment will be exchanged for webbing equipment at the Q.M. Stores tomorrow, the 19th instant, at 11.00 hours.

R.D. Heppenstall, 2nd Lt. Assistant Adjutant,
9th Bn. Gloucestershire Regiment (P).

BATTALION ORDERS BY LIEUT-COL. J. FANE, D.S.O.
COMMDG. 9th. Bn. GLOUCESTERSHIRE REGT. (P).
AUGUST 19th. 1919.

1163. DUTIES.
Bn. Orderly Officer for to-morrow — — — — — 2/Lieut. R.W. Smiles, M.M.
Next for duty — — — — — — — — — — — — — — Lieut. L.G. Holloway.

Bn. Orderly Sergeant for to-morrow — — — — Sgt. Ellis.
Next for duty — — — — — — — — — — — — — — Sgt. Plimsole.

No. 10, platoon, "C" Co. will provide the Guards for to-morrow.
No. 11,   "   "C" "   "   "   "   "   "   Thursday.

1164. PARADES.
Parades will be held under Company arrangements.

1165. GUARD PARADE.
Reference Battalion Order No. 708, d/20/5/19.
This parade will re-commence to-morrow, the 20th. inst., and will be continued daily at 09-30 hrs.

1166. TELEGRAMS.
No telegrams will be sent from any department of the Battalion without the approval of the Adjutant.

1167. G.H.Q. COLLEGES.- PAYMENT OF O.R's.
The following instructions regarding the payment of O.R's on Courses at G.H.Q. Colleges is published for information.
The College will keep its own Pay & Mess Book and Cash Account. When a man proceeds to the College for a Course of Instruction he should be treated, for the purposes of pay, as a man on detachment. Army Form O.1809.A. shewing rate of pay issuable, approx. credit, and the date to which paid and rationed will accompany the man on leaving his Unit, and from the information given thereon the College Commandant will compile Form 1 of the P. & M. Book.

1168. APPOINTMENTS.
Capt. G.J. Paul relinquishes the Appointment of Adjutant from this date.
Lieut. E.O. Pilcher to be Acting Adjutant vice Capt. G.J. Paul, to date 19-8-19.
Capt. G.J. Paul is posted to "A" Co. and will assume Command on return from leave.

1169. PROMOTIONS.
No. 260174, L/Sgt. W. Brooker is pro. T/Sgt. to complete Establishment.
 " 41 132 Cpl. H. Blair   "   " T/Sgt. "   "   "
 " 12900   "   J. Nelson   "   " T/Sgt. "   "   "
 " 50745,   "   W. Powell   "   " T/Sgt. "   "   "
 " 50711,   "   G. Knowles " Appd.Pd/L/Sgt.   "
 " 50910,   "   C. Mobbs   " Appd.Pd/L/Sgt.
 " 260065, L/Cpl. A. Lovell to be granted pay of rank vice Holder to U.K.

1170. TRANSFERS.
No. 50686, Pte. S. Hopkins is trans. from HQ.Co. to "C" Co. from this date.
 " 41132, Sgt. H. Blair   "   "   "   "C" "   "HQ."   "   "   "
 " 50737, Pte. H. Milligan is posted to "B" Co. from HQ.Co. "   "   "

(Sgd) R.D. HEPPENSTALL, 2/Lieut. A/Adjt.,
9th. Bn. GLOUCESTERSHIRE REGT.

NOTICE.

JEWISH SERVICES. - A Service will be held for all ranks of the Jewish persuasion every Saturday morning at the Synagogue, 5; Glockengasse, COLOGNE, (near the E.F.C?) at 11-00 hrs.

BATTALION ORDERS BY LIEUT-COL. J. FANE, D.S.O.
COMMDG. 9th. Bn. GLOUCESTERSHIRE REGT.(P).
AUGUST 20th, 1919.

1171. DUTIES.
Bn. Orderly Officer for to-morrow - - - Lieut. L.G. Holloway.
Next for duty - - - - - - - - - - - - 2/Lieut. B. Kembery.

Bn. Orderly Sergeant for to-morrow - - Sgt. Plimsole.
Next for duty - - - - - - - - - - - - Sgt. Buchanan.

No. 11. platoon will provide the Guards for to-morrow.
No. 12.   "   "   "   "   "   " Friday.

1172. PARADES.
Parades will be held under Company arrangements.

1173. VOLUNTEERS - OFFICERS.
Any Officer who has volunteered for the Army of Occupation and now wishes to withdraw his name should apply to this office forthwith.

1174. BOUNDS.- G.R.O. 3320 IS PUBLISHED FOR INFORMATION.
Owing to an outbreak of smallpox, Manchester and Salford are placed out of bounds to all troops and members of Q.M.A.A.C. proceeding on leave other than demobilization furlough. (A/572/138/9/0/M.)

1175. TRANSFERS.
No. 50737 Pte. H. Milligan is trans. to "A" Co. from "B" Co. from this date.
No. 201953 Pte. G. Cox is trans. from "B" Co. to "HQ" Co. from this date
No. 50597   "   P. Banthorpe "   " "B" "   " "HQ" "   "   "   "
No. 50824   "   B. Taylor is "   " "B" "   " "HQ" "   "   "   "
No. 50618   "   A. Clarke is "   " "A" "   " "HQ" "   "   "   "

(Sgd) R.D. HEPPENSTALL, 2/Lieut. A/Adjt.,
9th. Bn. Gloucestershire Regiment.

BATTALION ORDERS BY LIEUT-COL. J. FANE, D.S.O.
COMMDG 9TH BN. GLOUCESTERSHIRE REGT (P).
AUGUST 21st. 1919.

1176. **DUTIES.**
Bn. Orderley Officer for to-morrow - - - 2/Lieut. B. Kembery.
Next for duty - - - - - - - - - - - - - - Lieut. E.F.E. Peacock.

Bn. Orderly Sergeant for tomorrow - - - Sergt. Pixton.
Next for duty - - - - - - - - - - - - - -   "   Andrews.

No.12, platoon will provide the Guards for to-morrow.
No. 1   "   "   "   "   "   "   Saturday.

1177. **PARADES.**
Parades will be held under Company arrangements.

1178. **COURSE - P. & R.T.**
15137 Corpl Gardiner, E. "B" Co. who attended a course of training at the Second Army School of P. & R.T. received a Fair Report.

1179. **LEATHER EQUIPMENT.**
O.C. Cos. will render to the Q.M. by 10.00 hours the 23rd instant a certificate to the effect that all Leather Equipment in possession of O.Rs. of their Cos. has been exchanged for Webbing.

(Sgd) E.O. Pilcher, Lieut. A/Adjt.
9th Bn. Gloucestershire Regiment (P).

BATTALION ORDERS BY LIEUT-COL. J. FANE, D.S.O.
COMMDG. 9th. Bn. GLOUCESTERSHIRE REGT.(F)
AUGUST 22nd. 1919.

1180. DUTIES.
Bn. Orderly Officer for to-morrow — — — — — — Lieut. E.F.E. Peacock.
Next for duty — — — — — — — — — — — — — — Lieut. V.H. Robertson.

Bn. Orderly Sergeant for to-morrow — — — — — Sgt. Andrews.
Next for duty — — — — — — — — — — — — — — Sgt Eagles.

No. 1. platoon will provide the Guards for to-morrow.
No. 2.   "   "   "   "   "   "   Sunday.

1181. PARADES.
Parades will be held under Company arrangements.

1182. PROMOTIONS AND APPOINTMENTS.
50670. L/Cpl. F.J. Smith is promoted T/Cpl. Pd. from 21-8-19.
50688.   "   E. Goodchild   "   T/Cpl. Pd. "   -:-
50625.   "   G. Cheale   "   T/Cpl. Pd. "   -:-
50763.   "   J. Picken   "   T/Cpl. Pd. "   -:-

50596. L/Cpl. W. Brown is granted Pay of Rank from 21-8-19.
28692.   "   G. Holbrook   "   " "   "   "   -:-
50675.   "   A. Higgins   "   " "   "   "   -:-
12485.   "   E. Townsend   "   " "   "   "   -:-

50795. Pte. F. Saunders is appointed Unpd/L/Cpl. from 21-8-19.

(Sgd) E.O. PILCHER, Lieut. & A/Adjt.,
9th. Bn. Gloucestershire Regt.

NOTICES.

SPORTS FUND.

The subscriptions having been expended money is required to put the Sports Fund on a sound basis. It is suggested that each Officer pays 10 Marks per month, and each N.C.O. and Man 1 Mark per month. This money to be paid one month in arrear to the Sports Officer, commencing August 1st. 1919.

CONCERT.

There will be a Concert in the Battalion Recreation Hall on Saturday evening, commencing 18-45 hrs.

BATTALION ORDERS BY LIEUT.-COL. J. FANE, D.S.O.,
COMMDG. 9TH BN. GLOUCESTERSHIRE REGIMENT (P).
23rd AUGUST 1919.

1183. DUTIES.
　　Bn. Orderly Officer for tomorrow　-　Lieut. V. E. Robertson.
　　 "　　 "　　 "　　 "　　Monday　 -　2/Lt. E. C. Turner.
　　Next for duty　　　　　　　　　 -　2/Lt. W. Francombe.

　　Bn. Orderly Sergeant for tomorrow -　Sgt. Eagles.
　　 "　　 "　　 "　　 "　　Monday　 -　Sgt. Neale, F.
　　Next for duty　　　　　　　　　 -　Sgt. Dunn.

　　No. 3 Platoon, "A" Co., will provide guards for tomorrow.
　　No. 4　　 "　　 "　　 "　　 "　　 "　　 "　　 "　　Monday.
　　No. 5　　 "　　 "B"　 "　　 "　　 "　　 "　　 "　　Tuesday/

1184. DIVINE SERVICE.
　　Tomorrow the Battalion, less No. 1 Platoon of "A" Co. detached, will parade in Drill Order; formed up in line facing West, on the road leading to the Recreation Ground, at 11-30 hours; for Church of England Service, which will be held in the Protestant Church, Leichlingen, at 11-45 hours, followed by Holy Communion for all who wish to attend.

　　Roman Catholic Services will be held in the R.C. Church, Leichlingen, as follows:-

　　　　Holy Communion　　...　07-30 hours.
　　　　Morning Service　　...　10-00　 "
　　　　Benediction　　　　...　15-00　 "

　　Non-Conformist Service will be held in the Cinema at 10-30 hours.

1185. PARADES.
　　On Monday parades will be held under Company arrangements.

1186. MUSKETRY.
　　All other ranks of "A", "B" & "C" Cos. will fire the following practices during the ensuing week:-

　　　5 Rds grouping as in Practice I
　　　5　 "　application as in Practice III.
　　　10　 "　rapid as in Practice VI.

　　No. 1's and rangefinders of L.G. Teams will parade for revolver practice on "C" Co's. range at 09-00 hours on Monday & Friday under Lieut. Robertson.
　　　Practices:-　5 Rds deliberate & rapid, right & left hand.

1187. APPOINTMENT.
　　27970 Pte C. Mitchell, H.Q. Co., is appd. paid L/c. from this date.

1188. CLOTHING & NECESSARIES, ISSUE OF.
　　In future the following days only will be allotted to Companies for the issue of clothing & necessaries:-
　　　"A" Co.　Tuesdays, commencing 09-00 hours.
　　　"B" 　"　　　 "　　　　 "　　 10-30　 "
　　　"C" 　"　Wednesdays,　　 "　　 09-00　 "
　　　H.Q. 　"　　　 "　　　　 "　　 10-30　 "

1189. COURTS MARTIAL.
　　Ref. Bn. Orders Nos. 1114 & 1132.　The sentences therein stated have been commuted as follows:-
　　50615 Pte J. Cutler:- commuted from 60 days F.P. No.1 to
　　　　　　　　　　　　　　60 days F.P. No. 2.
　　260405 L/c H. Wellock- commuted from 40 days F.P. No. 1 to
　　　　　　　　　　　　　　40 days F.P. No. 2.

(Continued

1190. **IRREGULAR POSTING OF LETTERS (G.R.O.No.3334 of 20/8/19).**
It is observed that letters are being posted in large numbers by British troops at German Civil Post Offices and in street letter boxes. This practice is irregular. Letters so posted are often subjected to considerable delay.

(Sgd) E. O. PILCHER.

Lieut., A/Adjt.,
9th Bn. Gloucestershire Regt. (P).

BATTALION ORDERS BY LIEUT.-COL. J. FANE, D.S.O.,
COMMDG. 9TH BN. GLOUCESTERSHIRE REGT. (P).
25TH AUGUST 1919.

1191. DUTIES.
Bn. Orderly Officer for tomorrow — 2/Lt. W. Francombe.
Next for duty — 2/Lt. R.H. Warren, M.C., M.M.

Bn. Orderly Sergeant for tomorrow — Sgt. Dunn.
Next for duty — Sgt. Thorpe.

No. 5 Platoon will provide the guards tomorrow.
No. 6 " will be next for duty.

1192. PARADES.
Parades tomorrow will be held under Company arrangements.

1193. PARADE, WEDNESDAY.
The Bn. will parade on Wednesday next, 27th inst., on the Recreation Ground.
Time:- 10-30 hours. Markers report to R.S.M. at 10-15 hours.
Formation:- Mass, Facing East.
Dress:- All ranks Drill Order.
Company Commanders will be mounted (grooms will be in attendance.
Signallers under instruction will not parade but will carry out their training on the Recreation Ground.
The Band will not parade.
One Officer will parade with H.Q. Co.
2/Lt. B. Kembery will parade with "A" Co.
All employed O.Rs. who can be spared will parade.

1194. BICYCLES.
All bicycles will be taken to the Armourer's Shop for overhauling by 09-00 hours on Thursday next, 28th inst.

1195. STRENGTH.
Nos. 7 & 8 Platoons, "B" Co., rejoined the Bn. from Kalk Racecourse on 22nd inst.
No. 1 Platoon, "A" Co., rejoined the Bn. from Burscheid today, 25th inst.

1196. IDENTITY DISCS - WEARING OF. (G.R.O. 3310, 15/8/19).
With the introduction of Pay & Mess Book and the consequent withdrawal of A.B. 64, the latter will cease to be a means of a soldier's identification. Warrant officers, non-commissioned officers and men will therefore in future wear their identity discs at all times.

1197. TRAVELLING ON RAILWAYS. (G.R.O. 3340, 22/8/19.)
No civilians other than wives and relatives of British Officers, and ladies employed with the Rhine Army, whose position entitles them to officers' travelling accommodation, are allowed to travel in railway carriages reserved for British Officers. When wives or relatives travel in these carriages they will invariably wear the brassard issued to them from the Permit Office.

(Sgd) E. O. PILCHER, Lieut., A/Adjt.,
9th Bn. Gloucestershire Regt. (P).

-2-

N O T I C E.

AQUATIC SPORTS.

It is proposed to hold swimming sports at the baths, "C" Co., on Saturday, August 30th.

Entries to be made to 2/Lt. Rosbery before 18-00 hours August 27th.

First race, 16-00 hours.

The following are the events:-

1. Relay Race.   Teams of four: each man to swim 2 breadths.
2. Four Breadths.
3. Two   "
4. High Dive   (entrance fee half mark).
5. Plunge (Dive) (entrance fee half mark).
6. Longest distance under water.
7. Diving for plates (entrance fee half mark).
8. Officers' Race (4 breadths, handicap).
9. Polo - Six a side. Companies may enter one or more teams.
10. Life saving. (Entrance fee 1 mark). Each competitor to provide his own dummy, i.e.; a man who cannot swim.

11. Running Header.

The Band will play in the Square near Protestant Church, Leichlingen, to-morrow, from 17-30 to 18-30 hours.

BATTALION ORDERS BY LIEUT.-COL. J. FANE, D.S.O.,
COMMDG. 9TH BN. GLOUCESTERSHIRE REGT. (F).
26TH AUGUST 1919.

1198. DUTIES.
Bn. Orderly Officer for tomorrow   -   2/Lt. R. H. Warren, M.C., M.M.
Next for duty   -   2/Lt. B. Kembery.

Bn. Orderly Sergeant for tomorrow -   Sgt. Thorpe.
Next for duty   -   Sgt. Peet.

No. 6 Platoon will provide the Guards tomorrow.
No. 7 Platoon will be next for duty.

1199. PARADES.
Parades will be as detailed in yesterday's Bn. Orders.

1200. CLOTHING, ETC.
When an article of clothing equipment or necessaries is accidentally damaged or broken the remnants must be produced for exchange, - otherwise the man will be charged the full value of article damaged.

1201. PROMOTIONS & APPOINTMENTS.
50780 Sgt. S. Russon is appd. A/C.S.M. with pay 24/8/19 vice Ponting.
50444 Cpl. T. Ringrose prom. T/Sgt.   24/8/19 vice Russon.
37349 "   D. Godfrey   "   "   26/8/19 "   Neale, F.
50408 "   F. Broughton appd.L/Sgt.,pd., 21/8/19 vice L/Sgt Wharton.
50427 L/c H. Morgan prom. 2x T/Cpl   21/8/19 vice L/Sgt Wharton.
50842 "   H. Williams   "   "   24/8/19 "   Palmer.
50600 "   C. Birch   "   "   24/8/19 "   Tinsen.
50820 "   H. Timms   "   "   24/8/19 "   Ringrose.
50618 "   A. Caddick   "   "   26/8/19 "   Godfrey.
50708 "   F. Kemp   "   "   26/8/19 "   Large.
202494 "   Moody, A. appd. T/pd/L/c.   21/8/19 "   Morgan.
12521 "   E. Bowman   "   "   24/8/19 "   Williams
50897 "   Percox, C.   "   "   24/8/19 "   Birch.
32479 "   Wonks, G.   "   "   24/8/19 "   Timms
50885 "   Hayward, H.   "   "   26/8/19 "   Jenkins.
260278 "   Rees, L.   "   "   26/8/19 "   Caddick.

The u/m are appointed unpaid L/Cpls:-
50671 Pte J. Acton   50395 Pte B. Botcher.   50709 Pte F. Knowles
50643 " L. Evans   41094 " T. Chayney   40284 " T. May
50967 " Allet, J.   50462 " H. Bond   50467 " B. French
41085 " C. Tompkinson 50685 " J. Cain   50368 " Hale, G.
44933 " C. Hunt.

1202. TRANSFERS.
50444 Sgt. T. Ringrose is transferred from "A" to "B" Co.
50427 Cpl. H. Morgan   "   "   " "C" to "A" "

(sgd) E. O. PILCHER,   Lieut., A/Adjutant.
9th Bn. Gloucestershire Regt. (F).

BATTALION ORDERS BY LIEUT.-COL. J. FANE, D.S.O.,
COMMDG. 9TH BN. GLOUCESTERSHIRE REGT. (P).
27TH AUGUST 1919.

1203. DUTIES.
Bn. Orderly Officer for tomorrow — 2/Lt. B. Kembery.
Next for duty — 2/Lt. E. C. Turner.

Bn. Orderly Sergeant for tomorrow — Sgt. Peet.
Next for duty — Sgt. Brooker.

No. 7 Platoon will provide the Guards tomorrow.
No. 8 " will be next for duty.

1204. PARADES.
Companies will parade under Company arrangements.

1205. DUTIES AND ACCOUNTS.
2/Lt. G. A. Brinkworth, M.M., on return from leave will take over the duties of D.A.P.M/ and Civil Administrator.

2/Lt. E. A. Bresman, on return from leave, will take over duties of Band President, President War Savings Association, and Signalling Officer, and will serve on the Officers' Mess Committee.

2/Lt. R. D. Heppenstall will take over the Cinema A/cs. from 2/Lt. Warren.

The Lewis Gun Sergeant will be responsible for the training of the Lewis Gunners and will be under the supervision of the Adjutant.

1206. N.C.Os. CLASSES.
The N.C.Os. Class at present in existence will be known as "A" Class.

Another class, known as "B" Class — formed of L/cs. recently appointed & whose names have been notified to Companies today — will parade on the Recreation Ground daily, from tomorrow the 28th inst., from 09-30 to 11-00 hours.

The following programme will be carried out:-

	09-30/10-00	10-00/10-25	10-25/10-45	10-45/11-00
"A" Class:-	Drill	Musketry	Gas	Lecture
"B" Class:-	Musketry	Drill	Lecture	Gas

1207. OFFICERS' SERVANTS.
Attention is called to Bn. Order No. 979 of 14th ult. Os. C. Companies will ensure that this order is carried out.

1208. POSTAL ORDERS (Extract from G.R.O. 3344 dated 25/8/19).
No Officer or man may purchase an amount exceeding £5 in value in any one day. Issues above £1 may only be made on the certificate of the O.C. Unit that he is satisfied as to the necessity of the issue.

(Sgd) E. O. PILCHER, Lieut. & Adjt.,
9th Bn. Gloucestershire Regt. (P).

BATTALION ORDERS BY LIEUT.-COL. J. FANE; D.S.O.,
COMMDG. 9TH BN. GLOUCESTERSHIRE REGT. (F).
28TH AUGUST 1919.

1209. **DUTIES.**
Bn. Orderly Officer for tomorrow   -   2/Lt. E. C. Turner.
Next for duty   -   2/Lt. W. Francombe.

Bn. Orderly Sergeant for tomorrow   -   Sgt. Brooker.
Next for duty   -   Sgt. Buchanan.

No. 8 Platoon, "B" Co., will provide the Guards tomorrow.
No. 9 Platoon, "C" Co., will be next for duty.

1210. **PARADES.**
Parades tomorrow will be under Company arrangements.

1211. **INSPECTION.**
The Commanding Officer will inspect all riding horses and transport of the Battalion, less those on duty, on the Recreation Ground, at 10-15 hours tomorrow.

Draught horses will be harnessed but will parade without vehicles.

Saddle & pack horses will be saddled up.

Dress for personnel - Clean Fatigue.

1212. **LEAVE TO FRANCE & BELGIUM.**
Application for leave to France & Belgium must reach Orderly Room seven clear days before leave is required.

1213. **GERMAN NOTES (B.R.O. 891 of 27th inst.)**
All 50 mark notes issued by Reichsbank, bearing date 30th October 1918, will shortly be called in and exchanged for a newer issue. The actual date of recall will be notified later but in the meantime, to prevent financial loss, Os. C. Cos. will collect above-mentioned notes & hand same to the Adjutant so that they may be sent to the Field Cashier for exchange.

1214. **WASTE PAPER.**
All waste paper to be handed in to the Q.M. Stores at 10-30 hours on the 30th inst.

1215. **APPOINTMENT.**
No. 50846, Pte G. Wilkins, (H.Q. Co.) is appointed UMPS/L/c. from 27th inst.

1216. **REVERSION.**
No. 50302 Cpl. Sherwood, J., reverts to Private at own request 28/8/19; and is transferred to "C" Co.

(Sgd) E. O. PILCHER   Lieut. & Adjutant.
9th Bn. Gloucestershire Regt. (F).

CONCERT.

A Concert will be given by IENA ASHWELL'S CONCERT PARTY in Bn. Concert Hall on Monday, 1st prox., at 18-30 hours.

Tickets may be obtained by other ranks from C.Q.M.S. Prestridge, and by Officers & O.Rs. from Pte White, Education Office.

BATTALION ORDERS BY LIEUT.-COL. J. FANE, D.S.O.,
COMMDG. 9TH BN. GLOUCESTERSHIRE REGT. (P).
29TH AUGUST 1919.

1217. **DUTIES.**
Bn. Orderly Officer for tomorrow — 2/Lt. W. Francombe.
Next for duty — 2/Lt. L. G. Holloway.

Bn. Orderly Sergeant for tomorrow — Sgt. Buchanan.
Next for duty — Sgt. Stagg.

No. 9 Platoon will provide the Guards tomorrow.
No. 10 Platoon will be next for duty.

1218. **PARADES.**
Parades tomorrow will be under Company arrangements.

1219. **TITLES.**
It has been noticed that several men are still not wearing "Gloster" titles. This practice must cease forthwith and Company Commanders will ensure that all men of their Companies are provided with the proper titles.

1220. **TRANSFER.**
No. 50848 Pte A. Willis ("B" Co.) is transferred to H.Q. Co. from this date.

1221. **DISPOSAL OF CASUALS WHO DO NOT ACCOMPANY THEIR UNITS TO ENGLAND.**
(G.R.O. 3354, 27/8/19):— It is inevitable that on the departure of units from the Army of the Rhine a certain number of N.C.Os. and men in employments or on detached duties will not accompany their units to England.
The following instructions are therefore issued in order that trace of these men may not be lost, and that casualties affecting them may be duly reported:—
1. Every officer in charge of an Institution School, Club Detachment, etc., OR OTHER EMPLOYER, having under his orders any N.C.Os. or men who are not borne on the strength of a unit serving in the Rhine Army, will render on the first day of each month a nominal roll of such men serving to D.A.G. (Record Section), GHQ.
2. Casualties affecting the N.C.Os. and men under reference will be reported by the employer weekly, on Saturdays, to D.A.G., GHQ., A.F.B213 being used for this purpose.
3. In accordance with Rhine Army Letter No. A.602/6(01), dated August 8th 1919, each unit leaving the Army has been instructed to furnish a nominal roll of men who do not accompany it to England. A.F.B.103 of these men will be sent direct by the unit to D.A.G. (Record Section); G.H.Q. The Record Section will prepare A.F.O.1810, and will submit them to the proper Record Offices at Home.
4. The N.C.Os. and men will continue to be borne on the strength of their Units, and as soon as their services can be dispensed with they will be sent to the Rhine Army Reception Camp for despatch to England under the provisions of G.R.O. 2987.
5. Under no circumstances are N.C.Os. and men eligible for demobilization to be retained by employers.
These instructions are to be given the widest possible circulation, and will be repeated in all Formation and Unit Routine Orders.

1222. **PAYMENT TO TROOPS ON RETURN FROM LEAVE (D.R.O.908, 28/8/19).**
Further cash issues on men's return from furlough must be restricted to current earnings subject to necessary curtailment in cases of those in debt. Any additional payments will only therefore be made by Company Commanders after notification of balances by regimental paymasters in pay and mess books for period of expiry of furloughs. This however will not prevent special reference to regimental paymasters in urgent cases.

(Sgd) E.O. PILCHER,
Lieut. & Adjutant.
9th Bn. Gloucestershire Regt. (P).

**BATTALION ORDERS BY LIEUT.-COL. J. FANE, D.S.O.,
COMMDG. 9TH BN. GLOUCESTERSHIRE REGT. (P).
AUGUST 30TH 1919.**

1223. DUTIES.
Bn. Orderly Officer for tomorrow — 2/Lt. L. G. Holloway.
  "   "   "   "   Monday — Lieut. P. J. Hancox.
Next for duty — 2/Lt. H. R. Jones.
Bn. Orderly Sergeant for tomorrow — Sgt. Stagg.
  "   "   "   "   Monday — Sgt. Blair.
Next for duty — Sgt. Broughton.
No. 10 Platoon will provide the guards tomorrow.
No. 11   "   "   "   "   "   Monday.
No. 12   "   "   be next for duty.

1224. DIVINE SERVICE.
The Battalion will parade tomorrow in in Drill Order, formed up in line facing West, on the road leading to the Recreation Ground, at 11-30 hours, under command of Major H. B. Spear, for Church of England Service, which will be held in the Protestant Church, Leichlingen, at 11-45 hours, followed by Holy Communion for all who wish to attend.
Roman Catholic Services will be held in the R.C. Church, Leichlingen, as follows:-
    Holy Communion ... 07-30 hours.
    Morning Service ... 10-00 "
    Benediction ... 15-00 "
Non-Conformist Service will be held in the Cinema at 10-30 hours.

1225. PARADES.
On Monday parades will be held under Company arrangements.

1226. LEWIS GUN INSTRUCTION.
One Lewis Gun Class per Company, consisting of one Instructor and six O.Rs. per class, will commence on Monday next, 1st Sept.'19. These Classes will work according to Bn. Programme (copies of which will be circulated tomorrow) each day, Saturdays excluded, from 08-30 to 10-30 hours.
Companies will send nominal rolls to Orderly Room by 09-00 hours on Monday, 1st Sept.
N.C.Os. and men attending these classes should not be available for guard duties.

1227. MUSKETRY.
All O.Rs. of A, B & C Cos. will fire the following practices during the ensuing week:-
    5 Rds. Grouping as in Practice 2.
    5 " "Application" " " 4.
    5 " Rapid " " 7.
No. 1s and rangefinders will parade on the Bn. parade ground on Monday and Friday at 09-00 hours.
All Officers' servants will parade on Monday at 10-00 hours on Bn. parade ground for instruction in the use of revolvers.

1228. RHINE TRIP.
The following Officers & O.Rs. are detailed for a Rhine Trip on Monday, 1st Sept:-
    "A" Co.   2/Lt. R. W. Smiles and 15 O.Rs.
    "B" Co.   25 O.Rs.
    "C" Co.   Lieut. G. F. Pullen & 15 O.Rs.
    H.Q. Co.   Lieut. E. O. Pilcher & 5 "
These parties will march off to reach the station at 07-50 hours.
Waterproof sheets will be taken wrapped on the back of the belt.
Rations will also be taken.
Lieut. E. O. Pilcher will be in charge of the party.

1229. PROMOTIONS & APPOINTMENTS.
15137 Cpl. Gardner, E., prom. Sgt. 30/8/19 vice Neale, F.
50711 L/Sgt. Knowles, F.,   "   "   "   "   "   Jones.
41138 Cpl. Smith, W., appd. L/Sgt vice Sherratt 30/8/19
28614 "   Bownes, C.,   "   "   "   Knowles   "
32683 L/c Slater, G., prom. Cpl. 29/8/19 vice Sherwood.
50772 " Powell, S.,   "   " 30/8/19 " L/Sgt Knowles.
50459 " Leaver, H.,   "   "   "   "   "   Sherratt.
260065 " Lovell, A.,   "   "   "   "   Cook.
50596 " Brown, W.,   "   "   "   "   Gardner.
30743 Unpd L/c Norris, F., appd. Pd/L/c. 29/8/19 vice Slater.
260010 "   " Jones, A.,   "   30/8/19 " Powell
36835 "   " Reynolds, W., "   "   " Leaver.
26215 "   " Cooper, C.,   "   "   " Lovell.
263037 "   " Hunt, W.   "   "   " Phillpotts.
30567 "   " Nutt, H.,   "   "   " Brown
50471 "   " Hawkins, W., "   31/8/19 " Philips
50030 "   " Duffin, C., is appd. Pd.L/c. 30/8/19 vice Sessions
              and to be A/Cpl. unpaid.

1230. TRANSFERS.
15137 Sgt. Gardner, E., is transferred to "A" Co. from this date.
50459 Cpl. Leaver, H.,   "   "   "H.Q." "   "   "
41132 Sgt. Blair, R.,   "   "   "C"   "   "   "
37804 Pte Hector, W.,   "   "   "B"   "   "   "

(Sgd) E. O. PILCHER, Lieut. & Adjutant.
         9th Bn. Gloucestershire Regt. (P).

Army Form C. 2113.

P.W. 785

WAR DIARY
or
INTELLIGENCE SUMMARY.
(Erase heading not required.)

Northern Division (A)

Instructions regarding War Diaries and Intelligence Summaries are contained in F.S. Regs., Part II. and the Staff Manual respectively. Title pages will be prepared in manuscript.

Place	Date 1919	Hour	Summary of Events and Information	Remarks and references to Appendices
Recklingen	Sept 1st		B" Coy proceeded to DELLBRUCK to Guard the P.O.W. Camp. Lt. Holloway to U.K. leave	
"	2nd		Lt. V.E. Robertson proceeded to U.K. leave. Lt. Allen returned from leave 2/Lt. Todd M.C. rejoined from leave	
"	3		Capt. Paul rejoined from U.K. leave Lt. Col. Lane. D.S.O. proceeded on leave to U.K.	
"	4		Capt. Paul assumed command of A" Coy on return from leave	
"	5		2/Lt. Everall rejoined from U.K. leave	
"	6th		Lt. Bresmer rejoined from U.K. leave. 2/Lt. Jones proceeded on leave to U.K.	
"	7th		Lt. Handcox proceeded on leave to U.K.	
"	8th		Lt. Halward rejoined from U.K. leave	
"	9th		2/Lt. E.E. Turner and 2/Lt. Frascombe proceeded for Demobilization	
"	"		2/Lt. Stebbins rejoined from leave	
"	11th		Lt. Johnson rejoined from U.K. leave. Capt. L.S. Fee rejoined from leave	
"	12th		29. O.R's proceeded to U.K. for demobilization	
"	13th		Lt. Johnson. proceeded to U.K. for demobilization	
"	15th		Lt. Robertson proceeded to U.K. for demobilization	
"	16th		A" Coy 5. O.Rs 150 O.R's proceeded to LEVERKUSEN to take over Guards Etc from VIII. Cyclist Bn.	

Army Form C. 2118.

WAR DIARY
or
INTELLIGENCE SUMMARY.
(Erase heading not required.)

Instructions regarding War Diaries and Intelligence Summaries are contained in F. S. Regs., Part II. and the Staff Manual respectively. Title pages will be prepared in manuscript.

Place	Date	Hour	Summary of Events and Information	Remarks and references to Appendices
Fechingen	Sept 16		50 O'Ks proceeded to U'K for Demobilization	
"	19"		Lt Col Stone DSO returned from leave	
"	20"		10 O'Ks proceeded for demobilization 2/Lt Holloway 9 2/Lt Jones returned from leave	
"	21st		10 O'Ks proceeded for demobilization	
"	22nd		Lt Warren returned from U'K leave	
"	23rd		Lt Bressard proceeded for demobilization 15 O'Ks proceeded for demobilization	
"	26"		"C" Coy proceeded to Leverkusen	
"	27"		Demobilization stopped "B" Coy moved to Weisdorf from Deubruck	
"	28 t		n-l	
"	29th		n-l	
"	30th		n-l	
			Battalion Orders for Sept. attached	

Fechingen October 2nd 1919

Doug. W

BATTALION ORDERS BY LT.COL.J. FANE.D.S.O.
C'MG.9TH.BN.GLOUCESTER RGT.(PIONEERS).

SEPTEMBER 1st.1919.

331. DUTIES.

Bn.Orderly Officer for to-morrow.   ,,,   2nd.Lt.H.R.Jones.
Next for Duty.   ,,,   2nd.Lt.W.J.Noah M.M.
Bn.Orderly Sgt.for tomorrow.   ,,,   Sgt.Smith.
Next for Duty.   ,,,   Sgt.Godfrey.

No.12 Platoon will provide the Guards for to-morrow.
No.1 Platoon will be next for Duty.

332. PARADES.

Companies will parade under Company Arrangements.

333. COMMAND.

2nd.Lt.E.C.Turner will take over the Command and Pay of H.Q.Co.
from this date.

334. PAY OF TROOPS ON LEAVE TO U.K. (G.R.O.5537 published for information.
Reference G.R.O.5537 dated August 22nd. Further Cash issues on men's
return from Furlough must be restricted to current earnings,subject
to the necessary curtailment in cases of those in debt. Any
additional Payments will therefore only be made by Company Commanders
after Notification of balances by Regimental Paymasters in Pay
and Mess Books for period of expiry of furloughs has been received
This will not however prevent special reference to Regimental
Paymasters in urgent cases.

335. DISCIPLINE. (D.R.O.910 is published for information,)
The holding of mixed dances for British Soldiers and German
Civilians is prohibited.
In future no Officer or Other Rank will be allowed
to attend dances organized by Germans, or Vice versa.
This will be communicated at once t all ranks.

336. ATTACHMENT.
No.50601 Pte.Bond M.W. is attached to H.Q.Co.from "B" Coy from
this date.

337. AMENDMENT.
Reference Bn.Order No.1230 dated 30/8/19 for 37804 Pte.Hector
read 52039 Pte.Higgins F.

338. EDUCATION.
Education Duties and Correspondence will be handed over to the
senior Sgt.whilst Education Officers are on leave.
Orderly Officers will inspect the classes daily to see that they
are being carried on in a proper way, and will add a para. to this
effect on the Orderly Officers Report.

(Signed)E.O.PILCHER.Lieut.and Adjutant.
9TH.BN.GLOUCESTER RGT.(PIONEERS).

NOTICE.

Volunteers are required to form a choir for Sunday Services.
O.C.Companies will render a Nominal Roll to the Education Officer
by 0900 hours on Wednesday the 3rd.inst.

BATTALION ORDERS BY LT.COL.J.FANE.D.S.O.
COMMG. 9TH.BN.GLOUCESTER RGT. (PIONEERS).

SEPTEMBER 2nd. 1919.

1239 **DUTIES.**
Bn.Orderly Officer for tomorrow. .... 2nd.Lt.W.J.Noah.M.M.
Next for Duty. .... Lieut.G.F.Pullen.
Bn.Orderly Sgt. for to morrow. .... Sgt.Ellis.
Next for Duty. ---- Sgt.Andrews.
No.1 Platoon will provide the guards for to morrow.
No.2 Platoon will be next for Duty.

1240 **PARADES.**
Companies will parade under Company arrangements.

1241. **CASUALTY WIRE.**
Numerous instances have occurred recently of O.R.s returning from Leave, Hospital etc. and reporting direct to their respective Co. Offices. Some of these cases have not been shown on the daily Casualty Wire rerendered by Companies. O.C.Companies will ensure that all Other Ranks rejoining the Battalion report to Batt.Orderly Room and are also shown on the Casualty wire the day following the date of their rejoining.

1242 **BATHING IN THE RHINE.**
Owing to the number of deaths from drowning lately, bathing in the Rhine and all rivers is absolutely forbidden, except in the various baths which are moored on the Rhine Bank and reserved for Troops, and in such other places as may be reserved for Bathing, and so marked by Corps in whose area the Rivers run.

1243. **BATHS.**
From this date and until further orders the times and days for baths will be as follows:-
    Thursday 13-30 hours to 16-00 hours.
    Friday. 0900 " to 12-00 hours.
    "   13-30 " to 16-00 hours.
    Saturday. 0930 " to 1200 hours.

1244. **RATES OF EXCHANGE.**
The rate of Exchange for September is as follows:-
    5 Francs equals 2 shillings 11 pence. (France)
    5 Francs " 2 " 10 " (Belgium).
    2 Guilders " 2 " 6 " (Holland).
    10 Marks. " 2 " 1 penny. (Germany).

1245. **ATTACHMENTS.**
The following men are attached to the Transport for Pay, Rations and Discipline from this date.
    No.288006 Pte.A.Donaldson from "A" Co.
    No.40210 " E.Drew " "A" "
    No.50977 " A.Sykes. " "B" "
    No.40260 " S.Murford. " "C" "
    No.51801 " E.Liddington." "C" "

(Signed) E.O.PILCHER.Lieut. and Adjutant.
9TH.BN.GLOUCESTER RGT.(PIONEERS).

BATTALION ORDERS BY MAJOR H.B.SPEAR.
C.MG.9TH.BN.GLOUCESTER RGT.(PIONEERS).
SEPTEMBER 3RD. 1919.

1246 **DUTIES.**
Bn.Orderly Officer for tomorrow ..... Lieut.G.F.Pullen.
Next for Duty. ..... 2nd.Lt.B.Kembery.
Bn.Ordely Sgt.for tomorrow. ..... Sgt.Andrews.
Next for Duty. ..... Sgt. Hollands.
No.2 Platoon will provide the Guard for to morrow.
No. 3 Platoon will be next for duty.

1247 **PARADES.**
Companies will parade under Company Arrangements.

1248. **PARADES .. OFFICERS.**
All Officers will attend this Office at 1230 hours to morrow
the 4th.inst.

1249. **RECREATION GROUND.**
The Recreation Groung will not be available for the Battalion on
Fridays after 1800 hours ,after which hour the ground may be used
by Germans on that day only.

1250 **TRANSFERS AND ATTACHMENTS.**
The following O/R s will be attached to H.Q.Co.from this date.
    No.34098 Pte . Noon S. from "B" Co.
       39834 " Newman G. " "B" "
       36367 " Guy R. " "B" "
       50960 " Hitchings R. "B" "
       50589 " Betts W. " "B" "
The following O/R is transferred from "B" to H.Q.Co.
    No.27906 Pte Barnard J.
The following O/R is transferred from H.Q.to "C" Co.
    No.50344 Pte Rigby R.
A.F.B.122 s of the a/m men will be forwarded to H.Q.Co.Office
immediately,and in future this will always done by Companies
in the cases of men transferred or attached to H.Q.Co.

1251 **TRAVELLING ON RAILWAYS**
Complaints have been received that men,when travelling on the
Railway,are in the habit of using the emergency brake.
As this is the cause of considerable delay,all troops are to be
warned that this practice must cease.

(Signed) E.O.PILCHER. Lieut.and Adjutant.

9TH.BN.GLOUCESTER RGT.(PIONEERS).

BATTALION ORDERS BY MAJOR H.B.SPEAR.
CMMG. 9TH.BN.GLOUCESTER RGT.(PIONEERS).
SEPTEMBER 4TH.1919.
****

1252- **DUTIES.**
Bn.Orderly Officer for to morrow .... 2nd.Lt.B.Kembery.
Next for Duty. .... 2nd.Lt.W.J.Everall.
Bn.Orderly Sgt.for to-morrow. .... Sgt.Hollands.
Next for Duty .... Sgt.Eagles.

No.3 Platoon will provide the Guards for to morrow.
No.4 Platoon will be next for duty.

1253. **PARADES.**
Companies will parade under Company arrangements.

1254. **COMMAND.**
Major H.B.Spear took over the Command of the Battalion on the 3Rd.inst during the absence of Lt.Col.J.Fane on leave.

1255. **ATTACHMENTS.**
The following men are attached to H.Q.Co.from this date:
No.260119 Pte .Bryant P.H. from "C" Co.
50860 " Hadland G. " "A" "
52178 " Stubbs H. " "A" "
260365 " Howells J. " "A" "
32153 " Lickless " "C" "

1255 **OIL TINS.**
All Oil Tins in possession of Companies will be returned to Q.M.Stores by 10-00 hours on Saturday the 6th.inst.

1256. **RHINE ARMY CHAMPIONSHIPS. ELIMINATING COMPETITIONS.**
The Corps eliminating Competitions for the Rhine Army Championships will be held as follows:-
"9th.September Athletic Sports and Tug of War Events at P.and R.T.School, RIEHL, beginning at 14-30 hrs.
10th. Sept. Basket Ball & Cross Country run events in grounds just East of Casino at 17-30 hrs.
The Y.M.C.A. will provide a small canteen for refreshments at the ground at RIEHL. All Units are requested to repeat this notice in their Routine Orders.

1257. **PURCHASE OF SPORTING WEAPONS IN GERMANY.**
It is notified for the information of all concerned that although there is no objection to the purchase by Officers of Sporting weapons in Germany for taking home to England, yet, in view of the number of weapons confiscated from the Germans at the commencement of the occupation which have been irregularly taken by Officers, it is necessary that all weapons taken out of the area should be inspected, and that proof of legal ownership should be produced.
All Officers taking weapons out of the country will, therefore, obtain from their Commanding Officer a certificate to the effect that they have been purchased in Germany, and are the bona-fide property of the Officer concerned.

(Sgd) E.O. PILCHER, Lieut. & Adjt.,
9th. Bn. Gloucestershire Regt.(P).

N O T I C E.

"The Green Diamonds" will give a concert in the Battalion Concert Hall to-morrow the 5th. inst. at 18-30 hrs.

BATTALION ORDERS BY MAJOR M.B.SPEAR.
CMMG.9TH.BN.GLOUCESTER RGT.(P).
SEPTEMBER 5TH.1919.

1258 **DUTIES.**
Bn.Orderly Officer for to morrow — 2nd.Lt.W.J.Everall.
Next for Duty. — 2ndLt.R.W.Smiles M.M.
Bn.Orderly Sgt.for tomorrow. — Sgt.Eagles.
Next for Duty. — Sgt.Bownes.

No.4 Platoon will provide the Guards for to morrow.
No.9 Platoon will be next for Duty.

1259. **PARADES.**
Companies will parade under Company Arrangements.

1260 **TRANSFERS.**
The undermentioned N.C.O.s are transferred from "A" to H.Q.Co.
50803 L/c F.Steel.
50923 L/c F.Schofield.

(signed) E.O.Pilcher. Lieut.and Adjutant,
9TH.BN.GLOUCESTER RGT.(PIONEERS).

BATTALION ORDERS BY MAJOR H.B.SPEAR.
CMMG. 9TH.BN.GLOUCESTER RGT.(PIONEERS).
SEPTEMBER 6TH.1919.

1261 **DUTIES.**
Bn.Orderly Officer for to morrow.   2nd.Lt.R.W.Smiles.M.M.
"   "   "   "   "   2nd.Lt.W.J.Noah M.M

Next for Duty.   Lieut. Halward.
Bn.Orderly Sgt.for to morrow   Sgt. Bownes.
Bn.Orderly Sgt. for Monday   Sgt. Blair.
Next for Duty   Sgt. Plimsole.

No.9 Platoon will provide the Guards for to morrow.
No.10   "   "   "   "   "   Monday.
No. 11 "   "   be next for Duty.

1262. **DIVINE SERVICE.**
The Battalion will parade to morrow in Drill Order, formed up in
Line facing west, on the Road leading to the Recreation Ground
at 1130 hours, under Command of Major H.B.Spear, for Church of
England Service, which will be held in the Protestant Church,
Leichlingen, at 1145 hours followed by Holy Communion for all who
wish to attend.
Roman Catholics will parade on the Guard Mounting Parade Ground,
at 0945 hours for Service in the R.C. Church at 1000 hours. The
following R.C.Services will also be held:-
      Holy Communion .... 0730 hours.
      Benediction   1500   "
      Noncomformists will parade on the Guard Mounting Parade
Ground at 1015 hours for service to be held in the Cinema at 1030 hrs.

1263. **PARADES.**
On Monday Companies will parade under Company Arrangements.

1264. **MUSKETRY.**
"A" and "C" Companies will fire the following practices during
the ensuing week.
            -5 rounds application as in 15.
            15   "   Rapid   "   " 16.

1265. **DEMOBILIZATION AND COURSES.**
Attention is called to Bn.Order No.1157 dated August 18th. Names
of men due for Demobilization are still being submitted to this
Office as selected for courses or detachment. O/C Company's and E.O.
will ensure that this practice ends immediately.

1265. **PROMOTIONS AND APPOINTMENTS.**
No.50954 Cpl.Bennett L. promoted T/Sgt. vice Mills. 6/9/19.
No.12488 L/c Townshend E.   "   T/Cpl. 6/9/19. vice Bennett.
No.51982 u/L/c Savery W. appointed L/c 6/9/19   " Townshend.

1267. **ATTACHMENTS.**
No.31364 Pte.G.Clarke to be attached to H.Q. Co.whilst on Duty
at Ration Dump.

                (signed) E.O.PILCHER.Lieut.and Adjutant.

                        9TH.BN.GLOUCESTER RGT.(PIONEERS).
        N O T I C E.
        ****
It is proposed to hold a Whist Drive next Wednesday, September 10th.
at 1900 hours in the Recreation Room.
            Entrance Fee .... 2 Marks.
Tickets may be obtained from the Librarian up to Tuesday 9th.
September 9th.

W.D.

BATTALION ORDERS BY MAJOR H.B.SPEAR.
CMDG.9TH.BN.GLOUCESTER RGT.(PIONEERS).
SEPTEMBER 8TH.1919.

1268. **DUTIES.**
Bn.Orderly Officer for to morrow ...... Lieut.N.V.Halward.
Next for Duty. ...... Lieut.G.F.Pullen.
Bn.Orderly Sgt.for to morrow. ...... Sgt.Stagg.
Next for Duty. ...... Sgt.Buchanan.

No.11 Platoon will provide the Guards for to morrow.
No.12 " " be next for Duty.

1269. **PARADES.**
Companies will parade under Company Arrangements.

1270. **EDUCATION.**
Education programme for the remainder of the week will be as follows:
Tuesday)
Friday) A Company 0915 hours to 1030 hours.
Thursday) C " 1100 " to 1215 " .

1271 **APPOINTMENTS.**
Sgt. Dunn will take over Police Duties from to day vice Cpl.Dallimore

1272. **ATTACHMENTS.**
50896 Pte G.Harris to be attached to H.Q.Co.from "A" Co.from to day.
51483 " W.Damsell " " " " " A " " "

1273- **PROMOTIONS AND APPOINTMENTS.**
No.50623 Cpl. Cheale G. promoted T/Sgt. 7/9/19. vice Ellis.
50408 L/Sgt Broughton F. " " " Johnson.
41138 " Smith W. " " 8/9/19 " Boast.
12521 L/c Norman E. " T/Cpl. 7/9/19. " Cheale.
50897 " Percox S. " " " " Broughton.
50885 " Haward H. " " 8/9/19 " Smith.
50763 " Norris F. " " " " Mallett.
50386 u/L/c Swarbrick R. appointed P/L/c 7/9/19 vice L/c Norman.
59208 " Gotham F. " " " " Percox.
53286 " Price E. " " " " Finden.
28819 " Page C. " " " " Pilkington.
50472 " Shaylor W. " " " " Workman.
30705 " Fursden A. " " 8/9/19. " Hayward.
40170 " Currey W. " " " " Norris.
50606 " Bye J. " " " " Holbrook.

m1274. **PAY OF PERSONNEL ON DEMOBILIZATION.**
Each man proceeding for Demobilization will be in possession
of A.F.O.1809 Z.O/C Companies will take special steps to
ensure that no man goes to the Concentration Camp without this
Form, and that each man fully understands that,unless he is in
possession of one,he can draw no pay in England.
In Order to determine the state of a man's account ,at any given
time, the pay and Mess Book,will in future be kept in triplicate
one copy being retained by the Unit concerned.
(b) For the Current Period, the account of September will be shown
and if the state of the August Account is not known,a note to this
effect will be made on A.F.O.1809 Z.
(c) On no account is more than one name to be put on each A.F.O1809A

1275. **TELEGRAMS.**
Private and personal Telegrams are not to be despatched through the
Signal Service. They must be sent over the Civil Wires(Vide G.R.O.
3371 D/29/8/19).

1274. **OFFICERS ALLOWANCES.**
The Command Paymaster,Cologne invites any Officers,whose allowances
have not been credited up to date, to visit his Office at any conven
ient hour between 0900 hours and 2000 hours on Mondays or Tuesdays,
when he will investigate their cases. Officers will be able to see
their records.
All Officers should now have been credited with their allowances
up to July 31st.1919.

(signed) E.O.Pilcher Lt.and Adjt.

BATTALION ORDERS BY MAJOR H.B.SPEAR.
CMMG.9TH.BN.GLOUCESTER RGT.(PIONEERS).
SEPTEMBER 9TH.1919.
****

1275. **DUTIES.**
Bn.Orderly Officer for to-morrow.   Lieut.G.F.Pullen.
Next for Duty.   2nd.Lieut.B.Kembery.
Bn.Orderly Sgt.for to-morrow.   Sgt.Buchanan.
Next for duty.   Sgt.Godfrey.

"C" Co.will find the guards for to-morrow.

1276. **PARADES.**
The Battalion (less "B" Co.) will parade to-morrow on the Recreation Ground at 1030 hours. Formation:-Mass,Facing West. Dress. All Ranks Drill Order. Company Commanders will not be mounted. One Officer,and all Signallers not on Duty will parade with H.Q.Co.
2nd.Lt.B.Kembery will parade with "A" Co.
All employed O/Rs who can be spared will parade.

1277. **COMMAND.**
2nd.Lieut.W.J.Neah M.M. will take over the Command and Pay of H.Q.Co.from this date vice 2nd.Lt.H.H.Turner demobilized.

1278. **PROMOTIONS AND APPOINTMENTS.**
```
  250174 Sgt.Brecker W.  appointed A/CQMS. 9/9/19 vice Diamond.
   50585 Cpl.Bashford.   Promoted  Sgt.                Brecker.
   28614 L/St.Bownes       "        "                  Holland.
   56955 L/c Reynolds W.   "       Cpl.                Bashford.
   26215  "  Cooper C.     "        "                  Bownes.
   50905  "  Watson A.  appointed P/L/c                Reynolds.
   50795  "  Saunders P.   "        "                  Cooper.
```

1279. **TRANSFERS AND ATTACHMENTS.**
```
    50806 Pte.S.Smith.   transferred from "A" to H.Q. Co.
    50461  "  E.Osborne       "       "   "B"  "  "    "
    51965  "  A.Cole          "       "   "C"  "  "    "
    50404  "  A.Clinch.       "       "   "B"  "  "    "
    40256  "  W.Jeffs.        "       "   "A"  "  "    "
    50472 L/c W.Shayler.      "       "   "A"  "  "    "
    59390 Pte.S.Nagles        "       "   "C"  "  "    "
    52848  "  A.H.Cole.       "       "   "A"  "  "    "
    56022  "  A.Gillings  attached    "   "A"  "  "    "
    50711  "  H.Parsons       "       "   "A"  "  "    "
    59494  "  C.Hedges.       "       "   "A"  "  "    "
    50492  "  G.Blake.        "       "   "A"  "  "    "
  x 50986  "  H.Wheeler       "       "   "A"  "  "    "
    51767  "  H.Knight.       "       "   "A"  "  "    "
    39866  "  R.Haygarth.     "       "   "A"  "  "    "
    50513  "  W.Diggin        "       "   "A"  "  "    "
    50704  "  H.Iveny         "       "   "B"  "  "    "
    50856  "  C.J.Chick.      "       "   "C"  "  "    "
    50977  "  A.C.Sykes   returned to "B" Co.from H.Q.Co.
    50585 Sgt.Bashford.   transferred from "C" to "A" Co.
```

)signed)E.O.Pilcher Capt.and Adjt.

9TH.BN.GLOUCESTER RGT.(PIONEERS).

BATTALION ORDERS BY MAJOR H.B.SPEAR.
CMMG.9TH.BN.GLOUCESTER RGT.(P).
SEPTEMBER 10TH.1919.

1280- DUTIES.
Bn.Orderly Officer for to morrow .... 2nd.Lieut.B.Kembery.
Next for Duty. .... 2nd.Lieut.T.W.Everall.
Bn.Orderly Sgt.for tomorrow. .... Sgt.Godfrey.Andrews
Next for Duty. .... Sgt. Eagles.
"A" Co. will provide the Guards for to morrow.

1281. PARADES.
Parades to morrow will be under Company Arrangements.

1282. WATER SUPPLY.
Owing to the recent spell of dry Weather thw water supply of this district is exceedingly short. If the present daily amount of water hitherto used is kept up the supply will fail in two days time. Company Commanders will ensure that all men are aware of the extreme importance of this matter and that the minimum amount only of water is used.

1283. PROMOTIONS AND APPOINTMENTS.
50825 Sgt. Cheale appointed A/CQMSM 10/9/19 vice Bassett.
35652 Cpl. Boulton appointed A/Sgt. " " " Cheale.
50912 L/Sgt. Mobbs " " " " Plimsole
50445 L/Sgt. Odell " " " " Peet.
50852 Cpl. Cutler H. " " " " Kelly.
32479 L/c Monks G. " A/Cpl. " " Boulton.
265037 " Hunt W. " " " " Mobbs.
50567 " Nutt H. " " " " Odell.
50030 " Duffin C. " " " " Cutler.
50750 " Prince M. " " " " Workman.
260010 " Jones A. " " " " Clarke.
59208 " Gotham F. " " " " Clarke.
40170 " Curry W. " " " " Dallimore.
50606 " Bye J. " " " " Pearce.
50550 CBI Duffin C. " paid L/Sgt. " " Broughton.
50894 U/L/c Edward F. " L/c " " Monks.
50571 " Acton J. " " " " Hunt.
50595 " Betcher S.W. " " " " Nutt.
50702 " Knowles F. " " " " Duffin.
50643 " Evans L. " " " " Prince.
41894 " Chaney T. " " " - Jones.
40284 " May T. " " " " Gotham.
50967 " Allitt J. " " " " Curry.
50422 " Bond E. " " " " Bye.
50467 " French W. " " " " Jordan.
41035 " Thompkinson " " " " Mitchell.
51911 Pte. Dobbs A.G. appointed unpaid L/cpl.
30014 " Winney A. " " " " "
59831 " Backshall H. " " " " "
50705 " Jones W.H. " " " " "
51765 " Keylock T. " " " " "
55301 " Royal H. " " " " "

1284. ATTACHMENTS.
No.29490 Pte.Haynes J.attached to H.Q.Co.from "A" Co. from this date.
No.51697 " Pullen S. " " " " " " " " ".
No.17684 " Cornock J. " " " " " " " " ".
No.50512 L/c Margetts " " " " " " " "

(signed)E.C.PILCHER Capt.and Adjutant.

BATTALION ORDERS BY MAJOR H.B.SPEAR.
CMG. 9TH.BN.GLOUCESTER RGT.(P).
September 11th.1919.
****

1285- **DUTIES.**
Bn.Orderly Officer for to morrow.   2nd.Lt.T.W.Everall.
Next for Duty.   2nd.Lt. R.W.Smiles.
Bn.Orderly Sgt.for to morrow.   Sgt.Outler
Next for Duty.   Sgt.Gardner.

"A" Co.will provide the guards for to morrow.

1286. **PARADES.**
Parades to morrow will be under Company Arrangements.

1287 **WATER SUPPLY.**
The attention of all ranks is again directed to Battalion Order No.1282 of yesterday's date.

1288. **PROMOTIONS AND APPOINTMENTS.**
No.11702 Cpl.Herbert H. is appointed A/Sgt. vice Adamson.
No.50488 L/c Goodman E.   "   "   A/Cpl.   "   Herbert.
No.50625   "   Cain J.   "   "   P/L/Cpl.   "   Goodman.
No.50565   "   Hase G. :   "   "   "   East.

(signed) E.O.PILCHER Capt.and Adjutant.

9TH.BN.GLOUCESTERSHIRE RGT.(PIONEERS).

NOTICE.
****

A Concert by Miss Ada Moore will be given in the Battalion

Concert Hall on Saturday next the 13th.inst.

Full Particulars will be issued later.

AFTER ORDER.

1285. **TRANSFERS AND ATTACHMENTS.**
2835 Sgt. Dunn transferred from "A" to H.Q.Co.
50858 " Cutler " " "C" " "A"
50895 Pte Hearn D. is attached from "A" to H.Q.Co.

BATTALION ORDERS BY MAJOR H.B.SBEAR.
CMMG.OTH.GLOUCESTER RGT.(PIONEERS).
SEPTEMBER 12TH.1919-
****

1290. **DUTIES.**
Bn.Orderly Officer for to morrow.   2nd.Lt.R.W.Smiles M.M.
Next for Duty.   2nd.Lt.N.V.Halward.M.C.
Bn.Orderly Sgt.for to morrow.   Sgt.Gardiner.
Next for Duty.   Sgt.Eagles.

"A" Co.will find the guards for to morrow.

1291. **PARADES.**
Parades for to morrow will be under Co. Arrangements.

1292. **SPECIAL ORDER GEN.SIR W.ROBERTSON BART. G.C.B. G.C.M.G.**
K.C.V.O. D.S.O. A.D.C.   COMMANDING IN CHIEF,
BRITISH ARMY OF THE RHINE.
****
The following telegrams are published for the information of all ranks:-
From General Sir W.R.Robertson to the Secretary,Army Council
War Office,London.   21/8/19.
"All Ranks Rhine Army desire to express their pleasure at the historic visit of the Army Council,and hope that their Stay with the Army has been an agreeable one.

From the Secretary,Army Council,War Office London. To
Commander in Chief,British Army of the Rhine.
"Please convey to all ranks Rhine Army the thanks of the Army Council for their message of August 21st. The Council have greatly valued the opportunities of personal touch with the troops afforded them by their visit of which they retain the pleasantest memories. The Council were deeply impressed with the Soldierly bearing and the Fine spirit shewn by the troops under your command who worthily uphold the best traditions of the British Army.
          (signed)W.R.RObertson General.
                  Commanding in Chief,
                  British Army of the Rhine.

1293. **VICTORY RIBAND.**
This decoration may now be worn by all ranks entitled to it. An issue of the riband will be made in due course.

1294. **CAFES PASSES.**
Cafes and Restaurants are open to all Officers and W.O.s till 2300 hours daily,and to N.C.O.s and men in possession of a pass authorizing them to be absent from their quarters.
W.O.s are permitted to be absent from their billets until Midnight without passes.
Permanent Passes may be issued to N.C.O.s and men of good Character up to Midnight by C.O.s and daily passes up to 2300 hours or Midnight by Company Commanders.
These will be passed to Orderly Room for C.O.s sanction as before

1295. **APPLICATIONS TO REMAIN IN THE RHINE ARMY.**
Numerous applications are being received from Officers requesting that they may be allowed to remain in the Rhine Army instead of returning to England when their units are reduced to Cadres.
G.H.Q. state that such applications cannot be entertained and that it is no use forwarding them.

-2-

1296   PROMOTIONS AND APPOINTMENTS.
      35928 Pte. S.Clarke appointed U/L/c from this date.
      50963 "   A.Hill   "   "   " "   "
      51991 "   W.Newton   "   "   " "   "
      40269 "   C.Lee   "   "   " "   "

1297. TRANSFERS AND ATTACHMENTS.
      40251 Pte. G.Wise attached to H.Q.Co. from "A" Co.
      52053 "   R.Cowley   "   "   "   "   " "
      202490 "   Sims W.J.   "   "   "   "   " "

(signed) E.O.Pilcher.   Capt. and Adjutant.
9TH. BN. GLOUCESTER RGT. (PIONEERS).

BATTALION ORDERS BY MAJOR SPEAR.
CMMG.9TH.BN.GLOUCESTER RGT.(PIONEERS).
SEPTEMBER 13th, 1919.
* * * * * * * *

1298. DUTIES:-
    Bn.Orderly Officer for to morrow.   Lieut.N.V.Halward.
    Bn.Orderly Officer for Monday.   Lieut.G.F.Pullon.
    Next for Duty.   2nd.Lt.B.Kembery.
    Bn.Orderly Sgt.for to morrow.   Sgt. Eagles.
    Bn.Orderly Sgt.for Monday.   Sgt. Pixton.
    Next for Duty.   Sgt. Bownes.

    "A" Co.will find the Guards for to morrow.
    "C" " " " " " Monday.

1299. DIVINE SERVICE.
The Battalion will parade to morrow in drill Order, formed up in line facing west, on the Road leading to the Recreation Ground, at 1130 Hours, under command of Lieut.E.F.E.Peacock, for Church of England Service, which will be held in the Protestant Church, Leichlingen at 1145 hours followed by Holy Communion for all who wish to attend.
Roman Catholics will parade on the Guard Mounting Parade Ground at 0945 hours for Service in the R.C.Church 1000 hours. The following Roman Catholic Services will also be held:-
    Holy Communion..........0730 hours.
    Benediction ....1500 "
Noncomformists will parade on the Guard Mounting Parade Ground at 1000 hours for Service to be held in the Cinema at 1015 hrs.

1263. PARADES.
On Monday Companies will parade under Company Arrangements.

1264. MUSKETRY.
"A" and "C" Companies will fire the following practices during the ensuing week:-
    5 rounds application (Cover as in 11) Fixed Bayonets.
    5 " " (" " " 17)
    5 " Rapid (" " " 18).

1265. LEWIS GUNNERS AND REVOLVERS.
Lewis Gunners of "A" Co. will parade with Lewis Guns on "A" Company's range at 0900 hours on Monday and Thursday next.
No 1 s and Rangefinders will parade on "C" Company's Range at 0900 hours on Friday for Revolver Practice.

1266. EDUCATION PROGRAMME.
"A" and "C" Companies will parade at 1100 hours on Monday, Tuesday, Thursday, and Friday for Education.

1267. PROMOTIONS AND APPOINTMENTS.
    50763 Cpl.Picken J. appointed A/Sgt. 12/9/19 vice Stagg.
    50894 L/c Howard F. " A/Cpl. " " Picken.
    44535 " Hunt C. : P/L/c " " Howard.
    51911 " Dobbs. A. " " " " Swancott.

1268. TRANSFERS AND ATTACHMENTS.
    50960 Pte. Hutchings E.A. is transferred from "B" to H.Q.Co.
    36367 " Gay R. " " " "B" " "
    50513 " Diggin " " " "A" " "
    51911 L/c Dobbs " " " "A" " "
    27906 Pte. Barnard J. " " " "B" " "
    40361 " Perry E.J. " " " "C" " "
    52 178 " Stubbs H " " " "A" " "
    50589 " Betts W. " " " "B" " "
    50771 " Parsons H. attached to H.Q. Co.from "A" Co.
    201227 " Blackwell : " " "B" "
    51603 " Williams J. : " " "B" "
    50409 " Hughes "B"Co. ceases to be attached to H.Q.C

(signed) M.O.Pilcher. Capt.&Adj.

BATTALION ORDERS BY MAJOR H.B.SPEAR.
CMMG.9TH.BN.GLOUCESTER RGT.(PIONEERS).
SEPTEMBER 15 TH. 1919.
* * * * * * * *

1306. **DUTIES.**
Bn.Orderly Officer for to-morrow.　　2nd.Lt. XXXXXXX.Everall.
Next for Duty.　　　　　　　　　　　　2nd.Lt.N.A.Bresman.
Bn.Orderly Sgt. for to-morrow.　　　Sgt. Downer.
Next for Duty.
"C" Co. will find the Guards until further notice.

1307. **PARADES.**
Companies will parade as detailed.

1308. **DUTIES.**
Capt.C.S.Lee will take over the duties of P.M.C.vice
Capt.G.J.Paul from this date.
Lieut.G.F.Pullen will take over the duties of Musketry
Officer,Sports Officer and Entertainments Officer vice
2nd.Lieut.B.Kembery from this date.

1309. **GERMAN SERVICE RIFLES.** (O.R.O.2065 republished for information)
Officers and O/Rs are forbidden to take German Service
Rifles to the U.K.
It is notified however, that anyone requiring a German
Service Rifle can obtain one in England on application
to the War Office.

　　　　　　　　　　　　(signed) E.D.PILCHER. Capt.and Adjutant.
　　　　　　　　　　　　　　　　9TH.BN.GLOUCESTER RGT.(PIONEERS).

N O T I C E S.
* * * * * * * *

JEWISH SERVICE FOR NEW YEAR AND DAY OF ATONEMENT.
September 24th. Evening Service at 1800 hours.
　"　　　25th. First Day,New Year,at 1050 hours.
　"　　　26th. Second　"　　"　　"　　"　　"
October　3rd."Kol Nidrei" Service at 1800　"
　"　　　4th. Day of Atonement Service at 1000 hrs.
The Services will be conducted by the Revd.
H.P.Silverman C.F. Jewish Chaplain,Rhine Army, at the
Central Lerely Hall Y.M.C.A. 44 Friesen Strasse,Cologne.
****

The Chaplain wishes to acknowledge the following collections
made on Church Parade:-
August 10th."Gordon Boys Home" .... 117 Marks.
September 7th."Church of England
　　　　　Soldiers and Sailors Institute".. 205　　".

BATTALION ORDERS BY MAJOR H.B.SPEAR.
CMMG. 9TH.BN.GLOUCESTER RGT.(PIONEERS).
SEPTEMBER 16TH.1919.
****

1311. **DUTIES.**
Bn.Orderly Officer for to morrow   2nd.Lieut.E.A.Bresman
Next for Duty.   Lieut.G.F.Pullen.

1312. **PARADES.**
Companies will parade under Company Arrangements,

1313. **RATE OF EXCHANGE.**
The Rate of Exchange from the 16th.inst. are as follows:-
5 francs (France and Belgium) equals 2 shillings and 10d.

1314. **TRANSFERS AND ATTACHMENTS.**

50456	Pte.	Bettles H.	is attached to	H.Q.	Co.	from	"A"	Co.	
50451	"	Cassell	is returned from	H.Q.	"		to	"A"	"
202490	"	Simms	"	"	"	"	"	"	"
40451	"	Wise G.	"	"	"	"	"	"	"
50860	"	Hadland	"	"	"	"	"	"	"
52053	"	Cowley	"	"	"	"	"	"	"
36022	"	Gillings	"	"	"	"	"	"	"
50771	"	Parsons	"	"	"	"	"	"	"
50705	"	Jarrett	"	"	"	"	"	"	"

1315. **BLANKETS.**
All Companies will tender to this Office by 1100 hours
to morrow the 17th.inst. a return showing the exact
number of blankets in excess of One per man in possession.
This return will in future rendered weekly to the Q.M.
on Tuesday by 1200 hours.

                                (signed) E.O.PILCHER Capt.and Adjt
                                     9TH.BN.GLOUCESTER RGT.(P).

BATTALION ORDERS BY MAJOR H.B.SPEAR.
CMMG.9TH.BN.GLOUCESTER RGT. (P).
SEPTEMBER 17TH.1919.
****

1316— **DUTIES.**
Bn.Orderly Officer for to-morrow.   Lieut. G.F.Pullen.
Next for Duty.   2nd.Lt.T.W.Everall.

1317. **PARADES.**
Companies will parade under Company Arrangements.

1318. **BATHING.**
In future Clean Towels will be drawn before entering the Bath and not after.

1319. **PROMOTIONS.**

50738	Cpl.	T.Martin	appt.	A/Sgt.(with Pay)	17/9/19	vice	Eagles.
36935	"	W.Reynolds	"	"	"	"	"	Ringrose.
50386	L/c	W.Swarbrick.	"	A/Cpl.	"	"	"	Martin.
41085	"	C.Thompkinson	"	"	"	"	"	Jones.
50846	"	Wilkins	"	"	"	"	"	Reynolds.
50475	U/L/c	A.Hardiman	appointed Paid L/Cpl.		"	"	"	Swarbrick.
30014	"	A.Winney.	"		"	"	"	Thomkinson.
50705	"	W.Jones	"		"	"	"	Fursden.

1320. **TRANSFERS AND ATTACHMENTS.**

50684	Pte.	W.Harvey.W.	attached to H.Q. Co. from "C" Co.
52057	"	V.Haddrell	" " " " " " "
52058	"	A.Pearce	" " " " " " "
50944	"	S.Pullen	" " " " " " "

(signed) E.P.PILCHER. Capt.and Adjutant
9TH.BN.GLOUCESTER RGT.(PIONEERS).

N O T I C E.
*****

A Whist Drive will be held in the Recreation Room

on Saturday the 20th.inst.at 7 p.m.

Tickets may be obtained from the librarian Price 2 Marks.

BATTALION ORDERS BY MAJOR H.B.SPEAR.
CMMG.9TH.BN.GLOUCESTER RGT.(P).
SEPTEMBER 18TH. 1919.

1321 DUTIES.
Bn.Orderly Officer for to morrow 2nd.Lieut. T.W.Everall.
Next for Duty.   2nd.Lieut. E.A.Bresman.

1322. PARADES.
Companies will parade under Company Arrangements.

1323. BATHS.
Until the return of "A" or "B" Companies to Leichlingen the Battalion Baths will not be available on Saturdays.
Men who have not bathed to day (Thursday) will therefore bathe to morrow (Friday).

1324. MEDAL RIBAND--METHOD OF WEARING.
Medal Riband will be worn as prescribed in Dress Regulations and King's Regulations, Para 1736 i.e. on the left breast midway between the first and second buttons from the bottom of the Collar $1\frac{1}{2}$ ins. from edge of tunic.
It is noticed that in many cases Ribands are being worn immediately over the centre of the Breast Pocket, and when only one riband is being worn it is invisible when carrying the pack.
This practice must cease.

(signed) E.D.PILCHER. Capt.and Adjutant.
9TH.BN.GLOUCESTER RGT.(P).

N O T I C E.
****

A Whist Drive will be held in the Battalion Recreation Room on Saturday the 20th. inst. at 7 p.m.

Tickets may be obtained from the Librarian

PRICE........2 Marks.

AFTER ORDER.

1325. PROMOTIONS AND APPOINTMENTS.
No. 12521 Cpl. Norman E. appointed A/Sgt. (With Pay) 17/9/19 vice Sgt. Odell.

Battalion Orders by Major H.B.SPEAR.
COMMDG. 9TH. BN. GLOUCESTERSHIRE REGT. (P).
SEPTEMBER 19TH. 1919.

1325. **DUTIES.**
Bn. Orderly Officer for to-morrow----------Lieut. G.F.Pullen.
Next for Duty ------------------------------2/Lt. W.A.Bresman.

1326. **PARADES.**
Companies will Parade under Company arrangements.

1327. **POSTAL ORDERS AND WAR SAVINGS CERTIFICATES.**
Henceforth Sale of Postal Orders to any one individual, in any one day, will be limited to 10/- with extension to £1, if covered by Certificate of O.C. Unit as to necessity of issue.
Individual Officers may only putchase War Savings Certificates at Army Post Offices by means of Cheques or Cash in British Currency, unless the purchase is made through a War Savings Association.

1328. **ANTI-GAS PERSONNEL.**
Companies will render to Battalion Orderly Room by 12-00. hours on the 21st. inst. a Nominal Roll of all Gas N.C.Os. and state whether they are eligible for Demobilisation or not.

1329. **THE ATTENTION** of all Officers is drawn to the Notice which has been Posted up in the Officers Mess.

(Sgd). R. D. HEPPENSTALL 2/Lt. For Capt.&Adjt.,
9TH. BN. GLOUCESTERSHIRE REGT. (P).

N O T I C E.

A Whist Drive will be held in the Battalion Recreation

Room at 7 p.m. on Saturday the 20th. inst.

Tickets may be obtained from the Librarian - Price 2 Marks.

BATTALION ORDERS BY LT.COL.J.FANE D.S.O.

CMMG. 9TH.BN.GLOUCESTER RGT. (P).

SEPTEMBER 20TH. 1919.

****

1330 **DUTIES.**
Bn.Orderly Officer for to morrow.   2nd. Lt. E.A.Bresman.
Bn.Orderly Officer for Monday.   Lieut. E.F.E.Peacock.
Next for Duty.   Lieut. G.F.Pullen.

1331 **DIVINE SERVICE.**
Roman Catholics will parade on the Guard Mounting
Parade Ground at 0945 hours to morrow for Service in
in the R.C. Church at 10-00 hours.
The following R.C. Services will also be held:-
    Holy Communion........... 0730 hours.
    Benediction 1500   "
There will be no C.of E, or Noncomformist Parade to morrow
the 21st.inst.

1332. **PARADES.**
On Monday Companies will parade under Company Arrangements,

                    (signed) E.O.PILCHER. Capt.and Adjutant.
                             9TH.BN.GLOUCESTERSHIRE Rgt, (P).

N O T I C E.
K/E/K/K/K

A whist Drive will be held in the Battalion Recreation

Room to night at 7p.m.

Tickets may be obtained from the Librarian Price..2 Marks.

BATTALION ORDERS BY LT.COLONEL J.FANE D.S.O.
       CMMG.9TH.BN.GLOUCESTER RGT.(P).
           September 22nd. 1919.

- -

1333. DUTIES.
      Bn.Orderly Officer for to morrow........ Lieut. G.F.Pullen.
      Next for Duty.......................... Lieut.   Holloway.

1334. PARADES.
      Companies will parade under Company Arrangements,

1335. RATES OF EXCHANGE.(G.R.O.3424.)
      Owing to the needs of notifying the Home paymasters and
      other Authorities, the official rate has to be fixed several
      days beforehand; and the rapid fall in the value of the
      mark, resulting from trade and Speculative factors which
      cannot be foreseen, has made it impossible to prevent differences
      between the commercial and Official rates.
      To cash money at the commercial rate, and change it back
      directly or indirectly at the Official rate or vice versa
      is so obviously dishonest that it has not been considered
      necessary hitherto to draw special notice to it.
      Instances, however have occured in which the use of the
      Official rate has been abused, and all ranks are warned
      that any further cases of this kind will be severely
      dealt with.

1336. RATES OF EXCHANGE.
      The following rates of Exchange are fixed from September 16th.
           5 francs (France and Belgium) equals 2s-10d.

1337. PROMOTIONS AND APPOINTMENTS.
      No. 36899 Pte. Griffin G.A. is appointed U/L/C from this date.

1338. TRANSFERS AND ATTACHMENTS.
      No. 50607 Pte. A.E. Birtles transferred from "C" to H.Q. Co.
      No. 50517 "   C.T. Reynolds   "   " " " "A" "   "
      No. 52083 "   W.J. Hunt.   "   " " " "A" "   "

                            (signed) E.B.PILCHER. Capt.and Adjt.
                                  9TH.BN.GLOUCESTER RGT. (PIONEERS).

BATTALION ORDERS BY LT.COLONEL J.FANE D.S.O.
CMMG.9TH.BN.GLOUCESTER RGT.(P).
September 23rd. 1919.

1339. Duties.
Bn.Orderly Officer for to morrow..........Lieut.L.G. Holloway.
Next for Duty............................Lieut.E.F.H.Peacock.

1340. PARADES.
Companies will parade under Company Arrangements.

1341. LEWIS GUN COURSE.
No. 50738 Sgt.Martin "A" Co. qualified at the Lewis Gun
Course " held at the General Headquarters School of Musketry.

1342. DEMOBILIZATION--OFFICERS.
Any Officer,whether Volunteer or not who is desirous of
being demobilized,should submit to this Office at once
an application stating reasons.
Applications received at a future date will not be considered.

1343. FIRE ARMS ETC.
In future the Orderly Officer will inspect all parties pro-
-ceeding on Demobilization,and will render to this Office
a report to the effect that no man is in possession of any
unauthorized Firearms,Ammunition,or Grenades.

1344. TRANSFERS AND ATTACHMENTS.
No. 40264 L/c May T. is transferred from "C" to H.Q. Co.
as from to day.

(signed) E.O.PILCHER. Capt.and Adjutant.
9TH.BN.GLOYCESTER RGT. (P).

BATTALION ORDERS BY LT.COL. J. FANE D.S.O.
CMMG. 9TH.BN. GLOUCESTER RGT. (P).
SEPTEMBER 24th. 1919.

1345. DUTIES.
Bn. Orderly Officer for to morrow.   Lieut. P. Hancox.
Next for duty............................. Lieut. G.F. Pullen.

1346. PARADES.
Companies will parade under Company Arrangements.

1347. LEAVE.
In future no Officer, N.C.O., or man who is eligible for demobilization will be given leave to U.K.

1348. OFFICERS WIVES AND FAMILIES.
Officers Wives and Families, travelling from Stations in France to the occupied area, may obtain half rate fares on the French Railway Systems.
Application myst be made at the Booking Office of the Station of Departure.
Means of Identification of the applicant as belonging to the family of an Officer actually resident in Occupied Territory must be available for production if required by the French Authorities, before ticket at the reduced rate is issued.

(signed) E.O. Pilcher. Capt. and Adjt.

9TH. BN. GLOUCESTER RGT. (P).

BATTALION ORDERS BY LT.COL J.FANE.D.S.O.
CMDG. 9TH.BN.GLOUCESTER RGT.(P).
SEPTEMBER 25th. 1919.

1349- **DUTIES.**
Bn. Orderly Officer for to morrow..... Lieut. G.F. Pullen.
Next for duty............................ Lieut. P.J. Hancox.

1350. **PARADES.**
Companies will parade under Company Arrangements.

(signed) R.D. Heppenstall 2nd. Lt. A/Adjt.
9TH.BN.GLOUCESTER RGT. (PIONEERS).

BATTALION ORDERS BY LT.COL.J. FANE D.S.O.
CMMG. 9TH.BN.GLOUCESTER RGT.(P).
SEPTEMBER 26th. 1919.

1351. **DUTIES.**
Bn. Orderly Officer for to-morrow............. Lieut. P.J. Hancox.
Next for Duty................................. Lieut. L.G. Melloway.

1352. **PARADES.**
Companies will parade to-morrow under Company Arrangements.

1353. **LEAVE --OFFICERS.**
In future Officers available for leave and who do not wish to proceed, will be placed at the bottom of the Leave Roster from the date on which they refuse.

1354. **MARRIAGES BETWEEN BRITISH SOLDIERS AND GERMAN WOMEN.**
The Army Council have ruled that no Marriages can be permitted between British Soldiers and German Women before the Ratification of the Peace Treaty, and only then if and when the proper arrangements have been made by the German Government, as to the formalities and precautions to be observed. When these have been made instructions on the subject will be issued.

1355. **PROMOTIONS AND APPOINTMENTS.**
The undermentioned N.C.O.s are promoted to Temporary Rank as stated for the period of the Army of Occupation i.e. up to 30/4/20 with effect from date shown.

11702	A/Sgt.	Herbert E.	promoted Sergeant		11/9/19.
50763	"	Picken J.	"	"	12/9/19.
36835	"	Reynolds J.	"	"	17/9/19.
12521	"	Norman E.	"	"	17/9/19.
30567	A/Cpl.	Nutt H.	"	Corporal	10/9/19.
50759	"	Prince H.	"	"	10/9/19.
39208	"	Gotham F.	"	"	10/9/19.
50894	"	Harwood F.	"	"	12/9/19.
50386	"	Swarbrick W.	"	"	17/9/19.
50846	"	Wilkins E.	"	"	17/9/19.
50884	Pte.	Ivens	appointed U/L/c from this date.		

1356. **TRAVELLING.**
All Ranks are strictly forbidden to travel in the Brake Vans of trains. (G.R.O. 3445.).

1357. **LEAVE.**
All Leave is suspended forthwith owing to an anticipated Railway Strike.

1358. **DEMOBILIZATION.**
Lieut. G.F. Pullen and Lieut. P.J. Hancox will proceed with the Demob. Party parading at the Battalion Orderly Room at 1315 hours to No. 1 Concentration Camp, Cologne.

1359. **COLOGNE BOULOGNE EXPRESS.**
O/Rs travelling by the Cologne Boulogne Express will report at Rhine Army Reception Camp and will entrain and detrain at Coln-Deutz. Officers will entrain at Coln Main as usual.

1360. **DEMOBILIZATION.**
Men attested under the Derby Scheme, found unfit, and then called into the Army and are at present serving under the Terms of A.F.B. 2513 are not eligible for demobilization.
(Authority Rhine Army No. SZ.560 (M.O.B.) dated 19/9/19.).

(signed) E.O.PILCHER. Capt.and Adjt.
9TH.BN.GLOUCESTER RGT.(P)

BATTALION ORDERS BY LT.COL.J. FANE D.S.O.
CMMG.9TH.BN.GLOUCESTER RGT.(P).
SEPTEMBER 27th. 1919.

1361. **DUTIES.**
Bn. Orderly Officer for to morrow.......Lieut.L.G. Holloway.
Bn. Orderly Officer for Monday..........Lieut.G.F.Pullen.
Next for Duty..........................Lieut. P.J.Hancox.

1362. **DIVINE SERVICE.**
Roman Catholics will parade on the Guard Mounting Parade Ground at 0945 hours to morrow for service in the R.C. Church at 10-00 hrs. The following R.C. Services will also be held:-
    Holy Communion ......0730 hours.
    Benediction.........1500 "
There will be no C.of E. or Nonconformist Parades to morrow.

1363. **PARADES.**
Companies will parade on Monday under Company Arrangements.

1364. **BILLETS.**
O/C Companies will personally see that the billets and kitchens they vacate are clean. The T.O. will ensure that the different stables are clean and that the manure is removed.

1365. **TRAM FARES.**
It is notified for the information of all ranks that, from the date of the Ratification of Peace, free travel by tram for British Troops will cease. Full instructions will be issued later.

                            (signed)E.O.PILCHER Capt.and Adjutant.
                                 9TH.BN.GLOUCESTER RGT. (P).

N-O T I C E.

OPERA TICKETS.

The system of allotting seats for the Opera has been cancelled. In future seats may be booked by any Officer, W.O., N.C.O., or Man, by application at the Box Office either in person or by telephone. The booking will open 4 days in advance for each performance.

    Seats booked by telephone must be claimed 2 hours before the performance commenced either by a personal call at the Box Office or by a letter containing the money. Not more than two seats may be booked by any one individual.

Box Office is open daily at the following hours:-

0930 to 1300 hours. 1400 hours to one hour after the performance has started.
    (Telephone No. Coln 658.

BATTALION ORDERS BY LT. COL. J. FANE D.S.O.

CMMG. 9TH. BN. GLOUCESTER RGT. (P).

SEPTEMBER 29TH. 1919.

1366- **DUTIES.**
Bn. Orderly Officer for to morrow........... Lieut. P.J.Hancox.
Next for Duty. -;---------------------------- Lieut. L.G. Holloway.

1367. **PARADES.**
Companies will parade under Company Arrangements.

1368. **COURSE COOKERY.**
The undermentioned attended a Course at the School of Cookery of the British Army of the Rhine, and obtained good reports:-
No. 260267 Pte. Mc Kenzie G. "A" Co.
    50633   "   Dobbins   A. "C" "
    50732   "   Morgan   J. "HQ" "

1369. **AUDIT BOARD.**
An Audit Board, composed of the undermentioned Officers will assemble at 10-00 hours to morrow in "C" Co's Officers Mess to examine the accounts of the War Savings Association.
    President C.S. Lee.(Capt)   Member:- Lieut. L.G. Holloway.

1370 **KILLING OF GAME. (G.R.O.3461).**
It is notified that the hunting, shooting or killing of game (which includes hares and rabbits) by nets, snares or other methods, is prohibited in the Occupied Territory, unless the permission of the Owner or his representative has been previously obtained.   This prohibition applies equally to Crown, Government or Communal Ground.
Permission has now been given for those of the German Population who have obtained licenses to carry and use Sporting Weapons. It will therefore be necessary for Officers and O/Rs to lease shooting unless they have received express written permission from the owners or tenants of the Shooting in question to shoot free of charge.   All arrangements to lease shooting must be writing in proper form.   This order must be strictly complied with.

1371. **FISHING (G.R.O. 3462.)**
All Ranks are forbidden to fish in ponds connected to streams which act as breeding Pools.
Fishing is still permitted in Streams and in Stagnant Pools for course fish.

1372. **TRANSFERS AND ATTACHMENTS.**
No. 15435 Pte. Newport N. is transferred to H.Q. from "B" Co.
No. 40232 "   Candice E.   "   "   "   " "B" "
NNo. 50643 L/c Evans   L.   "   attached   "   " "C" "

(signed) E.O.PILCHER. Capt. and Adjutant.

9TH. BN. GLOUCESTER RGT (PIONEERS).

BATTALION ORDERS BY LT.COL J. FANE.
CMMG.9TH.BN.GLOUCESTER RGT.(P).
SEPTEMBER 30th. 1919.

1373. DUTIES.
Bn. Orderly Officer for to morrow..... Lieut.P.G.Holloway.
Next for Duty........................ Lieut.G.F. Pullen.

1374. PARADES.
Companies will parade to morrow under Company Arrangements.

1375. AGREEMENT OF SOLDIERS BALANCES. (G.R.O.3468).
It has been brought to notice that serious delays occur
in returning A.F.s W.3919 to Pay Offices, and in
numerous cases O.sC. have failed to return the form
at all.
As it is most important that the soldiers' agreement
to the balance of his account should be secured as early
as possible Os/c are instructed to take immediate
action immediately A.F.W.s3919 are received and to return
them to Paymasters within one week of day of receipt.

1376. SALE OF CIGARETTES.
On account of the trafficking which is taking place
in cigarettes, not more than 20 cigarettes will be sold
in any one day to any N.C.O. or man of the British Army of
the Rhine by any Canteen or institution.

1377. IMPORTATION OF MOTOR CARS INTO ENGLAND.
It is notified for information, that, as Motor Cars are
not now on list of restricted imports, Officers and
Other Ranks may at present take them to England from
Germany without conditions as regards re Sale.

        (signed) E.O.PILCHER. Capt.and Adjutant.

        9TH.BNGLOUCESTER RGT.(P).

Army Form C. 2118.

WAR DIARY
or
INTELLIGENCE SUMMARY.

(Erase heading not required.)

2/4 Br. Monmouth Regt (P)
"October" 1919.

Place	Date	Hour	Summary of Events and Information	Remarks and references to Appendices
LEICHLINGEN	3/10/19		Lt. H.C. HISCOCK takes off charge of Battalion. Auth: G.S. Div Letter No A.S./24/17 and Rhine Army No A.9/G (O1) of 27/9/19.	
"	9/10/19		A/Capt: E.O. PILCHER attended Regiment and A/Capt: G.J. PAUL with effect from 30/9/19.	
"	10/10/19		Two O.R. transferred to Class "Z" Army Reserve.	
"	11/10/19		"250" O.R. proceeded to U.K. for disposal.	
"	13/10/19		"72" " " " " "	
"	14/10/19		"38" " " " " "	
"	15/10/19		2/Lt R.W. SMILES rejoining Unit from Draft Conducting duties to U.K.	
"	17/10/19		2/Lt R.H. WARREN M.C. M.M. granted leave to U.K.	
"	20/10/19		Maj: H.B. SPEAR proceeded on leave to U.K. 2 O.R. to U.K. demob.	
"	22/10/19		2 O.R. to U.K. demob.	
"	23/10/19		Battalion H.Q. move by train to WIESDORF. 1 O.R. to U.K. demob.	
WIESDORF	24/10/19		10.45 hours from LEICHLINGEN. Relief conf'd M. 106.	
"	25/10/19		"	
"	26/10/19		2/Lt R.H. WARREN MC M.M. rejoined from leave.	
"	27/10/19		2/Lt L.J. WADDELL rejoining from Draft Conducting duties. 16 U.K. 10 O.R. demobbed.	
"	28/10/19		3 O.R. to U.K. demobbed.	
"	29/10/19		Lt L.G. HOLLOWAY proceeded to U.K. for disposal. 10 O.R. to U.K. disposal.	
"	30/10/19		2/Lt A.J. KNAPDOLL " " " " "	
"	31/10			

S. Fau Lt.Col.

www.ingramcontent.com/pod-product-compliance
Lightning Source LLC
Chambersburg PA
CBHW081529160426
43191CB00011B/1721